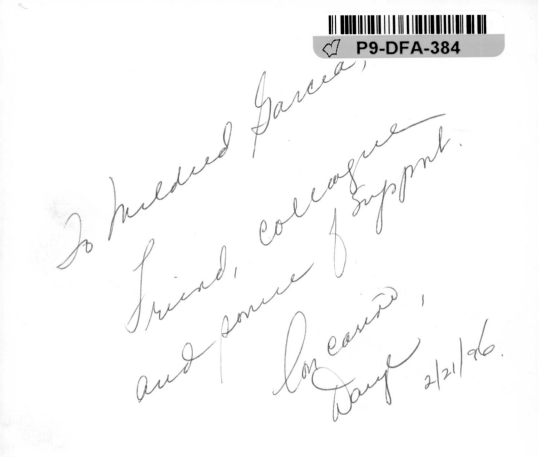

To Mildred Garcia,

Friend, colleague,
and source of support.

con cariño,
Daryl 2/21/96.

Strategic Governance

Strategic Governance
How to Make Big Decisions Better

by
Jack H. Schuster
Daryl G. Smith
Kathleen A. Corak
Myrtle M. Yamada

AMERICAN COUNCIL
ON EDUCATION
Series on Higher Education
ORYX PRESS
1994

The rare Arabian Oryx is believed to have inspired the myth of the unicorn. This desert antelope became virtually extinct in the early 1960s. At that time several groups of international conservationists arranged to have 9 animals sent to the Phoenix Zoo to be the nucleus of a captive breeding herd. Today the Oryx population is over 800, and nearly 400 have been returned to reserves in the Middle East.

© 1994 by American Council on Education/The Oryx Press
Published by The Oryx Press
4041 North Central at Indian School Road
Phoenix, Arizona 85012-3397

Published simultaneously in Canada
Printed and Bound in the United States of America

♾ The paper used in this publication meets the minimum requirements of American National Standard for Information Science—Permanence of Paper for Printed Library Materials, ANSI Z39.48, 1984.

Library of Congress Cataloging-in-Publication Data

Strategic governance : how to make big decisions better / Jack H. Schuster ... [et al.]. — (American Council on Education series on higher education)
    Includes bibliographical references and index.
    ISBN 0-89774-847-6 (alk. paper)
    1. Education, Higher—United States—Administration—Case studies. 2. Universities and colleges—United States—Planning—Case studies. 3. Decision-making. I. Schuster, Jack H. II. Series.
LB2341.S836   1994
378.1'000973—dc20   94-28927
                                                                               CIP

We dedicate this book to the memory of Howard R. Bowen (1908–89), gentleman and scholar, a skillful leader of the academy in many settings, and a resolute friend of the faculty. His memory continues as an inspiration to us all.

CONTENTS

• • • • • • • • •

LIST OF TABLES AND FIGURES

• • • • • • • • •

PREFACE

• • • • • • • • •

Campus planning and governance processes are often at odds with one another. That reality inhibits colleges and universities from fulfilling their potential in good times; in harder times, when higher education is being buffeted by a tangle of economic, political, and cultural pressures, the disjunction between planning and governance is a costly encumbrance.

Our research for this book was prompted by the suggestion that yet another model for strategic decision making was springing forth, one purportedly holding much promise. We sought to gather evidence about what was happening "on the ground." More important, we sought to discover whether the alleged new prototype was effective and what factors seemed to contribute to its success or failure.

Specifically, this book seeks to describe why the conflict between planning and governance exists, to identify the consequences of this habitual state of affairs, and to demonstrate how one approach—which we label "strategic governance"—can contribute to reconciling the competing demands of planning and governance. In short, our purpose is to show how "strategic governance" can help a campus adapt successfully to the rapidly changing environment.

The genesis of this project is traceable to the work of George Keller. In *Academic Strategy: The Management Revolution in American Higher Education* (1983), one of the most widely read books about higher education in the past decade or so, Keller warned higher education about the inadequacies of campus planning and governance in the face of rapidly changing environmental conditions. He went on to describe with enthusiasm a new kind of joint administration-faculty governance and planning unit (pp. 61–62). He labeled it the "Joint Big Decisions Committee" (JBDC). The central concept, as he explained it, was to bring together a small number of key administrators and faculty members to engage in a strategic planning process. He saw in this fresh approach a promising means for campuses to deal more effectively with changing conditions. This strategy, he argued, would help campuses avoid cumbersome, inherently inefficient "normal" planning procedures. Despite the attention Keller and others have given to such planning groups as putative "waves of the future" for campuses, these hybrid mechanisms had not been systematically investigated and evaluated. This we have sought to do.

We believe we have discovered some truths, or at least some principles, in eight case studies, some of which illustrate mechanisms that have worked well, and others which have not worked well at all. Of course, no small number of case studies, however carefully selected, could hope to demonstrate conclusively how campuses ought to proceed; the variety of higher education institutions is much too extensive to permit any such sweeping generalizations. Nonetheless, we believe that the cases explicated in chapters 3 through 10 strongly suggest some "do's" and "dont's." Even though the site visits were conducted several years ago and conditions have undoubtedly changed at those eight campuses, the lessons are no less relevant today. Beyond the cases that comprise the core of the book, our views about effective planning and governance are informed by a host of additional hands-on experiences: other studies we have conducted, accreditation activities, and consulting assignments. We would like to think that our insights can give campuses more confidence that their planning and governance processes and structures are reasonably well suited to the formidable tasks that await them.

INTENDED AUDIENCE

The audience we seek to reach spans all who are involved in higher education and care about how it can more effectively cope with the spiraling challenges of the 1990s and beyond. We envision that this book will be relevant to a mix of policy makers in, and observers of, contemporary higher education, in particular: faculty members striving to strengthen (or even to initiate) viable systems of shared governance; administrators desirous of charting a course for their institutions into the volatile future; the multifaceted planning community; and, more generally, proponents and students of organizational change.

ORGANIZATION OF THE BOOK

The book is organized into four parts. Part 1 provides the framework for our query. Chapter 1 establishes a context, identifying the momentous changes in higher education during the 1970s and 1980s and continuing into the 1990s. It introduces the separate domains of planning and governance and the increasing pressures on each. We explain the origins that prompted our inquiry and the means by which we sought to obtain and evaluate evidence.

In chapter 2 we describe the changing environment for campus governance and planning, illustrating how campus governance and planning efforts have evolved. We identify the four major forces or "imperatives" we see as shaping the campus response: the mandate for more efficient management; the push toward wider participation in decision making; the urgency of accommodating to a new environment, shaped particularly by demographics; and the salience of effective leadership—the prerequisite for enabling a campus to negotiate the new realities. The chapter concludes with a discussion of why "strategic planning councils"—our term for the administration-faculty entities designed to engage strategic planning—embody, at least in theory, characteristics desirable for meeting the formidable challenges.

In part 2 we examine the experience of four institutions that were among the earliest to develop strategic planning councils (SPCs). The establishment of these SPCs, we discovered, was motivated primarily by a concern to improve and to legitimate campus governance mechanisms. Chapters 3 through 6, respectively, describe the experiences at Princeton University, Northwestern University, Teachers College of Columbia University, and Ohio University.

Part 3 depicts newer initiatives, those undertaken in the 1980s. These initiatives emphasized the importance of planning and management rather than governance. The four institutions explored in chapters 7 through 10 are the University of Montana, Georgia Southern College [now University], Shippensburg University (PA), and West Virginia University. In all eight cases, regardless of the initial emphasis, both planning and governance were found to be inextricably linked—sometimes with success, sometimes not.

Part 4 identifies the lessons derived from the eight cases. Chapter 11 describes the characteristics and conditions pertaining to strategic planning councils that we found to be conducive to effective "strategic governance." The final chapter summarizes our argument and proffers our culminating observations about governance, planning, communication, and leadership.

Appendixes A and B provide basic comparative information about the eight campuses and their respective strategic planning councils.

ACKNOWLEDGMENTS

The authors express their appreciation to Teachers Insurance and Annuity Association-College Retirement Equities Fund, and in particular to Peggy Heim, longtime senior research officer at TIAA-CREF prior to her recent retirement, for the grant to transform our research into a book. The grant was especially important because it enabled the authors to converge from distant points at critical times.

We are grateful to Joy Rosenzweig and Lisa Wolf, two doctoral students at The Claremont Graduate School, who read the manuscript and offered very useful suggestions. We are particularly grateful to George Keller who was supportive of our project from its inception, who served as panel respondent when we first presented our findings at an annual meeting of the Association for the Study of Higher Education, and who subsequently read our manuscript and made important suggestions. Fay Rulau in the Center for Educational Studies at The Claremont Graduate School tirelessly processed many words through unending iterations.

David Smith, Patrick Olson, Donna Schaeffer, and Martha Estus assisted us with the graphics. We appreciate, too, the encouragement we received early on from Jim Murray of the American Council on Education and the editorial suggestions of Sean Tape of the Oryx Press.

We wish to thank the dozens of faculty members and administrators who found the time amidst busy schedules to participate in interviews for this project.

While it has perhaps become a cliché to thank families for their patience while the work of scholarship edges ever-so-slowly forward, we say to them again "thank you for your support."

Jack H. Schuster
Claremont, California

Daryl G. Smith
Claremont, California

Kathleen A. Corak
Minot, North Dakota

Myrtle M. Yamada
Honolulu, Hawaii

PART
1

··········

The Governance
Challenge

CHAPTER 1

· · · · · · · · ·

Setting the Scene for Strategic Governance

A management revolution has been underway in the United States. According to countless observers, the indicators are visible every where. Indeed, management "reform" is a theme that threads through—arguably is at the core of—the "excellence" literature on effective corporate management. The revolution is manifested in the prominence of "quality of work circles" and the ubiquitous "total quality management" and "continuous improvement" movements and the many variations on those themes. It is evident in the design of General Motors' mammoth Saturn plant in Tennessee and is a characteristic of such recipients of The Malcolm Baldrige National Quality Award as Federal Express and the Xerox Corporation (Garvin 1991).

In education, management reform lies at the crux of the "school restructuring" movement, emphasizing the merits of decentralization in the form of teacher empowerment and site-based management. All of these activities swirl around a central construct, a core value: enhanced employee responsibility and participation. But has this purported revolution penetrated the college campus? Has it affected the way institutions of higher education make important decisions? Perhaps that revolution had succeeded on campuses years ago. Perhaps, it might be argued, campuses have already functioned as an enlightened pathfinder. After all, colleges and universities are assumed to be a natural venue for "collegial" decision making. Or is participatory decision making on campuses more myth than reality—both then and now (Baldridge 1982; Bess 1988)?

Indeed, one of the intriguing developments in organizational behavior over the past two decades, so one argument goes, is that while corporate

3

America has gravitated toward a more collegial management style, colleges and universities, by way of contrast, appear to have moved toward a more hierarchical, old-style "corporate" mode of decision making. Thus, as corporate managers have become more aware of the advantages of empowering employees throughout the organization to help shape significant decisions, higher education's managers, née "administrators," have steadily sought, albeit in the face of adverse conditions, to assume a larger share of the power to make decisions.

If, in fact, the predominant management styles of the American corporation and of colleges and universities are on converging trajectories, how ironic! (Though lying outside the scope of this inquiry, we wonder whether this is really the case. If so, what is the significance of this development? And how is the quality of education affected by the methods colleges and universities use to reach important decisions?)

In the following sections, we set the stage for our concept of "strategic governance." First, we outline the major changes in the higher education environment that are creating new challenges for planning and governance on campus. Then we introduce the respective domains of campus planning and campus governance and the challenge of trying to synchronize those two multifaceted subsystems. Finally, we describe our efforts to find a solution— or, perhaps more modestly, to delineate approaches—that can diminish tensions between planning and governance processes, enabling campuses better to adapt to a highly volatile and complicated future.

THE ENVIRONMENT FOR HIGHER EDUCATION

Colleges and universities today arguably face a more problematic future than has been the case in some years. The litany of unknowns is broad and deep. And changes in the environment are occurring at an ever-increasing pace. At a recent annual meeting of the American Council on Education, Peter Vaill (1993) employed a vivid metaphor to serve notice to colleges and universities that they could expect no respite from relentless and rapid change. He likened the pace of societal changes to a scary ride in permanent white water, cascading through rapids filled with dangers and without a reasonable expectation of quiet water in which to take a breather after negotiating each set of rapids—because the rapids are never ending. The analogy may be overly dramatic, but the message is gripping; the rate of change—in demographics and technology to name just two areas—provides a formidable challenge to any organization. Among the forces that will press hardest on higher education are the following:

- An economy, prone to cyclical fluctuations, that at this writing is saddled with substantial budget deficits at the federal level as well as for many states, thereby severely constraining resources available for higher education, especially public sector institutions.
- A fundamental rethinking of how higher education is to be financed, raising anew basic questions about who pays and who benefits.
- A powerful assessment movement that, yet to lose momentum, demands demonstrable results in the improvement of learning.
- An invigorated effort to elevate the importance of undergraduate education, especially teaching.
- A struggle over curricular reform with mounting pressures to accommodate new scholarship that incorporates more inclusive approaches to knowledge (for instance, a less Euro-centric curriculum).
- A looming large-scale demand for new faculty by decade's end— prompted by a huge wave of retirements *and* by expanded college enrollments—coupled with a porous pipeline for supplying faculty.
- A heightened expectation that higher education can be better utilized to improve the nation's ability to compete effectively in an increasingly more competitive international economy.
- A physical plant, steadily deteriorating, that is in urgent need of rehabilitation, all in the face of anticipated steady increases in enrollments that will fuel pressures to upgrade existing facilities and expand current stock.
- An unremitting pressure (and a mounting moral imperative) to diversify higher education in all its aspects.
- The escalating specialization of scholarly activity that propels researchers deeper (but not often broader) and subjects the scholarly publishing enterprise and academic libraries to unprecedented pressures.
- An increasingly detailed set of governmental regulations that, whatever the social benefits, requires costly compliance activities—from standards for experimenting with animals to assuring physical access for disabled students and employees, from the disposal of hazardous waste materials to reporting on student loan defaults and student athlete graduation rates.
- The explosion of technology that is just beginning to transform modes of teaching and learning in profound ways.

Each of these "megatrends" subsumes a daunting array of interconnected issues. To respond effectively will require very large sums of money—new monies—and redeployed resources. The former is always hard to come by, and the latter is never easy to accomplish because any significant reallocation of scarce resources invariably takes a toll on the entire organization and its leadership.

What are the prospects that adequate resources will materialize? Can resources be marshaled that will not only be adequate to cope with the requirement to maintain operations, but will also be sufficient enough to enable campus leadership to prepare intelligently for the future?

In some respects there is little cause for optimism. Aside from vast sums appropriated for student financial assistance, higher education remains a politically handicapped contender for public monies. Its appeal extends just so far. And higher education's prospects for obtaining its "fair share" of government's disbursements (whether federal, state, or local) are undercut by the growing realization that other sectors of public life have urgent and politically compelling claims on the public treasury. Whatever the flaws of higher education—and they are many—"the system" probably functions better (on the whole) than many other sectors, most pertinently higher education's embattled cousins in elementary and secondary education. But other resource-starved domestic endeavors abound: health care, the environment, job creation, the decaying infrastructure, low-cost housing, public assistance, and the criminal justice system. Big ticket items all!

Thus the future for higher education is replete with challenges. Perhaps that has been invariably and inescapably the case over the decades (Cole 1993). It is clear, however, that higher education's leaders will need great skill and insight to negotiate a way through the awaiting hazards. It would appear that doing "business as usual" will be less viable than in the recent past. While higher education throughout its history has had to cope with wrenching changes—from explosive growth to painful retrenchment—it may well be that the confluence of external pressures and the tensions among higher education's principal constituencies now require a markedly different way of addressing the big, unavoidable decisions that must be reached.

What is called for, we submit, is a better means for defining big issues and a more effective process for making decisions about them (Lozier and Chittipeddi 1986). This will entail a planning process capable of anticipating and articulating the big issues as well as governance structures and processes capable of creating timely policies in a reasonably efficient and politically viable manner.

Under the conditions outlined earlier, it appears that many college and university presidents have been perplexed in developing a strategy to cope with uncertainties. The perplexity derives from two main sources. First, the future appears to be uncommonly difficult to read. The factors enumerated above are among the most important forces that are contributing to the hazy future. Beyond the challenge of setting a direction in the face of swirling crosscurrents, a second factor contributes to the perplexity: how to devise an appropriate governance apparatus. Put another way, how can campuses create mechanisms that both will be reasonably effective in determining priorities for the future *and* will be credible—that is, legitimate and acceptable—to the campus community?

The importance of this governance element should not be underestimated. The "best" plans and strategies are of little use if the campus community—especially the faculty—does not find them legitimate. And they will not be regarded as legitimate—and should not be—if the plans and strategies, regardless of content, are faulty with respect to the process that gives rise to them.

One widespread response to multiple pressures has been the substantial expansion of administrative positions. From an administrative perspective, this expansion has been essential to cope with increasingly complex demands. Financial pressures have led to burgeoning admissions (a.k.a., recruitment) and fundraising staffs. The ever-expanding list of regulatory requirements, state and federal, compel the hiring of implementers.

The most visible and symbolic manifestation of this phenomenon is the multiplication in the number of vice presidents over the past decade or so, often from two or three to six or eight (depending, of course, on campus size). From a faculty perspective, this expansion is typically characterized as "administrative bloat" or "administrative accretion." Accumulating evidence demonstrates that budgets for administration indeed have grown disproportionately to that of academic expenditures (Bergman 1991; Gumport and Pusser 1993). The swelling of administrative ranks contributes to faculty mistrust of decisions of consequence made unilaterally without adequate faculty participation. Indeed, surveys of faculty members consistently reveal a lack of confidence in administrators and a perception that "they" behave autocratically, a depressing point underscored in Table 1.1. Conversely, administrators, in our experience, are often exasperated by what they perceive to be the power and control of faculty: resistance to any reordering of priorities, entrenched "turfism," rejection of the dictates of the marketplace. They seldom voice their frustration "for the record"; political astuteness generally requires a less provocative stance. In sum, the gulf between administration and faculty very often is wide and deep.

THE PLANNING-GOVERNANCE TENSION

A campus's strategic planning and governance functions exist often, perhaps most of the time, in a state of tension, sometimes even in outright conflict. It is commonly thought that an effective planning process cannot afford the luxury of traditional decision making and, conversely, that governance which is shared meaningfully is incompatible with the requirements of a no-nonsense

---

TABLE 1.1

FACULTY ATTITUDES ABOUT ADMINISTRATION AND GOVERNANCE
ITEMS FROM RECENT NATIONAL SURVEYS OF FACULTY

1. "How would you rate the administration at your institution?"[a]

	Excellent	Good	Fair	Poor
All Faculty	6%	30%	35%	29%
Four-year institutions	4	27	36	32
Two-year institutions	9	36	34	21

2. Response of All Faculty to above item ("fair" and "poor" combined) for four surveys:[b]

   1969—46%
   1975—63%
   1984—66%
   1989—64%

3. "Do you feel that the administration at your institution is autocratic or democratic?"[c]

	Autocratic		Democratic	
	Very	Somewhat	Somewhat	Very
All Faculty	30%	39%	25%	6%
Four-year institutions	32	40	24	5
Two-year institutions	28	39	28	6

4. Responses of All Faculty to above item ("very autocratic" and "somewhat autocratic" combined) for three surveys:[d]

   1975—61%
   1984—67%
   1989—69%

5. Percent of full-time regular faculty who were "somewhat satisfied" or "very satisfied" with various dimensions of their job. . . ." (12 categories shown here from among 29 in survey)[e]

My job here overall	85%
Benefits	76
Workload	73
Mix of teaching, service, and administration	72
Quality of leadership in department/program	69
Quality of faculty leadership	68
Availability of support—services and equipment	60
My salary	58
Quality of chief administrative officers	57
Quality of research facilities	54
Relationship between administration and faculty	54
Research assistance I receive	50

Sources
a   Carnegie Foundation for the Advancement of Teaching, *Condition of the Professoriate* (Princeton, NJ: CFAT, 1989), Table 79, p. 107.
b   *Ibid.*, Chart 31, p. 123.
c   *Ibid.*, Table 80, p. 108.
d   *Ibid.*, Chart 32, p. 124.
e   National Center for Educational Statistics, *Faculty in Higher Education Institutions, 1988.* National Survey of Postsecondary Faculty, 1988 (Washington, DC: U.S. Department of Education, 1990), Table 5.1, pp. 60-67.

planning function. Why does this often disruptive tension exist? It is likely so because the two processes are driven by very different priorities and orientations. These tensions—their causes and dynamics—are examined in chapter 2; outlining effective strategies for reconciling these often-opposing forces is the purpose of chapters 11 and 12. But in setting the stage for strategic governance, it is useful to reflect on the current state of campus planning and governance.

Planning

In the 1970s and 1980s, in response to a swiftly changing environment for higher education, many campuses sought to become more efficient at "management" (a term, incidentally, that had been anathema to higher educationists prior to the 1970s). This effort commonly included changing from "long-range" planning to supposedly new and improved "strategic" planning. During that era, numerous campuses, probably most, finding themselves under intensifying financial and often political pressure as well, were obliged to devise new means for coping with changing and, generally speaking, harsher conditions. To address emerging conditions more effectively, campuses routinely developed new approaches to planning.

The 1990s have thus far led to even further belt-tightening in many venues, placing an ever-greater premium on how to accomplish more (or at least as much) with less. Greater efficiencies of all kinds are being required by cost-conscious legislatures and governing boards. Accordingly, the call for efficient management and effective planning has become increasingly insistent.

Governance

Meanwhile, the structures and processes of campus governance have frequently been found wanting. Existing governance arrangements have often been criticized—particularly the faculty's role in governance—for being too sluggish, too obstructive, and too predisposed to preserving the existing apportionment of jobs and resources. In a word, governance has long stood accused of not being equal to the hard, unpleasant tasks of realigning campus priorities in light of emerging demographic, economic, and political realities. In setting after setting, efforts have been launched to adjust the campus's resources to these new demands and to plan for a different kind of future. But these efforts, it appears, almost invariably have been initiated by campus administrations on whose shoulders fall the primary burden of adapting to a resource-scarce environment; it is a process that has produced serious strains in campus governance. These tensions, primarily between faculty and administration, were sometimes seen as undercutting efforts to make the necessary changes.

The widely perceived inadequacies of prevailing planning and governance modes have given rise to a key question. Can effective strategic planning be brought into synchrony with participative campus governance? Or, perhaps, has traditional campus governance become obsolete, simply unable, in its usual versions, to respond adequately to the emerging realities? Put another way, can a campus create structures and processes that will reasonably assure both effective planning *and* effective governance?

SEEKING A SOLUTION

A highly consequential challenge for the contemporary campus, accordingly, is to establish mechanisms and processes designed to bring the planning and governance domains into something approaching harmony with one another. It is not an easy task. But the failure to achieve an acceptable accord will severely handicap campuses in their efforts to prepare for the future intelligently and in such a way that natural tensions between the major constituencies—faculty and administration—are not exacerbated.

The Quest for "Strategic Governance"

This study is based on empirical research undertaken to determine whether models exist for successfully blending the requirements of planning and governance. As indicated in the Preface, we were struck by the suggestion in George Keller's *Academic Strategy* (1983) that a new model was emerging to help effectuate that blending. He labeled it a "Joint Big Decisions Committee." We sought, in consultation with him and others, to identify as many colleges and universities as we could find that purportedly had instituted a "JBDC." That proved to be a more challenging task than we had imagined. We applied Keller's criteria insofar as possible to identify campuses that had established JBDCs. These criteria were described by Keller as follows:

> This new kind of committee is usually composed of selected senior faculty members and key administrators, with some junior faculty, students, or trustee members sitting in at some institutions. The president is usually not a member. It is generally chaired by the chief academic officer. . . . The committee's work and membership are well known, but its deliberations are kept secret (61).

Keller's optimism ran high for this "new body," which he perceived to be "springing up like mushrooms in higher education" and which, furthermore, "has instantly become the center of power in most cases" (61).

Accordingly, our project set out to determine whether the allegedly fresh governance/planning "JBDC" model has to date proved to be a more effective means for campuses to make the "big decisions." Put another way, we wanted to determine whether these "strategic planning councils" (as we prefer to call them) show promise as a means for equipping campuses to deal more effectively with large-scale changing conditions. The answer is consequential because confidence in campus governance mechanisms is shaky at best and because many—probably most—campuses are being asked to achieve greater efficiencies. Accordingly, the question of whether proven approaches do exist for making better "big decisions" has become increasingly important.

Our scrutiny of strategic planning councils led to a consideration of the commonplace tension between the processes of planning and those of campus governance. The challenge was to determine whether these two basic processes or systems, rarely found to be in tune with one another, could be effectively linked through a mechanism such as a strategic planning council (SPC). We sought to discover, based on empirical evidence, whether SPCs could serve well the requirements of both the planning *and* governance. Did the experiences of the eight campuses we identified and visited provide evidence that such bodies worked well and, to the extent that they did, under what conditions were they successful? One result of our inquiry "on the ground," as augmented by our analyses of the general tensions between planning and governance (explicated in chapter 2), was to persuade us of the importance of bringing planning and governance—not, we submit, natural allies—into closer harmony.

Thus we found that our quest was to discover and describe the conditions for assuring what we came to call effective "strategic governance." By the term "strategic governance" we mean not merely campus governance that is reasonably responsive and efficient, but more than that. We have looked for approaches that successfully blend the requirements of intelligent strategic planning with those of legitimate, participative governance. We have tried, more specifically, to determine whether strategic planning councils are a useful model for making the "big decisions" that will guide a campus's direction and will order its priorities for years to come.

On the basis of initial inquiries at campuses, eight sites were identified that appeared to satisfy the criteria of having a "JBDC." Two parallel, related investigations were designed. Site visits were conducted during 1987 and 1988 and the case material—crucial for comprehending complex governance dynamics (Lee 1991)—was analyzed and reported. Both investigations attempted to assess the efficacy of the so-called Joint Big Decisions Committee model. For four of the campuses, the inquiry emphasized the governance aspects of the JBDC model (Yamada 1990; 1991). For the other four campuses, the emphasis was more on strategic planning (Corak 1990; 1992).

We settled on the term "strategic planning council" to refer generically to the committees we examined. We have introduced this term because it allows for the possibility that these bodies might in fact function in ways different from Keller's notion of a "JBDC." And we chose the term "strategic governance" to apply to the objectives and processes by which these (and other) campuses might engage in strategic planning and doing so with special sensitivity to the requirements of shared governance.

In sum, the argument on which the book is predicated is that revitalized structures and processes are required if higher education is to be able to cope successfully. What is needed is a reform that harmonizes planning and governance far better than the often dysfunctional fit. Our quest has been to determine under what conditions the strategic planning council—a vehicle for strategic governance—might be most effective.

The next chapter examines the forces within and upon higher education that are pressing colleges and universities to be more resourceful in their approaches to planning and governance. Our task in chapter 2 is to describe the conceptual tensions we began to see more clearly after analyzing the cases. The chapter attempts to outline ways in which efforts to bridge planning and governance present formidable challenges. Understanding these tensions became important in understanding both the cases and the lessons we derive in chapter 11.

CHAPTER 2

• • • • • • • • •

The Asynchronous Domains of Planning and Governance

With each decade and its particular challenges, higher education has sought to devise structures and processes that would be conducive to effective decision making. The stakes are high; the issues outlined in chapter 1 underscore the necessity of making sound decisions in an increasingly complicated and volatile environment. In this regard, higher education, of course, does not stand alone. The literature in management and organizational theory is replete with the same concerns. Nevertheless, the challenges to higher education's decision-making capacities are different—in considerable measure because of the distinctiveness (some would say peculiarities) of academic culture.

As higher education struggles to respond to changing circumstances, new approaches, theories, and models are constantly being tried. In the 1990s, Total Quality Management (TQM), or Continuous Quality Improvement, has swept from business to higher education in much the same way that strategic planning made that transition in the early 1980s. Skeptics and cynics might suggest that these approaches—like MBO (management by objectives) and PPBS (planning-programming-budgeting systems) before them—are false prophets, unable to deliver on their alluring claims and hardly worth the flurry of excitement they stir (Wildavsky 1973; Baldridge and Okimi 1982).

There is another way, however, to view this succession of decision-making disciplines. Each is part of the ceaseless effort to develop decision-making

13

models that will be responsive to the demands of the times and sensitive to the institution's own culture. As we have reviewed higher education's efforts over recent decades to create and re-create methods for making important decisions, we found that four issues persistently influence the way colleges and universities organize themselves for decision making. These issues, discussed in detail below, are sufficiently long-standing to be regarded as constants. In fact, they are so crucial that they should be regarded as imperatives. Put in other words, higher education's task has been, and will almost surely continue to be, to create a system for decision making that accommodates to and balances these imparatives.

FOUR IMPERATIVES FOR HIGHER EDUCATION DECISION MAKING

In the contemporary higher education setting, four pressures on decision making have become particularly prominent as campuses strive to carry out their missions. These imperatives tend to intertwine with one another, and they sometimes tug in opposite directions (for instance, the values of broader participation and greater efficiency). That is to say, they do not comprise a checklist of crisply defined objectives. Like organizational life, they are complex, messy, and strewn with ambiguities. But these values are basic, and they must be reckoned with if a campus is to be able to cope effectively. The four imperatives are the push for participatory governance, the mandate for efficient management, the urgency to adapt to a changing environment, and the salience of effective leadership. (See Figure 2.1.)

The Push for Participatory Governance

The move to expand participation in governance has been evident in higher education for decades. In the earliest literature on academic decision making, the collegial model was preferred as the most appropriate approach for the academy because of the nature of higher education as a community of scholars (Millett 1962; Etzioni 1964) and because of the importance of academic freedom and the autonomy required to preserve it. The value of participation was promoted by the American Association of University Professors in its 1940 Statement of Principles on Academic Freedom and Tenure and was developed in more detail in a series of statements on governance, most fundamentally the 1966 Statement on Government of Colleges and Universities (AAUP 1990; Statement 1966). (These statements prescribe standards for participatory decision making by faculty, administration, and governing boards.) Indeed, hierarchical models of decision making arguably have been rendered unworkable by a host of related factors, including the emergence of the organizationally complex contemporary university, the professional

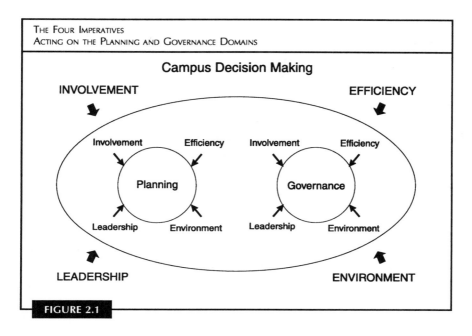

THE FOUR IMPERATIVES
ACTING ON THE PLANNING AND GOVERNANCE DOMAINS

Campus Decision Making

INVOLVEMENT   EFFICIENCY

Involvement   Efficiency   Involvement   Efficiency

Planning   Governance

Leadership   Environment   Leadership   Environment

LEADERSHIP   ENVIRONMENT

FIGURE 2.1

autonomy of faculty, and ever-accelerating specialization in the disciplines. As a result, campuses have struggled to accommodate faculty participation through a variety of forms (Duryea 1973; Floyd 1985).

In the late 1960s, largely because of student activism, the push for participation was extended by students. Student freedoms and responsibilities were articulated; the traditional conception of *in loco parentis* as the basis for defining institution-student relationships withered away (Stamatakos and Rogers 1984). While student participation in governance is no longer the force on campus that it once was, or a subject receiving more than scant attention in the literature, that era produced a variety of inclusive governance mechanisms and established the right of students to have a more meaningful voice.

At the same time, writers on governance focused increasingly on the need for governing boards to take more active responsibility for institutional policies. The student activism of the 1960s and 1970s frequently had targeted the role of trustees, catching many governing boards off guard. Following this period, calls from outside the campus for greater involvement by board members resurfaced and have remained persistent (Association of Governing Boards 1992).

In the 1980s the strategic planning movement introduced a new set of considerations, accentuating the need for institutions to understand their environment better. This movement reinforced the growing emphasis on wider participation. The literature brought to the fore the concept of "stake-holders," suggesting that a variety of constituencies, often situated beyond campus boundaries, had a legitimate stake in the decisions of colleges and universities. Such an inclusive concept reflected an understanding that campus decisions had an impact on—and therefore should be amenable to—parties other than the core, on-campus constituencies. Moreover, the stake-holder concept reflected an awareness that if institutions were to succeed in making fundamental changes, many constituencies would have to be support-ive. To illustrate, campuses that moved from single sex to coeducation learned that alumni support would be essential if so basic a change in mission were to succeed (Cameron 1983; Chaffee 1984; Powers and Powers 1984; Jones 1990).

In all, the demands of strategic planning required higher education to identify and respect important exogenous stakeholders. Thus, beyond the campus's boundaries, the parts played by alumni, legislative bodies, and surrounding communities were perceived as increasingly relevant and impor-tant. These external pressures served to bring higher education institutions, both public and private, back toward the founding conception of state-mandated charters predicated on a governing board's accountability to the state and to the larger community to achieve appropriate institutional stew-ardship.

On campus, meanwhile, the advent of collective bargaining for faculty (and staff, too) introduced dramatically new and often, at least initially, adversarial relationships that strained governance. And the role of staff in the governance process, with or without collective bargaining, received greater attention (Kemerer and Baldridge 1976, 1981).

Depending upon the particular context, successive decades have seen different groups of stakeholders receive prominent attention. In the 1960s the call for the formal participation of students was emphasized, and, indeed, several of the decision-making bodies included in this study emerged out of that movement. In the 1970s the pressure for student involvement, commu-nity involvement, and active board participation grew. In the 1980s, faculty members, seeking to reverse debilitating trends—declining resources for academic programs and a decade of badly eroding academic salaries—intensified their efforts to participate meaningfully in decision making. In the 1990s dwindling resources for higher education—occasioned in part by that sector's weakening claim for resources in competition with other social needs—have forced institutions to make critical choices among competing priorities. In this process, all stakeholders appear to be pressing more vigor-ously for a voice and a seat "at the table." Clearly, then, in recent decades the claims on participation have grown more intense, first in one direction, then in another, but always toward greater involvement, which is to say, toward dilution of the authority and power that might emanate from a single source.

The call for participation emerges, however, not only out of a political process in which various groups seek empowerment, but also out of a deeper understanding of academic culture and what complex organizations, especially professional organizations, must do to function effectively. As early as the 1950s the literature on organizations underscored the importance of individuals and groups having a stake in decision making (Lewin 1951). Today, the call for greater decentralization of decision making, expanded employee participation, and management by consultation permeates the higher education literature as well as the management literature more generally (Bess 1982; Austin and Gamson 1983; Powers and Powers 1984; Dill and Helm 1988; Schuster and Miller 1989; Cameron and Tschirhart 1992.) The call for expanded participation, once articulated most insistently for professional organizations (in which autonomy and expertise were seen as the compelling rationale for participation), has been extended to other employees more generally. The assumption underlying TQM and related movements is that all employees have an expertise to contribute to the organization (Seymour 1992).

These pressures for expanded participation have led to an increasing recognition that a clean separation of authority and power over specific domains is very difficult to achieve in practice. Dual models which once suggested that budgetary matters are purely administrative while leaving academic matters primarily to the faculty are clearly inadequate when a scarcity of resources requires decisions that squarely impact academic programs. Even the student life domain, which until recently has been the almost exclusive preserve of students and student life professionals, has captured the attention of campus administrators and faculty members as concerns about campus climate, harassment, fraternity life, and issues of alienation all extend student life into the academic arena and thereby affect the campus as a whole. Thus, not surprisingly, efforts to create bridges among and between constituencies have accelerated.

In the 1990s, the push for participatory governance will not abate, should not abate, and must be accommodated in the name of legitimacy.

The Mandate for Efficient Management

In part because of the image of collegial decision making as plodding and inefficient, the literature on higher education since the 1970s has often emphasized the need to improve the efficiency with which decisions are made. Indeed, during these earlier periods higher education was compared unfavorably to "sound business practice" in which careful attention to the bottom line and efficiency were considered hallmarks of good decisions.

During the last several decades, for various reasons, the slow pace of academic decision making has been identified as a serious problem. With George Keller's *Academic Strategy* (1983), this campus characteristic received heightened attention and became a matter of even broader concern. The environment of higher education was changing rapidly, and institutions were widely perceived as being poorly positioned to respond to those changes in a timely fashion.

The call for more efficient management also emerged from a critique that decision making, particularly faculty decision making, involved numerous committees—entities, according to critics, that failed to grasp the urgency for change and instead indulged in discourse to fine-tune a system already at risk of becoming inadequate if not irrelevant. Moreover, few if any of these committees had an overall understanding of the impact of their decisions on other bodies. Academic decisions were made based on academic criteria that were criticized as being largely unconcerned with financial realities. Correspondingly, financial and budgetary discussions were undertaken separate from considerations about the academic program. The fundamental challenge has been how to make significant decisions in a timely manner with the flexibility and participation required (Meeth 1974; Bess 1982; Alpert 1985; Chaffee 1985).

In the 1990s, the pressures to achieve greater efficiencies are relentless. The trick is to get there without sacrificing academic values and unavoidable complexity on the altar of efficiency.

The Urgency of Adapting to a Changing Environment

It is no accident that political models of organizations surfaced during a time when conflict—expressed through political interest groups and student activism—was rife. The changing environment of higher education forced many institutions to address both internal issues and an array of external issues— from the Vietnam War, to civil rights, to relationships with local communities. Campuses from Berkeley to Columbia were pushed to attend to the worlds outside higher education. Moreover, the venue of higher education became the focus of attention by critical outsiders, including disenchanted alumni and angry legislators. The boundaries between campuses and the outside world, once relatively impermeable, became more porous. With the deluge of literature in the 1970s and 1980s dramatizing changing demographics—particularly the decline of a traditional college age cohort and the increasing diversity of student bodies—campuses were asked to move from planning processes that had been largely internally focused to processes that engaged the external forces that would inevitably impact the campus in profound ways (Mortimer and Tierney 1979; Crossland 1980; Meredith 1985).

The notion that higher education should—or could—function in ways buffered from external realities had slowly and painfully given way to the realization that grappling directly with changes in the environment was unavoidable (Kerr 1973). The literature, once predominantly emphasizing the necessity of *responding* to changing conditions, began to shift to advocate that the campus stance should be fundamentally *proactive*. That is, what had been perceived as threats to institutional well-being could be transformed into opportunities if the institution could position itself appropriately (Drucker 1980; Chaffee 1985; Cope 1987; Schmidtlein and Milton 1989).

In the 1990s, the external realities—from the characteristics of would-be students to international competitiveness to assessment-minded policy makers—are shaping the academy in profound ways. The challenge is to respond to those realities proactively while still protecting academy autonomy.

The Salience of Leadership

Throughout these recent decades, discussions about leadership have remained continuous even as changing notions of effective leadership have been introduced (Cohen and March 1974). While some authorities (Calder 1977; Birnbaum 1985) continue to suggest that we overestimate the power and effectiveness of a single leader, and while other research on leadership points out that the context of leadership strongly impacts who or what is effective, the importance of skillful leadership nonetheless persists as an imperative of effective decision making (Bennis 1992).

Contemporary research on strategic planning emphasizes that the support and guidance of leaders is essential to an effective planning process (Ackoff 1970; Heydinger 1980; Jones 1990; Schmidtlein 1990). The literature on becoming an effective leader and sustaining leadership qualities is endless (Covey, 1991; Bennis 1992), and the role of presidents, in particular, continues to be depicted as critical to the health of an institution.

The primary change during the last several decades has been a retreat from the belief that a single leader can serve as organizational savior in all times and situations to a more nuanced notion of successful leadership as a fundamentally interactive phenomenon—a function of a good match between institutional needs, individual strengths, and the context in which decisions are being made (Yukl 1981; Fiedler and Chemers 1984; Chemers 1993). In addition, the notion of leadership has expanded to focus on leadership at multiple levels in the institution and as emerging from a variety of organizational roles (Kerr and Gade 1986; Gardner 1989). Faculty leadership, union leadership, and administrative leadership at all levels—not just presidential leadership—need to be addressed to assure effective academic decision making and planning.

In the 1990s, skillful leadership is arguably more of an imperative than ever before. Yet it is all the more difficult to achieve because of the forces that limit a leader's degrees of freedom and power.

ACCOMMODATING THE IMPERATIVES

Simply put, the literature in higher education would seem to suggest that involvement, efficiency, environmental monitoring, and leadership are the keys to effective decision making in the contemporary college or university. These four imperatives, however, emphasize different elements of the governance and planning processes that, in reality, are often in tension with one another.

On most campuses, through the usual governance mechanisms, a reasonably articulated decision-making process is available for making important internal decisions. These processes focus in large part on faculty academic decision making, administrative decision making, collective bargaining (if applicable), and the ways in which these basic areas get coordinated, divided, and shared. Through these governance entities budgets, faculty appointments, program evaluations, and salaries are routinely negotiated.

At the same time, institutions are being pushed to formalize planning processes. The forces at work are formidable. They include environmental changes that require a fundamental rethinking of institutional purposes, practices, and responses to the larger society. Accreditation agencies increasingly urge or mandate a workable planning process. Strategic planning efforts in some form, then, are all but universal. These planning processes generally incorporate opportunities for broad consultation of important stakeholders, focus heavily on the world beyond campus boundaries, and are committed to the proposition that efficiency in response to a changing environment is very important.

Given those pressures, what do we find taking place on many campuses? It is commonplace to see large task forces drawn from a variety of constituencies (including board members, alumni, students, staff, faculty, and administrators) attempt to coordinate a highly complex process of committees, focus groups, and environmental scanners with the ambitious goal of formulating a strategic approach for the twenty-first century. It is a process that often is convoluted, however well intentioned, and can take a full year or much longer to give rise to a "Grand Plan."

In effect, many campuses have created parallel processes: one for governance, to attend to the normal run of institutional decision making; the other for "grand planning," to formulate a more visionary and global outlook for the institution, its mission, and its relationship to the environment. The former process relies heavily on faculty and administrative involvement; the latter often entails broad-based constituent participation. The first focuses mostly inward on the institution itself, the second predominantly on the institution's place in the larger world. The former focuses heavily on organizational practice, the latter on articulating loftier mission and purpose. All of this is to say that the orientations—the centers of gravity—of the governance and planning processes are quite different. At the same time, as we have suggested earlier, all is not well within the respective domains of governance and planning.

Governance

Many campuses have been struggling to address dissatisfactions with governance by redefining administrative and faculty roles as well as by paying more attention to the role of staff in institutional decision making. It well may be that even student involvement, a topic that once commanded the scene, will return in the next few years as a more serious agenda item. There is also increasing recognition that even on small campuses the right and left hands of governance are not always coordinated. Thus, faculty sitting on budget committees may not have adequate perspective on discussions in educational policy committees and vice versa (Bess 1982; Floyd 1985). Not only does there seem to be a lack of coordination and communication among committees, there is also inadequate communication within particular constituencies. That is, the mere fact of participation on committees, representing a faculty or administrative perspective, does not ensure that the "representative" has either discussed or informed the rest of the constituency about the issues under discussion.

Planning

There are a number of problems with typical planning processes. Planning activities often become a means of creating a wish list for new resources that may not be grounded in current realities. In addition, planning activities are frequently criticized for being tremendously time consuming. And not uncommonly the result is a report that may not ever be acted upon, that is, actually result in decisions that significantly change the institution (Schmidtlein 1990).

Efforts to broaden the base of participation by administration or faculty necessarily devolve on a representative (or unrepresentative) few. As a result, any changes have to filter through the normal governance structure. Ironically, then, planning, which was set up to position an institution to respond to a changing environment, often becomes a once every five- or ten-year exercise that is tiring and of questionable practicality. Thus while the process of rethinking the mission of an institution in light of changing circumstances and new opportunities can be exciting and stimulating, the planning process itself is inevitably labor intensive and time consuming. It is not a process that can be repeated very often, and it is often seen as being impractical and even irrelevant (Steiner 1979; Bean and Kuh 1984).

TENSIONS BETWEEN GOVERNANCE AND PLANNING

In many ways, the processes of planning and governance, as suggested above, embody two very different orientations to decision making. Moreover, it is not clear that currently prevailing approaches to planning or governance, conducted independently of each other, are—or can be—at all satisfactory; they must be coordinated. The reality is that serious organizational tensions inevitably afflict the domains of planning and governance—and perhaps especially the intersection of the two activities.

Three such tensions bear particular scrutiny. First is the tension between and among the four imperatives. Second is the tension between superficial representation and genuine participation. A third tension is evident between two fundamentally different perspectives of planning and governance.

Tension among the Four Imperatives

The four imperatives—involvement, efficiency, the environment, and leadership—press on institutional decision making at all levels in ways that are not always complementary, indeed, in ways that are often in conflict. Figure 2.2 represents a somewhat simplistic visual representation of the relationships between the imperatives. The importance of greater involvement and participation in decision making is compelling. Nevertheless, this imperative falls at odds with other imperatives, particularly efficiency.

Consider *the tension between involvement and efficiency*. The traditional model of the visionary leader who changes institutional direction to take advantage of external opportunities requires a hierarchical organization, one in which authority is vested at the top. Such a model is not very compatible with academic culture. The only other models in which relatively few decision makers can quickly act are found in very entrepreneurial *or* highly decentralized settings. In most colleges and universities, particularly public ones, neither of these conditions is present. To encourage involvement and ownership of change requires broad-based decision making within and perhaps outside the institution. Such participation necessarily requires time, including extensive communication to inform, involve, and convince individuals and groups that the change is necessary or desirable. This is true whether those to be involved are part of the traditional decision-making structures, which are not often notable for their efficiency, or whether the

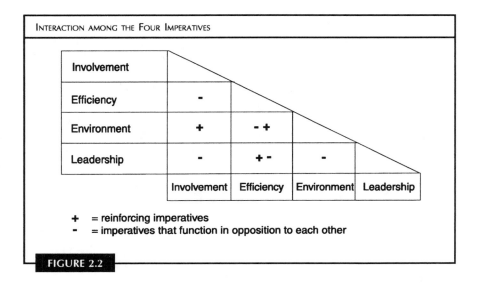

INTERACTION AMONG THE FOUR IMPERATIVES

	Involvement	Efficiency	Environment	Leadership
Involvement				
Efficiency	-			
Environment	+	- +		
Leadership	-	+ -	-	

+ = reinforcing imperatives
- = imperatives that function in opposition to each other

FIGURE 2.2

leaders of governance are reaching out to involve constituents who exist outside of the decision-making structures, or outside of the institution.

Traditional decision-making authority on campuses vests in faculty and administrative structures that recommend or make decisions about programs, budgets, and so forth. Problems arise when *strategic* questions need to be addressed by broadly involving the institutions' many constituencies. The traditional decision-making bodies are marginalized whenever new bodies generate strategic perspectives. At the same time, restricting strategic discussions to traditional decision making narrows perspectives. No easy solution is found in creating new planning bodies designed to incorporate broad-based constituent representation. The number and level of those who inevitably must decide to implement any recommendations that come out of planning processes is naturally limited by practicality. It is not uncommon to create planning processes in which only a few key faculty or administrators are involved. It is rare to include all groups in the discussion. To do so would be both cumbersome and inefficient. This tension is not easily resolved and yet finding a balance is fundamental to strategic decision making.

Thus, *leadership, in whatever form, is in tension with participation.* Efforts to give more participants a genuine voice in the process often seem to compromise the prospects for visible and effective leadership. There is no shortage of outspoken participants who believe that their perspective should prevail, that their views should affect the decision-making process. At the same time, efforts to limit participation of important stakeholders will necessarily limit the possibility for fundamental change. Power and authority are simply too diffuse in colleges and universities to permit extensive unilateral decision making. The proper balance between leadership and broad-based participation is elusive—but necessary.

Consider next *the relationship between involvement and responding to a changing environment*. Here, the relationship is probably more complementary. That is, responding to a changing environment requires greater involvement to build support and also to be able to "read" the environment. As institutions have been impacted by events around them, the boundaries between colleges and universities and the outside world have become more permeable and have required better communication and involvement of many more groups and individuals. Nevertheless, as previously observed, the necessity to respond becomes more complex as involvement grows. Even here, the relationship is not simple.

Turning to *the relationship between efficiency and leadership* we easily could have suggested a more positive relationship. Certainly, the more traditional notions of "strong" leadership lead to a more positive relationship between the two. Today, however, as noted earlier in the chapter, conceptions of leadership underscore involvement, participation, and constituent support. Efficiency is compromised to achieve effectiveness. Nevertheless, strong leadership can be used to guide, direct, and even focus complex decision-making processes (Bennis 1992; Chemers 1993). A more accurate depiction might then include both a positive and negative relationship between the two as indicated in Figure 2.2.

In many ways the rapidly changing *environment* in which colleges and universities find themselves is part of the reason fueling the imperative of *efficiency. But the relationship between the environment and efficiency is complex.* A curriculum project that requires five years may be rendered obsolete by the time it takes effect. Thus, we have suggested a positive relationship between the two. At the same time, however, the very nature of change in the environment requires more involvement and discussion than might be possible in a short time frame.

The "messages" that we get from changing conditions are not always clear and the response not always obvious. During the early 1980s, the declining number of 18-21 year olds was a "fact" that many interpreted would require scaling back and scaling down in preparation for declining enrollments. While the overall number of this age cohort did in fact decline, enrollments in higher education grew because of increases in the number of adult learners. Moreover, in some parts of the country the traditional age cohort did not decline because of immigration patterns and differential birth rates among various population groups. Even here, "reading" the environment requires an astuteness that can be enhanced by discussion and involvement.

Last, we suggest that *the environment presents a challenge to leadership.* While the salience of leadership becomes more pronounced, the possibility of successful leadership becomes more difficult to accomplish. Indeed, prevailing notions about the omnipotence of leadership have been undermined in recent decades due to the increasingly complex and unstable environments that confront organizations of all kinds. The assumptions are no longer credible that crises routinely can be anticipated and averted merely by means of effective leadership or that flawed leadership is the predominant cause of organizational failure. Such oversimplified assumptions are no longer tenable in today's "white water" world. Nevertheless, the demands on leaders for wise and swift responses grow unabated. Thus a certain humility about the power of leadership is necessary while at the same time the need for astute, decisive leadership has become even more salient.

These tensions impact planning and governance processes and thus create a complex interplay of tensions that challenge the current environment for making strategic decisions at the institutional level. It is a powerful challenge, and one that must be resolved.

The Tension between Superficial Representation and Genuine Participation

One of the limitations inherent in most decision-making processes is that representation does not necessarily guarantee that stakeholders will perceive that they actually had a voice. Accordingly, placing one dean, one vice president, one alumni member, one student, and so on, on a planning committee does not necessarily reassure or inform constituencies of their purported participation. Thus most efforts to secure broad participation through simple representation, while looking splendid on paper, are likely to be regarded as superficial—unless the representatives are conscientious and effective in communicating with their respective constituencies.

These tensions appear not only between planning and governance but within each of these domains as well. That is, the tensions among involvement, representation, and leadership exist *within* the planning and governance domains as well as between them. They are inherent and long-standing tensions that exist in organizations that value professional autonomy or believe in the necessity to expand decision making to make better and more responsive decisions.

Differing Perspectives between Planning and Governance

The tensions between the traditional mechanisms of strategic planning and governance can be explained by those domains' differing perspectives. Consider three basic ways in which the two perspectives are at odds with one another. First, they have roots in two fundamentally different orientations or worldviews. This can be expressed in terms of the difference between an orientation to divergent thinking (exploring wider implications and possibilities) versus convergent thinking (focusing on solutions) (Chaffee 1985; Jones 1990; Schmidtlein 1990).

Second, the differing perspectives can be captured by looking at the predominant orientation to time. Strategic planning looks more to the future, while governance's orientation is more grounded in the present.

A third orientation suggests that planning quite often assumes resource enhancement while, in this day, governance is often focused on limitations and hard choices among competing priorities. That is, strategic planning, by its nature, orients its participants to think broadly about expanding possibilities; the planning process often seeks to enhance opportunities through access to new resources or markets discovered via an extended process of information gathering and consultation. In contrast, governance is often focused on day-to-day operations, decisions that tend to be constrained by current resources and limited also by time restraints defined by timelines such as the budget cycle.

The opposing orientations between planning and governance have usually resulted in the use of quite separate structures, processes, and participants. These parallel but not well coordinated domains help to explain why governance, on the one hand, too often seems mechanical and uninspired while planning, on the other hand, too frequently seems unrealistic or too global in reach. How to reconcile the two domains, with their markedly different valences—that is, how to have them adequately inform one another and utilize the strengths of each—and also to reconcile the tensions between and among the four imperatives that press hard on both governance and planning constitutes this book's central inquiry.

THE LOGIC OF ALTERNATIVE STRUCTURES

Many campuses are struggling to devise institutional structures and processes that can adequately respond to and balance the imperatives described in this chapter. Given the tensions inherent in these imperatives and the fundamentally different outlooks that characterize traditional strategic planning and governance activities, it is not surprising that many governance and planning efforts have met with limited success when attempting to reach "big decisions"—the strategic decisions that will set a course for the campus.

The case studies in the following chapters describe campus efforts, in recent times and in varying contexts, to create a single structure and a process that would be capable of responding more effectively to the four imperatives: the call for broader participation, for timely decisions, for responsiveness to the external environment, and for a setting conducive to strategic leadership, particularly presidential leadership.

In suggesting the need to create "joint big decisions committees," Keller can be seen as attempting to combine the features of governance and planning in an integrated model of decision making that could better respond to the imperatives of our time in as parsimonious a process as possible. While attractive in theory, this approach must be examined to determine whether and under what conditions such an approach actually works (Powers and Powers 1984). The eight case studies presented in the following pages, grounded in 131 interviews conducted at those campuses, provide insights into the effectiveness of joint committees—what we have termed "strategic planning councils." We explore their potential for effectively blending campus planning and governance activities. We seek to determine whether the differing perspectives of governance and planning can be integrated in a way that capitalizes on the strengths of each and suppresses their weaknesses. It is this blended, balanced approach to governance and planning—what we describe as strategic governance—to which our quest now turns.

PART
2

·········

The Early Initiatives:
Accent on Governance

CHAPTER

· · · · · · · · · ·

Princeton University's Priorities Committee

Founded in 1746, Princeton University is the country's fourth oldest university, after Harvard, William and Mary, and Yale. Originally located in Elizabeth, New Jersey, where its first president was also pastor of the town's Presbyterian church, the college moved to Newark in 1747 and then to Princeton in 1756.

Chartered officially as the College of New Jersey, Princeton was known initially as Nassau Hall, a name derived from its principal building, and later as Princeton College for its location. The title of Princeton University was officially adopted in 1896 at its sesquicentennial.

Princeton's location combines the advantages of a small town environment with accessibility to larger metropolitan areas. The town of Princeton, surrounded by the farmlands of central New Jersey, adjoins the main campus on three sides. Both New York and Philadelphia are easily accessible.

The university's ties to the past are clearly visible on its main campus with its wealth of architectural styles from the oldest colonial buildings to the predominantly Gothic dormitories. Nassau Hall, the oldest building on campus, housed the entire college for nearly half a century. It was one of the largest buildings in the colonies and played a role in colonial history, surviving bombardments during the Battle of Princeton in 1777 and serving as home for the Continental Congress in 1783. Princeton's town square is modeled after Colonial Williamsburg, and an abundance of traditional architecture is evident throughout the town.

The contemporary university enrolls approximately 6,200 students (4,500 undergraduates and 1,700 graduate students). Since becoming coeducational in 1969, representation of women in the student body has increased to more than 40 percent. The university offers instruction in the liberal arts and sciences and in three professional schools: the School of Architecture, the School of Engineering and Applied Science, and the Woodrow Wilson School of Public and International Affairs. Students come from all 50 states and from more than 50 foreign countries. Admission to Princeton is highly competitive. Approximately 1,100 entering freshmen are chosen from more than 12,000 applicants annually.

The university employs a single faculty to teach both graduate and undergraduate students. Approximately 68 percent of its professorial faculty is tenured. Princeton's approximately 800 faculty (600 full-time, 200 part-time) members includes many eminent scholars and researchers who receive numerous national and international awards annually and includes several Nobel Prize recipients.

Princeton University has enjoyed a history of stable leadership. Its president at the time of this study (1987), William G. Bowen, began his tenure as president in 1972. Before becoming president, Bowen, an economist, had served the five previous years as provost of the university and had been a member of the faculty since 1958. He succeeded Robert F. Goheen who had served as the university's president for 15 years. Neil Rudenstine, provost at the time of this study, was completing his ninth year in that post, having served previously as dean of the college, dean of students, and professor of English literature. Aaron Lemonick, dean of the faculty since 1973, was first appointed to the physics faculty in 1969 and served previously as dean of the graduate school. Incumbents in many other key administrative positions had served in those capacities for more than 10 years. In its governance, Princeton equaled stability.

Princeton's governance arrangements are atypical. The university has no established faculty senate. The faculty, meeting as a body, vote on pertinent academic issues. The faculty consists of the president of the university, the academic officers, the professors, the associate professors, the assistant professors, and when on full-time appointments, the lecturers and instructors. The president (or, in his absence, the provost) presides at meetings of the faculty. Regular meetings of the faculty are conducted once a month during the academic year. Much of the business of the faculty is transacted through 17 standing committees. The standing committees propose and/or review programs, policies, and procedures concerning the academic life of the university.

ESTABLISHMENT OF THE COUNCIL OF THE PRINCETON UNIVERSITY COMMUNITY AND THE PRIORITIES COMMITTEE

Until 1969, the governance structure at Princeton University consisted solely of the faculty standing committees and general meetings of the faculty body.

The 1967-68 academic year proved to be highly volatile. Long-accepted governance arrangements were challenged head-on. Student concerns over the university's relationship to the Institute for Defense Analyses, arrangements for counseling students about the draft, regulations regarding visitors in dormitories, and terms for re-admission of graduate students who had been forced to leave Princeton because of the draft were hotly debated issues. On May 2, 1968, heightened tensions culminated in a demonstration involving over 800 individuals demanding that the university's policies on these matters be changed. In the course of debating these issues, university procedures for setting policy were called into question. The leaders of the May 2 demonstration denounced several past decisions of the administration as "irresponsible" and urged that "we must restructure the decision-making process so that those who live in the university and are most seriously affected by the decisions which control its future are themselves the ones who make these decisions."

With the support of President Goheen and the approval of the Board of Trustees, the Special Committee on the Structure of the University was established in May 1968. The 16-member committee included 8 members of the faculty, 3 graduate students, 4 undergraduate students, and the president of the university (ex officio). Members of the committee were elected by their constituencies.

The special committee examined the university's decision-making procedures in eight areas: rules of conduct, research contracts, the university's affiliations with other institutions and organizations, relations with the local community, conflicts of interest, the budget, development plans, and investments.

The special committee proposed the restructuring of several standing committees to allow for greater participation by students and nontenured faculty. By the spring of 1969, students had attained membership on the standing committees on undergraduate admission, the library, the course of study, examinations and standing, and discipline. Students also established committees parallel to the faculty committees on the course of study and undergraduate life. Faculty membership on the standing committees was also changed to specify the membership of a minimum number of nontenured faculty on each committee.

The special committee also proposed the establishment of the Council of the Princeton University Community (CPUC) as a mechanism for greater student and faculty input into nonacademic issues. The CPUC was charged with three major responsibilities: 1) to consider and investigate any question of university policy, any aspect of the governing of the university, and any general issue related to the welfare of the university and to make recommendations regarding any such matters to the appropriate decision-making bodies; 2) to make rules regarding the conduct of resident members of the university community exclusive of rules regarding academic subjects; and 3) to oversee the making and applying of rules regarding the conduct of resident members of the university community. This proposal was accepted by the university and the charter of the Council of the Princeton University Community (CPUC) was adopted in June 1969.

Except as noted, members of the Council of the Princeton University Community are elected by their constituencies. The membership of the 51 member CPUC consists of the President of the University, the Provost, 4 other officers of the university as appointed by the President, 15 members of the faculty, 12 undergraduate students, 7 graduate students, 4 alumni, and 7 staff members. The business of the CPUC is transacted by six charter committees: Executive Committee, Committee on Rights and Rules, Committee on Governance, Committee on Priorities, Committee on Resources, and Judicial Committee. Special committees are established by the council as needed. Members of the charter committees need not be, and frequently are not, drawn exclusively from members of the council.

The establishment of the CPUC resulted in the abolishment of two standing committees of the faculty, the Committee on Honorary Degrees whose responsibilities had been reassigned to CPUC's Committee on Governance and the Committee on Public Speaking and Debate whose responsibilities were partially reassigned to the Standing Committee on Examinations and Standing. Additionally, the membership of the Standing Advisory Committee on Policy was changed to consist of the six faculty members of the Executive Committee of the CPUC.

The Priorities Committee

The Committee on Priorities is one of the six charter committees of the Council of the Princeton University Community. The committee, chaired by the provost, has 16 regular members: three administrative officers, each serving ex officio (the provost, the dean of the faculty, and the financial vice president and treasurer); six members of the faculty with at least one representative from each of the four academic divisions (at least one of whom must be a nontenured member); four undergraduate students, two graduate students; and one staff member. Faculty are appointed for three-year terms; students and staff are appointed for one-year terms but typically serve two terms. All members are appointed by the provost. Faculty and staff members are appointed with advice from department heads; student members are selected with advice from the elected representatives of the undergraduate and graduate student governments.

The primary function of the Priorities Committee is to advise the president on the budget for the succeeding fiscal year and on long-range plans for resource allocation. The committee's role is to make recommendations that establish in a *broad way* the priorities that govern the use of university resources. It does not perform a line-by-line budget review or involve itself in the day-to-day management of the university. It does not recommend the actual allocation of funds within major budgetary units; these functions are performed by the university officers responsible for those units. Thus while the Priorities Committee may recommend increases in the total number of faculty positions, the assignment of these positions to specific units is determined by the dean of the faculty in consultation with the academic department heads. Similarly, the Priorities Committee recommends the funding level for salary increase pools but individual faculty and staff salaries are determined by department heads with the approval of appropriate university officers.

The Priorities Committee also reviews proposals for funding increases submitted by individual university units such as the library, computing services, athletics, facilities, and administrative and support services. To arrive at a balanced budget, the Priorities Committee reviews both funding requests and increases in student fees (tuition and room and board). The areas reviewed by the Priorities Committee in determining 1987-88 budget recommendations included faculty staffing, facilities, library, athletics, administrative and support services, support for research, computing, salary pools, undergraduate financial aid, student fees, and other charges. Priorities Committee recommendations for the 1987-88 budget included 1) increasing total staffing by 7.0 full-time equivalent (FTE) positions (4.5 FTE in faculty positions; 2.5 FTE in graduate assistant positions); 2) establishing the salary increase pool at $7.8 million, including increases in wages for student jobs; 3) providing additional funding, above normal adjustments for inflation, for the library ($75,000), computing services ($350,000), facilities maintenance ($115,000), athletics ($200,000), and administrative and supporting services ($125,000); and 4) increasing undergraduate student fees (tuition, room and board) by $938 and graduate student tuition by $770.

Over the years, a rhythm for the committee's work has emerged. It usually convenes in October and continues twice-a-week meetings until Christmas vacation. Sessions in October and November are devoted mainly to reviewing requests from individual budgetary units and evaluating those needs and the possibility of deferring requests or making budget reductions. Written requests are submitted to the Priorities Committee by the university officers responsible for those units. Meetings between those officers and the committee are then scheduled.

Initial budget projections for the succeeding year are reviewed in early December. Budgetary units are examined to discover where reductions could be effected or where increases were required, resulting in a set of budgetary recommendations—for tuition and other charges as well as for major categories of expenditures—that could be expected to produce a balanced budget. The tentative recommendations are reviewed with the CPUC before the holiday recess. The committee reassembles in early January to review its tentative recommendations in the context of four-year budget projections that are provided by the provost's office. Final recommendations, including four-year projections, are incorporated into a final report to the president. Every effort is made to reach a consensus within the committee on its final recommendations. Perhaps remarkably, all but one of the final reports issued since the committee's inception have been submitted to the president with the unanimous support of the committee.

While the deliberations of the Priorities Committee are confidential, the committee communicates regularly with the university community. Copies of the written budgetary proposals submitted by the individual units are made available to the community. Periodic progress reports are made to the CPUC, other groups, and through the daily student newspaper, to the wider community. The committee also sponsors at least one public meeting to which members of the university community are invited to discuss the university's financial situation and priorities.

Profile of Interview Subjects

To examine the impact of the Priorities Committee on governance and planning at Princeton University, a total of 15 semi-structured hour-long interviews were conducted with 13 administrators, faculty, and students at Princeton during March of 1987. The interviewees included six administrators (four senior; two mid-level), three senior faculty, one junior faculty, two undergraduate students, and one graduate student. Nine of the 13 interviewees were either current or past members of the Priorities Committee. The average tenure at Princeton University of the interviewees, excluding the students and junior faculty member, was 20 years. Six of the interviewees were with the university prior to the establishment of the Priorities Committee and two were members of the special committee that proposed the establishment of the Council of the Princeton University Community and the Priorities Committee. The interviewees were therefore well qualified to discuss the operation of the Priorities Committee and its impact on the decision-making processes at Princeton University.

IMPACT OF THE PRIORITIES COMMITTEE

The establishment of the Priorities Committee has had a wide-ranging impact on the campus. The committee's effects are evident in the governance of academic and administrative/financial affairs, on the planning and communication processes, as well as on the campus's sense of community.

Governance of Academic Affairs

Princeton University has a long tradition of faculty control over academic affairs. Decisions about the academic program are reviewed primarily by the faculty standing committees on the course of study, examinations and standing, and the graduate school and are voted on by the faculty as a whole. Faculty influence over the academic program is exercised by its individual members, the academic departments and programs, faculty standing committees, and the faculty as a whole. Individual faculty members determine course content, teaching methodology, and evaluation of students. Departments prescribe the course of study for departmental majors, decide what courses are to be offered each term, and propose new courses and programs. Faculty standing committees, within their areas of responsibility, propose and review changes that affect the general requirements of the academic program including the number and distribution of courses, competence in English composition and in a foreign language, regulations for changes in candidacy for a degree, transfers, registration, and so forth. Standing committees also review proposals for new courses and for the establishment of new departments and programs. Recommendations of the standing committees are acted on by the faculty as a whole.

The 13 individuals interviewed unanimously agreed that academic decisions are ultimately determined by the faculty. A senior faculty member with almost 30 years experience at Princeton University commented that Princeton's tradition was one of strong faculty influence over academic programs and curriculum, stronger than in many other institutions. A senior administrator concurred: "Faculty are the ultimate arbiters of academic matters. Only departments can propose curriculum; only the full faculty can approve."

The extent of faculty control over the curriculum, however, was not seen as being absolute. Thus, while acknowledging that final approval of curriculum decisions rests with the faculty as a whole, a junior faculty member commented about the "black box" nature of major academic program decisions, contending that these decisions were essentially made by the president, provost, and selected senior faculty. A senior administrator corroborated this contention by describing the academic decision-making process as one in which new program decisions in effect are made by the dean of the faculty, the dean of the college, the dean of the graduate school, the provost, the chair of the research board, and the president—and then voted on by the faculty. Another senior administrator, while downplaying administrative influence in academic decisions, nevertheless described the close interaction between faculty and administration on program decisions and remarked that the deans of the college and graduate school play important roles in curricular decisions. All interviewees, however, agreed that final approval of academic program decisions rests with the faculty as a whole, with initial reviews of proposals conducted by the appropriate standing committee.

The faculty standing committees and the CPUC are viewed by members of the Princeton community as two separate structures with no overlapping responsibilities. Indeed, in an effort to eliminate the possibility of overlapping responsibilities, the Faculty Standing Committee on Honorary Degrees was abolished with the establishment of the CPUC and that standing committee's responsibilities were reassigned to the CPUC's Committee on Governance.

The Council of the Princeton University Community and its Priorities Committee were established primarily to allow greater faculty and student influence in nonacademic areas. The Priorities Committee, specifically, is concerned with the development of the university's budget and its long-term consequences. While the Priorities Committee has no direct influence over the establishment, discontinuance, or review of academic programs, its budget decisions certainly affect the operations of those programs. Two senior administrators commented that while the Priorities Committee does not decide on new program initiatives, if these initiatives required additional resources, the Priorities Committee would have a say in the funding of those programs.

Governance of Administrative/Financial Affairs

The impact of the Priorities Committee is most evident, as would be expected, on the decision-making processes involving the budget. Prior to the establishment of the Priorities Committee, there were no formal mechanisms for faculty or student input into budget decisions. Previous budget decisions were described by a senior faculty member as being made by a "floating group of notables" consisting of senior administrators and selected senior faculty with the composition of the group changing from decision to decision. Another senior faculty member described governance at Princeton prior to the creation of the Priorities Committee as a "highly benevolent despotism" with budget decisions essentially being made by the dean of the faculty and the financial vice president. A long-time senior administrator and faculty member described the previous budget procedure at Princeton as a simpler process in which the president, dean of the faculty, and treasurer would develop the budget and make budget recommendations to the board of trustees. A senior faculty member commented that this simpler system with its "primitive" level of participation could not survive the rapidly increasing size of the institution (he recalled that enrollment expanded from 4,200 in the early 1960s to 5,600 by the late 1960s) and the push for greater participation in decision making characteristic of the late 1960s at Princeton and elsewhere.

As described by a senior administrator, the establishment of the Priorities Committee resulted in

> broader-based participation into the budget process with the new process providing a mechanism for faculty, student, and staff input into areas in which no formal channel for such participation had previously existed.

Consequently, the establishment of the Priorities Committee, with its membership of administrators, senior and junior faculty, students, and staff, dramatically changed the mix of participants in budget decisions. It provided, for the first time, a formal voice for these various constituencies into budget decisions.

Perhaps the most profound impact of the establishment and operation of the Priorities Committee on administrative and financial affairs was to formalize the budget process. As noted by a senior faculty member, the Priorities Committee process created a new "formalized, continuous, accountable budget process." Another senior faculty member contended that the Priorities Committee process forced the administration to be more explicit and provide detailed reasons for budget recommendations. An administrator agreed that the Priorities Committee process required administrators to be more systematic about the budget process and decisions. He felt that consequently more thought and justification went into budget decisions. Indeed, another senior administrator argued that the operation of the Priorities Committee brought credibility to the budget process by forcing members of the community to provide detailed data and rationales for their proposals.

Governance: A Redistribution of Influence

The activities of the Priorities Committee directly influence budget decisions at Princeton University. To the extent that academic program initiatives require additional resources, Priorities Committee recommendations also influence academic affairs. Within these two areas, to what extent has the Priorities Committee affected the distribution of influence among the various participants?

As previously noted, the CPUC and its committees were established to provide greater student and faculty input into campus decision making. According to a senior faculty member, the establishment of the Priorities Committee was perceived to have weakened the role of administrators in budget decisions because of the larger participation it mandated. He claimed, however, that while the administrative role certainly became more complex and decision making became a longer, more time-consuming process, the administrative role was not necessarily rendered weaker. In fact, he contended, the presence of more constituencies in the decision-making process tended in some ways to strengthen the administrative role as administrators assumed the responsibility for reconciling the views of the various constituencies.

However true that may be, the 13 interviewees unanimously agreed that the establishment and operation of the Priorities Committee increased the influence of faculty in the budget process. The six faculty members constitute the largest group represented on the Priorities Committee. A current Priorities Committee faculty member remarked that the faculty members of the Priorities Committee clearly dominated the process because of "their numbers, the nature of faculty, and some feeling of intimidation on the part of the student members." A student, serving her second year on the committee, concurred that faculty tended to dominate the committee. Further, she felt that the faculty members of the committee exercised a definite influence on the budget decisions based on their knowledge of the academic programs. An administrator observed that faculty members constitute the largest single bloc within the committee. Consequently, he maintained that faculty have the capacity to make important contributions to the decision-making process as their concurrence is necessary to approve the budget allocations. A senior faculty member commented that the faculty "feel they have quite a lot of influence" and that this feeling was as important as the actual influence. Both a senior faculty member and a senior administrator point to the absence of tension within the faculty regarding the Priorities Committee as an indicator of general satisfaction with the level of faculty influence in budget decisions.

While the faculty members of the Priorities Committee are viewed as dominating committee deliberations, the three student members of the committee interviewed for this study clearly felt that student views were taken seriously by other committee members. A student member remarked that student representation on the Priorities Committee was not just "token representation." Indeed, she commented that as all decisions of the Priorities Committee are reached by consensus, a lot of give and take occurs to prepare a final package that can be accepted by all committee members. Consequently, she believed that the views of every member of the committee received serious consideration. Other committee members confirmed this view. A senior administrator allowed that it was sometimes a little irksome to "trade wisdom with someone whose only credential is being admitted to Princeton" (the olden days have not vanished altogether!) but conceded that student input was solicited and respected.

While faculty influence in budget decisions increased with the operation of the Priorities Committee, the role and influence of administrators was not severely diminished. The administrative role in the budget process is described by interviewees as one of guiding or leading the process. The three administrative members of the Priorities Committee are the only long-term continuing committee members because the faculty, student, and staff members generally serve terms of one to three years. Consequently, a senior administrator and member of the Priorities Committee observed that while administrators do not dominate the deliberations of the committee, they are more experienced at it and are responsible for educating the new members of the committee. A student member of the Priorities Committee described the role of administrators as one of steering the proceedings:

> Administrators raised and answered more questions partially because they are more experienced and knowledgeable. They try to direct the discussions and have an idea of where the budget should go but are never overbearing about it and never insist that their proposals be accepted.

Additionally, all of the interviewees credited the role of the administration in initially reviewing proposals and preparing the data for the Priorities Committee as a major influence in the process.

A senior administrator viewed the distribution of influence between administrators and faculty as being very fluid and dependent on availability of resources. He observed:

> If things are going well, more authority over the budget rests with the administration. During times of scarcity, participation levels and faculty input increase resulting in greater faculty influence on decisions.

This might be seen as counterintuitive insofar as conventional wisdom holds that faculty members tend to avoid making tough reallocation or downsizing decisions, thereby ceding to administrators greater influence over "decisions that hurt." Princeton's Priorities Committee therefore may be an exception to the common perception.

Planning

The Priorities Committee was not established in conjunction with Princeton University's strategic planning efforts but in response to student unrest in the late 1960s. It is viewed, however, as one of three bodies at Princeton responsible for planning for the future. The other two bodies are the Committee on Plans and Resources of the Board of Trustees and the Office of the Provost. The deliberations of the Priorities Committee are conducted within the context of planning data provided by various university administrative offices. General data regarding the state of the economy as it affects operational expenses, for example, inflation rates, energy costs, and so forth, are taken into account. Tuition and fees at comparable institutions are examined in setting limits on fee increases. Four-year budget projections are traditionally developed by the Priorities Committee to assess the long-term consequences of their budget recommendations and to illuminate conditions, other than the specific recommendations, that could affect the institution's subsequent budgets. Through its budgetary responsibilities, the committee clearly influences the determination of both short- and long-term institutional priorities and direction.

Fostering a Sense of Community

The Priorities Committee has had a generally positive impact on governance at Princeton University. As noted by a senior administrator, the substantial contribution of numerous participants into budget decisions has served to "legitimize" the budget process. Indeed, a senior faculty member commented that controversy over budget decisions has been "quite muted" since the establishment of the Priorities Committee.

A positive attitude towards Princeton University, its administration, faculty, staff, and students was evident among the 13 individuals interviewed. The attitude is presumably a function of the type of institution Princeton is, its history and traditions, and the faculty and students it attracts. However, the general conviction that the Priorities Committee process presented an opportunity for substantive input from faculty, students, and staff into the budget process apparently serves to reinforce the positive attitudes that all interviewees showed towards the institution and their role within it. The Priorities Committee must therefore be credited with contributing positively to campus morale.

As noted by an administrator, the operations of the Priorities Committee provide an "obvious mechanism" for consultation and a resulting sense of joint decision making and thus give everyone greater confidence in the system. A faculty member echoed these sentiments by observing that the Priorities Committee creates a feeling of participation within the university community. One senior administrator dissented in part, declaring that the Priorities Committee process was generally a "waste of time," but even he conceded that the element of participation is useful:

> There's a lot of pretending. There are also a group of intelligent people sitting around the table talking about important issues. That's useful. It's also the most expensive seminar that has been given.

Another important consequence of the Priorities Committee is its positive impact on the relationship between the faculty and the administration. All of the individuals interviewed agreed that a good relationship exists between the two groups at Princeton University. They all commented that the academic officers of the university, including the president, held professorial positions in departments and continued to teach undergraduate or graduate courses on a regular basis. Consequently, an "us versus them" mentality is noticeably lacking at Princeton.

While the Priorities Committee is not seen as having created these good relations, the committee is credited by five of the nine interviewees who serve or had served on it with promoting a positive relationship. As a senior faculty member put it, the university enjoys a long tradition of good relations between administration and faculty and while the operation of the Priorities Committee is not responsible for creating this relationship, it certainly helps to sustain it. Another senior faculty member characterized the relationship between faculty and administration as "extraordinarily good" and credited the Priorities Committee as one of many committees that contributed to these good feelings. A senior administrator, while crediting the Priorities Committee with fostering positive relationships between faculty and administration, cautioned that unless done competently, the process could break down and create larger problems for the university.

Improving Communication

The operation of the Priorities Committee provided the campus community with greater information about the budget processes and decisions of the university. A senior faculty member contended that an important consequence of the committee's establishment was a wider dissemination of information through periodic progress reports to the CPUC and other groups and through the daily student newspaper.

The earlier analogy comparing the Priorities Committee to a very expensive seminar reveals another consequence of the operation of the committee. Participation in the Priorities Committee serves to educate its members about the budget process. The continued operation of the Priorities Committee is creating an increasingly larger group of individuals knowledgeable about the budget process. As a senior faculty member observed:

> There are a growing number of people who have served on the Priorities Committee, who understand the process, and who can explain it to their colleagues.

Additionally, two interviewees believed that by increasing understanding about the budget process, the Priorities Committee enhanced the ability of the university to respond to crises. A senior administrator commented that

> When it works well, you build a group of faculty and students who understand budget considerations with better sensitivity to budget prob-

lems. So, in times of budget crises, the community is more knowledgeable and able to assist and trust the administrators and the process.

A senior faculty member remarked that a positive aspect of the operation of the CPUC and its committees is that a system is already in place for discussing tough issues when they arise: "Solving problems is not complicated by the need to first decide who should be involved in the discussion."

EFFECTIVENESS OF THE PRIORITIES COMMITTEE

The Council of the Princeton University Community and its Priorities Committee were established to facilitate and increase faculty and student input into nonacademic areas. The Priorities Committee, specifically, was created to allow greater input into the development of the university's budget and to shape the budget's long-term consequences. While the Priorities Committee has no direct influence over academic program decisions, its budget decisions certainly affect the operations of academic programs.

How effective has the Priorities Committee been in influencing nonacademic matters? The Priorities Committee was unanimously viewed by the interviewees as a "major center of campus influence," particularly with respect to budget decisions. Most tellingly, as noted by a senior administrator, the recommendations of the Priorities Committee have always been adopted by the president and the trustees.

Committee membership is valued not only because of the committee's impact on budget decisions but also for the opportunity to interact on a regular basis with senior administrators at Princeton, including the provost and the dean of the faculty. Committee members do pay a price; members typically have not served multiple terms because of the large workload associated with membership on the committee.

It must be remembered that the role of the committee is to make recommendations that establish in a broad way the priorities that govern the use of university resources. The Priorities Committee thus fixes the total pool of money available for various general purposes; these include such crucial matters as faculty salary increases, faculty staffing, student financial aid, and graduate student support. However, the committee's overall impact is more difficult to assess. This is because the Priorities Committee also functions within limits established by trustees' guidelines and by senior administrators. Indeed, since much of the university's budget is fixed, one faculty member estimated that the Priorities Committee only dealt with a tiny fraction— perhaps only 1 percent—of the university's annual budget.

Disagreement exists over the extent to which the Priorities Committee served as a rubber stamp for administrative decisions. One senior administrator contended that the Priorities Committee did not decide issues; it was "pushed and cajoled" into making budget decisions that were not substantially different from those that would have been made unilaterally by the administration. Further, he observed that the Priorities Committee functions within limits set by the president and senior administration. A senior faculty member estimated that most of the decisions of the Priorities Committee fell within 2 percent of what the administration would have decided. However, he believed this congruence to be the result of the development of a broad understanding among committee members rather than the result of administrative manipulation.

Indeed, 10 of the 13 interviewees believed that while the Priorities Committee process was clearly guided by the administration, with the administration providing the data and rationale for the proposals under review, the Priorities Committee did not serve as a rubber stamp for administrative decisions. A student member of the committee commented that a genuine opportunity for discussion and interaction is available in committee meetings. A faculty member echoed these sentiments noting that proposals with strong Priorities Committee opposition were dropped from consideration. Further, one administrator recalled several instances in which support was increased for proposals above levels anticipated by the administration because of insights provided by the Priorities Committee.

Quality of Decision Making

With two exceptions, the individuals interviewed strongly believed that the Priorities Committee enhanced the quality of budget decision making at Princeton University. A senior faculty member suggested that both the quality of decisions and the decision-making process improved significantly as a result of the establishment of the CPUC and the Priorities Committee. He recalled that at the time of the first Priorities Committee deliberations the associate provost felt that the budget decisions were better made because all recommendations had to be explicitly "spelled out" to the committee. The faculty member contended that the need to support recommendations before the Priorities Committee required administrators to be better prepared and to "think harder" than was previously required. The general consensus of the interviewees was that budget decisions were more informed and more thoughtful; the operation of the Priorities Committee resulted in higher quality decisions.

One senior administrator, however, commented that he could not believe that a mechanism had not existed prior to the Priorities Committee for reaching good decisions, and thus, he doubted that quality had been enhanced to any great extent. Another administrator, while agreeing that the quality of decisions had been improved by the operation of the Priorities Committee, suggested that the extent of any improvement was not great:

Decisions may have been different without the Priorities Committee, *on the margin*, and probably not as good, *on the margin*, as might have been made centrally.

Another administrator commented that he believed the quality of decisions to be "terrific"—with one qualification. He observed that

members sometimes tended to compromise in reaching decisions by trying to accomplish as much as possible for as many as possible. It was therefore hard [for the committee] to make sharp determinations of policy.

A senior administrator with 19 years of experience at Princeton placed the question of quality within the context of the times. He observed that prior to the establishment of the Priorities Committee, Princeton was a smaller place. The budget problems of the early 1960s were relatively small with budget surpluses in many years and an abundance of federal money. The budget process could afford to be more informal and less participatory. In all, the old process produced quality decisions for its era.

But by the late 1960s, Princeton had grown, the climate was more turbulent, and the need for participation was greater. Additionally, budgets were becoming increasingly more complex. The old informal system was not working, and a new mechanism was needed—one that was more inclusive and that provided a more orderly process for hearing and weighing budget requests. He firmly believed that Princeton could not have survived the problems of the 1970s and early 1980s without a process like the Priorities Committee, and thus felt that, within this context, the Priorities Committee process improved the decision-making process and the quality of decisions.

Factors Contributing to the Effectiveness of the Priorities Committee

Several factors contributed significantly to the success of the Priorities Committee. First, the Priorities Committee enjoyed the support and commitment of senior-level administrators from its inception. President Goheen served as an ex officio member of the Special Committee on the Structure of the University that proposed the establishment of the Council of the Princeton University Community and the Priorities Committee. William Bowen (then the provost) and a senior faculty member are credited as the principal drafters of the charter for the CPUC. Provost Bowen then chaired the Priorities Committee until he became president of Princeton University in 1971. Presidential support of the Priorities Committee is most evident in the fact, as noted, that all recommendations of the committee have been accepted by the president since its inception. Further evidence of senior-level support of the

Priorities Committee can be inferred from regular committee attendance by the administrative "varsity"—the dean of the faculty, the vice president of administrative affairs, the financial vice president and treasurer, and the budget director. In addition to the provost serving as chair of the committee, the associate provost serves as secretary for the committee.

Second, skillful leadership of the committee is viewed as essential to its effectiveness. A senior administrator contended that "intelligent, wise, thoughtful leadership" was crucial. He opined that without skillful and strong leadership, the committee could fractionate and the process might disintegrate. Another administrator remarked that the single most important factor in the effective operation of the committee was the presence of a chair able to lead the group and sensitive to its role and discussions. In addition to adept personal leadership, administrators need to provide realistic guidelines and set parameters for committee deliberations and decisions. Further, administrators must provide committee members with accurate and adequate information. This administrative involvement ensures that informed decisions will result from committee deliberations.

Third, committee membership is also deemed to be crucial. As one interviewee put it, for the committee to be effective, its members must be "serious, intelligent, competent, responsible, respected" members of the university community. And, according to the consensus, the committee has been generally blessed by such members.

Fourth, as one senior administrator contended, the relative homogenous nature of the university was also essential to the effectiveness of the committee. He remarked that it would be difficult to achieve consensus on the committee if the university were not relatively homogenous or if it were much larger and more complex. Another senior administrator agreed. He suggested that the presence of a single faculty was a crucial factor—that a mix of professional and liberal arts faculty likely would be unable to reach consensus. A senior faculty member also cautioned against exporting Princeton's system to other universities unless the other institutions "have the same elements— people who know each other and wish each other well." A senior administrator argued that the chances of a system like Princeton's working well at other institutions was "very small"; there were numerous potential obstacles—the importing institution might be too complex, the committee leadership might be inadequate, the institution and its committee might lack the analytical capacity to review financial data, or the committee might be used merely as window dressing for administrative decisions. He remarked that other Ivy League institutions had established more participatory systems at about the same time as Princeton but that Princeton's was the only one still operating.

Prior to this site visit to Princeton University, President Bowen and Provost Rudenstine announced their intent to leave Princeton to join the

Mellon Foundation. (Rudenstine was later appointed president of Harvard University in 1992.) A presidential search process was underway as the interviews were being conducted. When questioned about possible changes in the Priorities Committee due to the forthcoming change in administration, a faculty member remarked that the Priorities Committee was part of the "established bureaucracy" at Princeton; he would be surprised if the new leaders "do away with the system." A senior administrator commented that the reason the Priorities Committee has existed so long is because "people believe in it and believe it's necessary." Because of this, he believed that the system, or something like it, would continue under a new administration.

CONCLUSION

The Priorities Committee at Princeton has functioned effectively for over two decades. Created for a focused purpose, its effects have been widespread. There are differences of opinion concerning whether the committee's impact is substantial or, rather, is seriously circumscribed by guidelines propounded by the governing board and senior administration. Nevertheless, the committee is generally perceived as having had a constructive impact on governance, planning, and communication.

It may be that pre-existing characteristics at Princeton—including its relatively small size for a university, its great affluence providing a buffer against excruciating decisions, its tradition of close faculty-administration relations—were conditions present for the Priorities Committee to take root and thrive. Whether or not Princeton's distinctive environment is a prerequisite for the success of a mechanism like the Priorities Committee, that is to say, whether or not the Priorities Committee is exportable, the committee's effectiveness at Princeton cannot be gainsaid.

CHAPTER 4

· · · · · · · · ·

Northwestern University's Budget and Resources Advisory Committee

On May 31, 1850, a physician, three attorneys, two businessmen, and three clergymen met in an office above a hardware store in Chicago, then a struggling frontier town. They were determined to provide for the young men of the Northwest Territory access to a higher form of education than was then available. The institution that they envisioned, Northwestern University, was officially chartered in 1851. On the date of its founding, Northwestern had no faculty, students, campus, or buildings, and only $9.92 in the treasury.

In 1853, John Evans supplied $1,000 in cash and assumed a mortgage for the balance of the $25,000 necessary to purchase the original 380 acres of land along Lake Michigan as a site for the new university. Because of his contribution, the community that grew up around the university was named Evanston. In 1855, with the completion of its first building, Northwestern's College of Liberal Arts opened with two faculty members and ten students. By 1900, Northwestern was a university composed of seven graduate and undergraduate schools with 2,700 students. Northwestern's growth in those early years was achieved mainly by the acquisition of a group of professional schools including a School of Law and medical and dental schools.

Today, Northwestern is a large, private research university located on two lake-front campuses in Evanston and Chicago. Northwestern offers more than 150 undergraduate and graduate programs through 12 academic divisions: College of Arts and Sciences, School of Speech, School of Music, J. L. Kellogg Graduate School of Management, McCormick School of Engineering and Applied Science, Graduate School, Medill School of Journalism, School of Education and Social Policy, School of Law, Medical School, Dental School, and University College. About two-thirds of all degrees and four-fifths of post-baccalaureate degrees granted at Northwestern are in professional fields.

Northwestern University enrolls approximately 15,000 students (7,400 undergraduates and 7,600 graduates). Admission to Northwestern is highly competitive with approximately 1,800 entering freshmen selected from an annual pool of some 11,000 applicants. Students are enrolled from all 50 states and more than 70 countries.

The university employs approximately 1,700 faculty (1,350 full-time, 350 part-time); 70 percent of the full-timers are tenured. Northwestern has a single faculty for undergraduate and graduate education. Consequently, all faculty members are expected to perform research as well as teach, the majority at both the undergraduate and graduate levels. Faculty members are the recipients of numerous professional awards annually including Guggenheim, National Endowment for the Humanities, Rockefeller Foundation, and Ford Foundation fellowships.

The two chief executives of Northwestern University, prior to the appointment of a new president in February of 1985, served long tenures in that position. The longest tenure of any Northwestern president was that of J. Roscoe Miller, president from 1949 to 1970 and chancellor from 1970 to 1974. Miller's presidency was marked by growth in funding, faculty, salaries, and facilities. During Miller's tenure, the university grew from 800 faculty and an annual budget of $17 million to 1,200 full-time faculty and an annual budget of $109 million.

Robert Strotz was appointed to succeed Miller as president in 1970 and served in that post until early 1985. Strotz had come to the university as a faculty member in the economics department in 1947 and had served as dean of the College of Arts and Sciences from 1966 until his appointment as president.

The early years of President Strotz's administration were financially stable for the university. However, beginning in 1972 various faculty groups, concerned about continued projections of costs rising faster than income along with declining undergraduate and graduate student enrollment, urged the administration to devote more attention to long-range financial planning. The administration, however, resisted these faculty recommendations, choosing instead to rely on its policy of "grassroots opportunism"—described as a flexible quest for excellence by seizing targets of opportunity—to guide its financial and development activities.

Concerned over a perceived lack of institutional leadership, in 1976 a faculty committee was formed to investigate collective bargaining at Northwestern. While the committee concluded that strengthening faculty governance, not collective bargaining, was needed, anxiety over Northwestern's financial condition mounted. These fears were realized over the next five years as Northwestern's budget situation worsened.

Beginning in 1978, Northwestern experienced a sustained period of budget deficits. While the 1977-78 and 1978-79 deficits were budgeted deficits, a three-year plan to restore balanced budgets, adopted in 1979, failed to achieve its goals as expenditures continued to exceed revenues in the next three fiscal years. The 1981-82 year ended with a deficit of $8.8 million. In 1982, in opposition to faculty arguments for a gradual reduction of the deficit, the board of trustees, concerned with the university's credit rating, directed President Strotz to correct the deficit in a single year and mandated that the 1982-83 budget be balanced. The budget was balanced by resorting to tough measures: increasing tuition, instituting a hiring freeze, decreasing central administration costs mostly through personnel layoffs, decreasing funds for maintenance, and providing only minimal faculty and staff salary increases. These measures brought the trustees their prize; the 1982-83 year closed with a surplus of $1.4 million.

The period of sustained deficits and budget cuts and the resulting turmoil and heated debates over eliminating the deficits sorely tried the presidency of Robert Strotz. Declining faculty morale and confidence in Strotz's ability to correct the budget situation without harming the institution resulted in an overwhelming vote of no confidence against Strotz by the faculty of the College of Arts and Sciences. In September of 1983, Strotz announced his desire to be relieved of his responsibilities as president. In early 1985, Strotz was named chancellor, and Arnold Weber, previously president of the University of Colorado, succeeded him as Northwestern's new president.

GOVERNANCE AT NORTHWESTERN UNIVERSITY

The University Senate, various university committees, the academic deans' council, and the associated student government comprise the major governance bodies at Northwestern University. The University Senate's membership is large; it includes all professors, associate professors, assistant professors, and various officers of administration. The senate, which meets quarterly, is presided over by the president of the university. The senate considers matters of general interest to the university and matters that affect more than one school. It may make recommendations involving educational policy, recommend candidates for honorary degrees, or elect committees of faculty members to consider policies within the powers of the senate.

The General Faculty Committee (GFC) is one of eight university committees. As the only totally elected all-university faculty committee, the GFC functions in effect as Northwestern University's faculty senate. It is composed of 21 members, including 18 elected as representatives from the various schools and three at-large members. Members of the committee are elected for staggered three year terms. It is charged with representing the faculty of the university and presents recommendations to the faculty at large (that is, the university senate), the president, or other members of the administration on behalf of the faculty.

The seven remaining university committees are Budget and Resources Advisory Committee, Educational Policies Advisory Committee, Faculty Planning Committee, Policy Advisory Council, Research Policies Advisory Committee, Staff Advisory Council, and University Faculty Reappointment, Promotion, Tenure, and Dismissal Appeals Panel.

THE BUDGET AND RESOURCES ADVISORY COMMITTEE

The Budget and Resources Advisory Committee (BRAC) was established in 1970 by resolution of the University Senate. Its charge was "to participate with and advise the chancellor, president, and other administrative officers of the university in every phase of preparing the annual budget and to participate and advise in preparation of the long-range (five-year) budget."

The committee is composed of seven faculty members: three members of the General Faculty Committee and four members-at-large. Faculty are nominated by the chair of the General Faculty Committee for BRAC membership and are appointed by the GFC to serve three-year staggered terms. Faculty are selected for BRAC membership to provide a balanced representation from the various schools at Northwestern and are normally selected from the senior faculty. The president, the provost, the senior vice president for business and finance, the vice president for administration and financial planning, and the assistant vice president for planning, analysis, and allocation attend all BRAC meetings and participate in deliberations, but they are not voting members of the committee.

Since its inception, BRAC has concentrated on reviewing the overall budget of the institution and on recommending funding for general categories of expenditures, for example, compensation pools, maintenance, general support services, and central administrative services. BRAC is not involved in the allocation of resources within the university to individual schools or departments.

During the Strotz administration, the Budget and Resources Advisory Committee conducted numerous meetings. During periods of financial stress more than 18 three-hour meetings with senior administrators were held annually. Additional meetings were held with only committee members in attendance or with the deans of various schools. All budget items were open for discussion. Many meetings were devoted to line-by-line examinations of the administration's proposed budgets.

Under the Weber administration, BRAC meetings have been reduced to five or six meetings annually and are scheduled in conjunction with a more formalized budget calendar. Initial meetings are devoted to an examination of the past year's budget and revisions of the present year's budget. Subsequent meetings focus on general budget categories and the budget for the following year. Funding for the faculty salary increase pool, tuition, and financial aid levels are areas discussed annually by BRAC. The other areas reviewed by the committee for the 1986-87 budget included support accounts, deferred maintenance, liability insurance, and funding for guest lecturers.

While BRAC deliberations are confidential, the committee reports regularly to the General Faculty Committee. It also issues an end-of-the-year report to all faculty summarizing BRAC's activities, recommendations, and subsequent decisions by the administration regarding the coming year's budget. (The committee was renamed the Budget and Finance Committee in 1988, one year after the site visit.)

Profile of Interview Subjects

To study the impact of the Budget and Resources Advisory Committee on governance and planning at Northwestern University, a total of 23 semi-structured hour-long interviews were conducted in March 1987. The interviewees included 10 administrators (seven at senior level, including the president, the current provost who had been in office for only three months, the previous provost who had served as provost during the Strotz administration, and three at mid level), 11 faculty members (all full professors), and 2 undergraduate students. Seven of the 23 individuals interviewed were either current or past members of the BRAC. Excluding the students, their tenure at Northwestern ranged from 1 to 30 years with an average of 14 years. Sixteen of the interviewees had joined the university prior to the establishment of the Budget and Resources Advisory Committee.

IMPACT OF THE BUDGET AND RESOURCES ADVISORY COMMITTEE

BRAC's impact can be discerned in many aspects of campus life. Its direct influence over academic affairs, determining the budget, and planning is marginal. BRAC, however, does provide a vehicle for faculty input into the budget process (if not substantial influence) and for better communications between faculty and administration.

Governance of Academic Affairs

Northwestern University has a strong tradition of faculty control over academic affairs. Everyone interviewed unanimously agreed that academic decisions are controlled by the faculty. A senior administrator contended that faculty logically decide academic matters because they possess the "decisive, critical information on questions of program and curriculum." The dean of one of the schools concurred that curriculum matters were really the faculty's prerogative. A senior faculty member agreed that academically the university was run by the faculty and maintained that within the academic domain, no issue existed over which the faculty felt they did not have sufficient control. Another senior faculty member described faculty input as "paramount" in academic decisions.

Faculty control academic affairs centrally through their membership in the University Senate and the activities of the Educational Policies Advisory Committee (EPAC). The University Senate recommends general educational policy. BRAC's direct influence on academic decision making is minimal. This is because the EPAC deals with curriculum, instruction, and other matters of educational policy. EPAC membership consists of nine faculty and student members, at least five of whom are faculty members. Faculty members are appointed by the president for three-year terms; student members are appointed by the Associated Student Government for one-year terms.

Effective control over academic affairs rests within Northwestern's schools and colleges. Only actions that involve the interests of another school or college require the approval of the University Senate. Faculty within the individual schools and colleges have wide powers over academic matters. Under the terms of the University Statutes (established by the board of trustees), the faculty of each college or school determines admission requirements, prescribes and defines the course of study, determines degree requirements, recommends candidates for degrees, and establishes rules and regulations for student discipline.

The influence of colleges and schools over academic affairs results from Northwestern's long tradition of school autonomy and powerful deans. As mentioned earlier, the university's evolution from the original liberal arts college to a major research university was accomplished mainly through the acquisition of strong professional schools. Northwestern was described by a senior faculty member as a "collection of fiefdoms" with strong school structures. Consequently, the faculty influence over academic decisions is exercised mostly at the school level. A senior faculty member described the curriculum approval process for undergraduate courses as originating within a departmental faculty curriculum committee and ending with that school's curriculum committee. Graduate courses require the additional approval of the Graduate School.

The Budget and Resources Advisory Committee has no direct impact on academic decision-making processes and decisions at the university. BRAC's charge restricts its activities to the development of the university budget. Its focus on general budget issues—for example, faculty salary pools and central administrative services—additionally limits its influence on academic affairs. However, as all budget decisions impact the operation of academic programs, BRAC indirectly influences academic affairs at the university.

Governance of Administrative and Financial Affairs

The Budget and Resources Advisory Committee was established to advise senior administrators on the preparation of annual and long-term budgets of the university. It is the only university committee with budgetary responsibilities, and thus it is the only committee with potential to influence the development of the budget. However, BRAC's influence over budget decisions is not large; indeed, 19 of the 21 nonstudent interviewees characterized BRAC's direct influence on the budget to be minimal.

Perhaps the major impact of the committee on university administrative and financial affairs was to widen participation in budget processes and decisions. A current administrator and former BRAC chair recalled that prior to the establishment of the committee there was no formal mechanism for faculty input into budget decisions. Additionally, even senior administrators are said to have had little input as budget decisions during the Miller presidency were made primarily by him.

One senior administrator described BRAC as providing a vehicle for faculty reaction and views about budget strategies. All interviewed administrators and faculty agreed that BRAC successfully fulfilled this objective. A faculty member who had been at Northwestern for over 25 years remarked that there was more faculty input into budget decision making since the establishment of the committee.

Another major impact of the Budget and Resources Advisory Committee was to validate the budget process. The establishment of the committee provided a formal mechanism for faculty to interact with administrators on budgetary issues. A senior administrator contended that this interaction "validates the credibility" of the budget process to the faculty.

Governance: A Redistribution of Influence

Established to provide a formal mechanism for faculty input into budget decisions, BRAC, as noted, has had very little direct impact on academic affairs at the university. Academic affairs continue to be controlled by the faculty through their schools and colleges. Consequently, BRAC's activities have not significantly affected the distribution of influence among the various participants in academic affairs.

But has the establishment and operation of the committee affected the distribution of influence among the various participants in the budget-making process? Specifically, has the operation of BRAC enhanced the influence of the faculty in budget decisions?

It appears that the committee has led to greater faculty input into budget decisions. The committee provides a formal mechanism for faculty input into budget decisions. As a senior faculty member commented:

> The name of the game [in any university] is keeping the faculty informed and giving the appearance that faculty input is sought. BRAC provides the structure for doing so.

In this sense, faculty influence has increased because of the operation of BRAC. A senior administrator and former faculty member suggested that BRAC gave faculty "significantly more influence than they had before." In fact, he reported, the administration resisted the establishment of the committee and tried to contain its influence. Another senior administrator agreed that BRAC had generally enhanced faculty influence. A senior faculty member agreed that faculty influence improved substantially with the committee's establishment. She contended that without BRAC, faculty at Northwestern were relegated solely to a reactive mode. BRAC's establishment, at a minimum, allowed faculty to bring issues to the attention of the administration.

There were different perceptions about how the faculty role had changed with the new Weber administration. One senior faculty member contended that BRAC had been more influential in budget decisions under the Strotz administration. Another senior faculty member perceived a significant improvement in faculty influence over budget decisions under the previous president and a slight deterioration of that influence under the current president. A senior administrator concurred that faculty "probably had more influence on budget decisions in the past than now."

But others had a different perspective. One senior faculty member disagreed, arguing that the previous administration had mostly disregarded faculty input. Another faculty member concurred, contending that President Weber sought more faculty input than did President Strotz and took that advice more seriously. She believed that the old administration was not very comfortable with the operation of BRAC and, in contrast to the new administration, did not take the committee seriously.

While BRAC has provided a means for expanding faculty influence in budget decisions, it has not significantly decreased the influence of the administration over these decisions. As a senior faculty member asserted, the administration "holds the upper hand" in most decisions at Northwestern. Indeed, because BRAC's role is limited to providing reaction to a budget that has been prepared by the president and his senior administrators, the inescapable conclusion is that administrators exercise decisive control over consequential financial decisions.

The existence of BRAC did nothing to expand the influence of students on budget decisions. Their influence had been, and continues to be, nonexistent in these matters. Indeed, the two students interviewed saw no need for student input into the budget process. They reported that while students desired a stronger role in curriculum decisions, they had no desire to take part in budget decisions.

Planning

The impact of the Budget and Resources Advisory Committee on planning at Northwestern University is marginal. As noted, BRAC's purview is limited to reviewing annual and multi-year budgets that have been prepared by senior administrators. While budget decisions certainly influence the development of institutional programs and activities, BRAC's impact on the actual development of these budgets is slight.

Additionally, the governance structure at Northwestern divides various planning-related activities among three committees. The Budget and Resources Advisory Committee is the only committee with budgetary responsibilities. The Faculty Planning Committee recommends long-range institutional policies affecting the future direction and development of the university, while the Policy Advisory Council recommends long-term university goals, program development, human resources allocations, and investment priorities. This separation of responsibilities further limits BRAC's ability to influence planning.

The April 1982 report of the Budget and Resources Advisory Committee expressed the committee's continued frustration in convincing the university to develop long-range budgets "which could express the priorities of the university and provide a framework for evaluating allocations in the short-run budget." It reported that while BRAC had repeatedly urged multi-year budgeting, it had never been implemented by the administration.

In 1986, President Weber reported on Northwestern's strategic planning efforts over the previous 18 months. The comprehensive set of goals and programs, called the "Framework for Distinction," outlined university-wide priorities and plans for achieving academic excellence in teaching and research. The framework was developed with input from the Policy Advisory Committee, other faculty, students, members of the board of trustees, and alumni. The BRAC had no formal role in the development of the framework.

Improving Campus Climate

On a more positive note, the Budget and Resources Advisory Committee is credited with improving the climate of the university community by improving faculty-administrative relationships at Northwestern. The committee prevented major confrontations by providing administrators with an "early warning system." The establishment of the committee was also viewed as a sign that administrators were willing to listen to faculty and thereby helped to ease tensions between the two groups.

There were dissenters. Three of 13 interviewees who commented on the relationship between the faculty and the administration characterized that relationship in negative terms. One, a senior administrator, submitted that committees like BRAC serve to "heighten conflict" and create an "adversarial relationship" between the two groups. Another senior administrator reported that BRAC's operation was not helpful in easing relationships during tough times as committee members were seen by dissatisfied faculty to have been co-opted by the administration. A senior faculty member and former BRAC member suggested that the committee did not help relations between faculty and administration in the past because committee members felt they were not getting accurate information and were thus wasting their time.

One interviewee believed that the Budget and Resources Advisory Committee exerted no influence over the relationship between faculty and administration. Nine of the interviewees, however, argued that BRAC had served to improve these relationships. A senior faculty member and former BRAC member argued that the existence of BRAC prevented major confrontations between faculty and administration, serving as a "lightening rod in both directions." He opined:

> There's no question that relations are far better off for the existence of those committees and for the fact that they are taken seriously.

Another senior faculty member reported that BRAC fostered good relations between faculty and administration by providing a "good sign that the administration was willing to listen to faculty to discuss something as sensitive as the budget." A senior administrator with 11 years of experience at Northwestern reported that the faculty-administration relationship benefited by the committee's existence, especially during periods of high tension on campus. He remarked:

> Without committees, we would have been an anarchy. The committees provided an outlet for discussion and confrontation.

Another senior administrator commented that committees like BRAC served to foster good relations between faculty and administration. Further, he argued that "if we did not have it, we would have to invent it."

Improving Communication

The Budget and Resources Advisory Committee serves as an important source of communication between administrators and faculty. A senior faculty member conceded that while BRAC is not a major source of influence at Northwestern, it is at least a major center of communication. Another senior faculty member described BRAC as being "immensely useful in providing a point of contact between administration and faculty." A former administrator suggested that university committees like BRAC are the "best communication link from the administration to the faculty." Another senior administrator agreed:

> I think that it's [BRAC] very important because it's an opportunity [for the administration] to communicate with the faculty to give them a sense of direction and a sense that the University is being managed in a very systematic and professional way.

Indeed, all 21 of the faculty and administrators who were interviewed agreed that providing a communication link between the faculty and central administration was an important function of the committee.

A senior faculty member, while acknowledging the importance of such communication, voiced concerns that instead of providing for meaningful communication, BRAC was used primarily as a "sounding board" for administrative ideas and decisions. Another senior faculty member worried that under the Weber administration, BRAC was used more as a "source of affirmation for administration decisions rather than as a deliberative body."

In that vein, another senior administrator described BRAC's most important role as that of a "sounding board." Another mid-level administrator saw BRAC as a vehicle for building support for administrative initiatives, summing up:

> The committee has access to what the administration is thinking about relative to faculty salary increases, tuition increases, student aid issues, so it's a very important communication process. In the past, it probably had more influence on the outcome. Now it's tilted more to being a way for the administration to communicate and build up support for the direction it is presently taking.

EFFECTIVENESS OF THE BUDGET AND RESOURCES ADVISORY COMMITTEE

The Budget and Resources Advisory Committee, as noted, was established to provide formal faculty voice in the preparation of the annual and long-range budgets of the university. While BRAC, as the only recognized university committee with budget advisory responsibilities, may have the potential to influence the development of Northwestern University's budget, it is a potential that is mostly unrealized. A senior faculty member and recent chair of the General Faculty Committee remarked that BRAC was not effective in influencing the university's budget and that BRAC had no real role in setting budget priorities. A mid-level administrator (one of the first BRAC chairs) observed that while BRAC had "some influence" over the development of the annual budget, it was not a major influence. A senior administrator contended that BRAC is "not a joint decision-making group" but is a vehicle for "reaction and input" into budget strategies. The current chair of the faculty senate acknowledged that while BRAC has "no real participation in setting the university's budget," it is seriously "listened to" by the administration though "clearly in an advisory capacity."

Only 3 of the 21 nonstudent interviewees at Northwestern believed that BRAC was influential in budget decisions. Two of the senior faculty members contended that BRAC had once exerted a "strong impact" in shaping the budget—prior to the Weber administration. Both believed this impact has diminished under the new administration. A third faculty member, a former senior administrator, was the only interviewee to contend that BRAC was influential in the "central development of the budget." These three constitute a distinct minority.

Several examples illustrate BRAC's minimal influence over the budget. In 1978, to avoid continuing budget deficits, BRAC advocated reduction or elimination of programs and activities over several years. This advice was not followed. In reviewing the 1982-83 budget, BRAC presented a list of proposals for the reorganization, contraction, and elimination of administrative units. While a few of the proposals were implemented, the majority were not. For the 1983-84 budget, the administration called for $3 million in budget cuts in academic and administrative areas from the base 1982-83 budget. The BRAC sought meaningful involvement in this budget-cutting process, but the committee reported that it was "informed that we could not usefully participate" in the process.

Development activities and priorities are another example of BRAC's unsuccessful attempts to influence university policy. Since 1978, BRAC has consistently urged the administration to curtail its "grassroots opportunism" development policy—a strategy that emphasized development activities for specific schools and activities—and instead to focus on an institution-wide campaign to build the operating budget of the university. This advice was consistently ignored until recently.

BRAC's influence is perhaps most notable with respect to faculty salaries. One school dean thought that the only area in which BRAC had a reasonably serious impact was in salary pool allocations. A senior faculty member argued that BRAC was instrumental in keeping faculty salaries from "lagging further behind than they did."

BRAC's overall influence, as noted earlier, is perceived to have changed with the new administration. A senior faculty member, and former General Faculty Committee chair, remarked:

> Previously, BRAC had a strong impact in shaping the budget. It really was involved in making the budget. It will not be involved to the same degree now.

Another faculty member and former member of BRAC agreed:

> Previously, BRAC was influential in decisions. The new president has greater control over the budget. . . . He may use it [BRAC] more as a source of affirmation for administrative decisions than as a deliberative body.

Although many of BRAC's recommendations were not accepted, all the administrators and faculty interviewed agreed that BRAC received a serious hearing from the administration. In spite of its inability to secure acceptance of many of its proposals, eight of the interviewees believed that BRAC's influence over budget decisions and processes cannot be ignored. A senior faculty member contended:

> BRAC has made a positive contribution. Their influence has been felt. The university [administration] pays attention to BRAC. If BRAC is unhappy with something, notice is taken. BRAC does make a difference.

Another senior faculty member and a former BRAC member argued that BRAC has been "taken seriously" by the administration. He believed that BRAC was a major influence when problems and major disagreements existed.

Quality of Decision Making

Perhaps the Budget and Resources Advisory Committee's most important contribution, despite minimal influence on final budget decisions, was enhancing the "quality" of those budget decisions. Most of the interviewees— nine of the 13 who commented on the quality of budget decision making— agreed that BRAC had had a positive impact in that regard. As a senior faculty member reported, the establishment and operation of BRAC:

> ... enhanced quality through providing more input and in agitating and
> making necessary changes. . . . Quality is much better now than before.

One senior administrator argued that BRAC's most important role was that of "quality control" over budget decisions and priorities. He argued that decisions were not only substantively better because of BRAC's involvement but also politically better because the opportunity for formal faculty input into the process fostered easier acceptance of budget decisions by the general faculty.

Two senior administrators dissented, however. One administrator (with one year's experience with BRAC) felt that BRAC had not improved the quality of budget decisions. Another administrator, with an 11-year tenure at Northwestern, concluded that on the whole, BRAC's influence on the quality of decision making was neutral—sometimes good, sometimes bad. He contended that President Strotz had made bad budget decisions because of BRAC's influence, especially in heeding the committee's advice to grant large faculty salary increases and to increase tuition; the result, he said, contributed to Northwestern's budget deficits.

Factors Limiting the Effectiveness of the Budget and Resources Advisory Committee

Several factors contribute to the Budget and Resources Advisory Committee's lack of substantial influence over its life span. Perhaps the major factor limiting BRAC's influence is Northwestern University's structure and tradition of strong school autonomy. A dean of a professional school with a three-decade tenure at Northwestern characterized the university as a "decentralized" institution where deans have substantial discretion. BRAC has no role to play in the allocation of resources to or within individual schools. Those decisions are made by the president in consultation with the deans of the schools. Consequently, budget decisions that directly affect the operation of academic programs are made well beyond BRAC's limited scope of influence.

Second, the composition of the committee's membership also serves to limit its effectiveness. The all-faculty membership, nominated by the chair of the General Faculty Committee, is selected to provide a balanced representation from the constituent schools. As a senior administrator commented, however, BRAC's members are selected for their representativeness, not their competence. Indeed, Northwestern's tradition of strong schools is seen as being responsible for shaping a faculty perspective limited to their respective schools or, in the words of one senior administrator, "parochial." Another senior administrator lamented that a "series of very bad faculty leaders" [of BRAC] had "kept energy focused on 'wrong' issues." A senior faculty member judged the effectiveness of BRAC to be "highly dependent on the chair and his interests." Still another senior administrator concurred:

> . . . leadership of BRAC is critical to its role and influence. The chairperson must be energetic in drawing up meeting agenda and in engaging administration to provide the necessary information to the committee in advance of the meetings so that meaningful dialogue may occur.

Third, lack of senior leadership support also limits BRAC's effectiveness. The committee is a creation of the faculty, motivated initially by concern over projected budget deficits and a perceived lack of institutional leadership. A senior administrator recalled that BRAC encountered resistance from the administration, especially from the president, in its early years, resistance aimed at containing BRAC's influence. The current administration has shown no interest in increasing the function of the committee. As noted by two senior administrators, BRAC is not a "decision-making body"; it is instead a "vehicle for faculty reaction and input into budget strategies."

SUMMARY

Northwestern's Budget and Resources Advisory Committee can be said, at one level, to function effectively. It was created with a limited purpose in mind, and it appears to fulfill that limited purpose reasonably well. BRAC is most certainly not a means for addressing issues of strategic planning, and it positively does not afford faculty entrée to that domain. It does provide faculty with a say in the year-to-year budget deliberations, but primarily as a sounding board, as a mechanism for communicating to the administration that aspects of the budget are badly off the mark. In those instances, the faculty's reactive voice appears to exert a positive influence, to provide a means for enhancing the "quality" of budget-related decision making—albeit at the edges.

Thus BRAC functions on a relatively small playing field. What it does within its restricted purview, it does reasonably effectively. But BRAC is no model for balancing the needs of strategic planning and governance. It never was intended to be.

CHAPTER 5

Teachers College's
College Policy Council

Teachers College was founded in 1887 by the philanthropist Grace Dodge and the philosopher Nicholas Murray Butler. The origins of Teachers College can be traced to the Kitchen Garden Association which was incorporated in 1880 to promote domestic industrial arts training for young women. In 1884 the Industrial Education Association replaced the Kitchen Garden Association and trained both young men and women in household and manual arts. The Industrial Education Association was transformed into the New York College for the Training of Teachers in 1887. When it received its original provisional charter from the Regents of the University of the State of New York in 1889, the college employed a faculty of 13 and enrolled 150 students. The college was granted its permanent charter in 1892 under the corporate name of Teachers College.

Teachers College moved from its downtown New York location to its present site in upper Manhattan in 1893. Soon after, the property adjacent to Teachers College's new location was purchased by Columbia University. The Teachers College campus today consists of several large buildings occupying a city block on West 120th Street opposite the main campus of Columbia University.

In 1892 the trustees of the college offered to turn Teachers College over to Columbia University "only to have the proposal rejected . . . on the grounds that 'there is no such subject as Education and moreover it would bring into the university women who are not wanted.'" However, with the support of Columbia's President Frederick Barnard, Teachers College was formally affiliated with Columbia University in 1898. The affiliation has been maintained through successive agreements between the respective trustees of Teachers College and Columbia University. Under the present arrangement,

Teachers College functions as Columbia's graduate faculty of education. Although a part of the university for academic purposes, Teachers College remains a separate corporation responsible for its own financial support, budget, plant, personnel policies, and internal organization and administration.

In addition to teachers' training, Teachers College introduced some of the earliest advanced programs of nursing, health, nutrition education, and applied psychology. Today, Teachers College is an independent graduate school preparing students for careers of professional service in schools, colleges, universities, hospitals, clinics, business organizations, day-care centers, community agencies, government bureaus, and research facilities. Teachers College offers more than 90 graduate programs leading to master's or doctoral degrees through five academic divisions: Philosophy, the Social Sciences, and Education; Psychology and Education; Educational Institutions and Programs; Instruction; and Health Services, Sciences, and Education.

Teachers College (or "TC," as it is almost universally known) enrolls approximately 4,000 students. Fifty-one percent of the college's students have been admitted to doctoral study or are studying beyond the master's degree; the remaining 49 percent are in master's or nondegree programs. Less than 40 percent of the students matriculate on a full-time basis. Students are enrolled from all 50 states and over 70 countries.

The faculty of the college, in 1987, consisted of approximately 140 full-time employees of professorial rank, 76 percent of whom were tenured. Teachers College also employed an equal number of adjunct professors, visiting professors, lecturers, and instructors.

The college has endured long-term, continuing enrollment and financial problems. Enrollment remained stable during the late 1960s and early 1970s at approximately 5,500 students annually. Between 1976 and 1986, however, TC experienced a 25 percent decline in enrollment. During that same period, the number of faculty at Teachers College was reduced by 17 percent.

In 1974, Lawrence Cremin assumed the presidency of Teachers College. President Cremin was an alumnus of the college and a senior faculty member at TC prior to his appointment. While Teachers College managed to operate in the black during the first two years of his presidency, the next six years ended in deficits.

In 1981, P. Michael Timpane joined Teachers College as dean of the college. He succeeded Lawrence Cremin as president in 1984. Teachers College's financial situation did not improve significantly during President Timpane's tenure and has managed in most years to just break even. Its financial independence from Columbia University and its lack of an undergraduate student base, coupled with declining enrollments, limit its efforts to achieve financial stability.

GOVERNANCE AT TEACHERS COLLEGE

Although affiliated with Columbia University for academic purposes, Teachers College, as noted, is a separate corporation with an independent board of trustees. While all degrees are granted by Columbia University, TC is solely responsible for its own financial support and operation.

Governance at Teachers College is shared by several groups, among them, the trustees, the president and other senior administrators, the faculty, and the College Policy Council. Teachers College has no established faculty senate. Much of the faculty business is conducted through five standing committees: the Faculty Executive Committee, the Faculty Advisory Committee, the Faculty Personnel Committee, the Faculty Salary Committee, and the Faculty Committee on Academic Affairs.

Unlike the various faculty committees, the College Policy Council has a broad-based membership, as outlined below. Membership in the College Policy Council is the primary means for professional staff and students to participate in college governance.

THE COLLEGE POLICY COUNCIL

The establishment of the College Policy Council (CPC) in 1972 was a major outcome of student demonstrations at Columbia University in the late 1960s and early 1970s. Those demonstrations led students at Teachers College to push for more involvement in college governance. A committee was appointed by then President John Fischer to examine governance at TC. The committee, consisting of an associate dean, a faculty member, and a student, reported that many of the policy decisions at Teachers College were being made without the involvement of the college's various constituencies. The committee recommended establishing a representative council to serve as the policy-making body for the institution. The College Policy Council was subsequently constituted and began functioning in the fall of 1972.

The CPC's history has been complicated, even convoluted. The Statutes of Teachers College (March 7, 1985) stipulate the operation of three governance bodies: the College Policy Council, the Faculty Advisory Committee, and the Faculty Executive Committee. The Faculty Advisory Committee serves as a grievance body for academic appointees; the Faculty Executive Committee operates as Teachers College's faculty senate. The College Policy Council has four major responsibilities: 1) to consider, formulate, and define policies regarding the purposes, priorities, and general allocation of the resources of the college; 2) to consider and act upon proposals for institutional policies of the college as they relate to programs, personnel, organization, operation, and finance; 3) to advise the president, the dean, and the vice president for finance and administration in the preparation of the annual budget; and 4) to establish regulations concerning student academic discipline. The council also assists in the initial search for the president and the dean of the college and conducts periodic reviews of major administrative officers and academic programs.

The 40-member College Policy Council is the only governance body at Teachers College with representation from the various constituencies—administrators, faculty, students, and professional staff. Chaired by the president, the council consists of the following members:

- Ten *administrators*, all serving ex officio: the president, the dean, the vice president for finance and administration, the vice president for development and external affairs, the controller, and the five directors of the instructional divisions.
- Eighteen *faculty members* (functioning also as the Faculty Executive Committee): five elected at large; 13 elected to represent the five divisions.
- Nine *student members*: eight elected members plus the chair of the student council.
- Three elected members from the *professional staff*.

A 14-member Executive Committee of the College Policy Council serves as its steering committee, sets the agenda for council meetings, and acts on behalf of the council between meetings. It is composed of five faculty, two professional staff, three student members who are appointed from among the elected members of the CPC, and four administrators. The Faculty Executive Committee (as distinguished from the Executive Committee of the CPC) designates the faculty members to sit on the CPC Executive Committee; the Professional Staff Advisory Committee designates the representatives of the professional staff; and the student senate designates the student representatives. The president, the dean, the vice president for finance and administration, and the vice president for development and external affairs serve as ex officio members of the executive committee.

Prior to the establishment of the CPC, two faculty committees—the Faculty Executive Committee (FEC) and the Faculty Advisory Committee—had been the major governance bodies at Teachers College. The Faculty Advisory Committee served as the grievance committee for academic appointees. Its role was unaffected by the establishment of the College Policy Council.

The Faculty Executive Committee's major responsibilities involved curriculum and general academic matters. Its membership and responsibilities were expanded to form the College Policy Council; consequently, with the establishment of the College Policy Council, the Faculty Executive Committee ceased to function as a separate committee for a while. It later reappeared as faculty dissatisfaction with the CPC grew.

Originally, CPC meetings were held twice a month. As prescribed by current bylaws, the council, at the time of this study, held regular meetings four times during the academic year. Meetings of the CPC are open to any Teachers College member and minutes of the council are distributed to all faculty. Nonmembers may participate in council discussions only at the invitation of the council.

Profile of Interview Subjects

To examine the impact of the College Policy Council on governance and planning at Teachers College, a total of 14 semi-structured hour-long interviews were conducted in April 1987. The interviewees included seven administrators (including the president), five full professors, one associate professor, and one student. Of the 14 individuals interviewed, 13 were either current or past members of the CPC. Excluding the student, the tenure at Teachers College of the interviewees ranged from 3 to 37 years with an average of 18.5 years. Most of the interviewees—9 of the 14—had joined TC prior to the establishment of the CPC.

IMPACT OF THE COLLEGE POLICY COUNCIL

The CPC's impact can be discerned, in greater or lesser degree (mostly the latter), in various aspects of the college's life. These include its effect on the governance of academic affairs and administrative/financial affairs, on planning and communication, on the distribution of influence among constituencies, and on campus climate more generally.

Governance of Academic Affairs

The faculty of Teachers College play a central role in determining the academic affairs of the college. The statutes of Teachers College grant faculty the ultimate authority to fix requirements for student admission, programs of instruction, and student academic discipline, and to recommend the conferring of degrees and diplomas. Proposals relating to the academic program are reviewed primarily by two faculty committees—the Faculty Executive Committee and the Faculty Committee on Academic Affairs.

Proposed program changes are submitted to the Faculty Committee on Academic Affairs by faculty after reviews by departmental and divisional program committees. The recommendations of the academic affairs committee are submitted to the 18-member Faculty Executive Committee for consideration. The Faculty Executive Committee is responsible for receiving, considering, discussing, and acting on concerns and proposals as they relate to the educational program of the college.

The College Policy Council also has some responsibilities in the academic affairs realm. It reviews institutional policies relating to programs of the college, and it has authority to establish regulations concerning student academic discipline. Indeed, its purview over student academic discipline directly conflicts with the faculty's authority in that area. Consequently, a strong potential for tension exists between the purely faculty bodies and the CPC itself.

Prior to the establishment of the CPC, the Faculty Executive Committee exercised substantial influence over academic issues. A senior faculty member and division director reported:

> When the Faculty Executive Committee was really the Faculty Executive Committee, before the CPC [was created], if you wanted to construct a new program and even new courses, you would have to go to the Faculty Executive Committee and defend yourself and prove that this was a viable program. . . . It was done on a collegial level but the questions were very severe and there was much less overlap than there is now.

As noted, however, the original Faculty Executive Committee temporarily ceased to exist with the establishment of the CPC.

In its early years of operation, the College Policy Council was more actively involved in academic affairs. A senior faculty member recalled that between 1972 and 1979 the College Policy Council functioned as an active "legislative body" and examined "the whole gamut of issues—curriculum, appointments, budget, instruction, and research."

The role of the College Policy Council, however, did not remain consistent over the years. An administrator commented that "enthusiasm for CPC had diminished." Another senior faculty member reported a definite change in the College Policy Council beginning in 1980. He characterized the change as one from an "active participative body to a pro forma body" with meetings reduced from 12 or 14 a year to merely 3 or 4 in recent years. Indeed, a senior administrator stated that in recent years the College Policy Council had taken only two formal actions every year:

> One is to approve the academic calendar for the following year. The second is to review the budget of the College and recommend it or make other commentary on it to the Board of Trustees. . . . There are not many real issues joined.

The re-emergence of the Faculty Executive Committee was viewed by all the faculty interviewed as an attempt to recapture faculty control over academic issues. A senior administrator described control over academic affairs as a:

> function that has been given back to the faculty. The faculty set up an academic affairs committee which has gradually been rebuilding.

Another administrator reported:

> When it turned out that CPC didn't do that job [rigorous review of program/course changes] because it wasn't a collegial body, course overlap proliferated, and [there were] lots of other things that faculty sensed were out of control. Those things are now [what] they are trying to get back under control, like the Academic Affairs Committee.

A senior faculty member described faculty authority today over course changes or the development of new courses as "complete." Another senior faculty member concurred and maintained that there is "very strong faculty input and very strong faculty participation in decision making" regarding curriculum issues. He maintained that faculty exercise "an awful lot of autonomy in creating courses." This authority, however, is tempered by budget considerations.

Teachers College's continuing financial problems limit faculty influence and correspondingly increase the influence of administrators. A senior faculty member reported that the staffing of new courses and programs are now approved by an administrative advisory group called the "Deans and Directors"; consequently, "D & D" plays a significant role in curriculum decisions. He commented:

> There are some very important budgetary and curriculum decisions that are made in D&D because [D&D] has an effect on personnel.

An administrator contended that faculty influence over academic matters is greatest in regard to issues that can be resolved within a single program but diminishes as issues move away from the program level:

> As issues emerge which move away from the program, usually they pertain to the budget, then faculty influence diminishes rapidly; division directors become more powerful. It's harder for a division director to say, you teach this, you teach that. It's almost unthinkable. But it's very easy for a division director to say I'm not going to support a new position and in the process you're saying, you can't teach this. . . . So policy issues, as you move away from the department, become clouded in exigencies. So therefore, administrators take over responsibility for planning academic affairs.

All 14 of the individuals interviewed agreed that the College Policy Council had little impact on academic decision-making processes and decisions at Teachers College. Instead, faculty and administrators, acting outside the CPC, exerted the greatest influence over academic issues.

Governance of Administrative/Financial Affairs

A major responsibility of the College Policy Council is to advise the president, the dean, and the vice president for finance and administration in the preparation of the annual budget. The advisory nature of the CPC was clearly recognized by all 14 individuals interviewed.

The impact of the College Policy Council on budget decisions can best be described as minimal. The interviewees unanimously agreed that the CPC had very little influence over the development of the budget. The CPC review of the budget is mostly characterized as form without substance. As a senior administrator commented:

> In fact, the College Policy Council does not spend much time reviewing the budget and its decisions are relatively pro forma.

Two administrators stated candidly that CPC's role in the budget process was mainly to "legitimize" the budget by providing the appearance of community input. Another administrator agreed, suggesting that CPC's actions served only to "mobilize prestige":

> A lot of what happens here happens because a prestige structure sanctions it and things follow that. In that sense, CPC is an important part of that process.

Nevertheless, a major influence of the College Policy Council on administrative and financial affairs was to open up the budget process. A senior faculty member reported that the College Policy Council made the budget-making process "a very, very public matter" since prior to the existence of the CPC "the faculty and the community in general were hardly advised at all about what was happening" regarding the budget.

In addition to advising the campus community about the budget process, the College Policy Council provides an open forum where representatives of the various constituencies can discuss issues. It thus fosters a sense of participation in college decision making. An administrator reported that the CPC provides "at least one forum where everybody sits together." Similarly, a senior faculty member described the CPC as giving "people a forum for having a sense of participation."

Governance: A Redistribution of Influence

The College Policy Council was established to provide a vehicle for participation by faculty, staff, and students in the major decisions affecting Teachers

College, including program and budget decisions. However, as suggested above, a consensus among interviewees holds that the College Policy Council exerts minimal influence over academic and budget decisions. Despite its lack of influence, has the College Policy Council affected the distribution of influence among the various constituencies within these two key areas?

For one thing, the College Policy Council provided students a formal voice in college decision making for the first time. While the interviewees agreed that student representatives to the CPC were "listened to seriously" during CPC deliberations, students by all accounts exerted little influence over decisions ultimately reached by the council. For example, student members on the CPC have consistently and strongly opposed tuition increases proposed in the annual budgets and accordingly have voted as a bloc against approval of budgets. Every year, however, the budget was passed by the CPC without revising proposed tuition increases. A senior faculty member claimed that students were never intended to exert any influence over college decisions:

> [The CPC] served a function in giving students a "sense" of participating although I don't believe it was anyone's intent at any time to give students an actual voice or actual power in the participation. I think that this is sort of a legacy from the sixties and seventies. . . . But since in fact, to my knowledge, no one else is involved really in making these decisions, there is absolutely no reason why students should be. And they are not.

The seven individuals questioned about the impact of the College Policy Council on faculty influence agreed that the role of faculty in college governance had been severely diminished. A senior faculty member suggested:

> The major result of the CPC was to dilute the faculty voice in governance. . . . Faculty unrest has come about because of the fact that the faculty had given up so many of its powers to the CPC.

Another senior faculty member described the faculty as being "disenfranchised." A senior administrator concurred:

> It has led to a disempowerment of the faculty. . . . I think what happened was that CPC took up so much time and energy that the faculty has been spread very thin over its assignments, and I think faculty feel a large amount of frustration about that and blame a lot of that on CPC.

This pervasive feeling of faculty disempowerment led the faculty in the spring of 1986 to create an ad hoc committee to examine governance at Teachers College. In April 1987, the faculty overwhelmingly voted to formally separate the Faculty Executive Committee from the College Policy

Council. The Faculty Executive Committee was henceforth to operate as an independent group involved exclusively with faculty-related matters. Additionally, the FEC members would no longer serve as the faculty members of the CPC. During the 1987-88 year, the nine carry-over FEC members would remain on the CPC. The matter of CPC membership past the 1987-88 academic year was to be discussed at a later date.

The chair of the Faculty Executive Committee commented:

> The CPC doesn't serve us [faculty], it cannot serve us. . . . If the faculty want to accomplish what they want to accomplish, the organization of the faculty will have to be strengthened.

An administrator viewed the faculty action as taking "back to themselves some of the power they gave to the CPC." Another administrator believed that the faculty action would result in the Faculty Executive Committee serving as a "more potent force" in college decision making.

The College Policy Council's impact on the administrative influence in college decision making is best described as negligible. A group called the "Deans and Directors" ("D&D") serves as the senior administrative advisory group to the president, and this group has the greatest impact on decision making. D&D is composed of the five directors of the instructional divisions, the three vice presidents, and the directors of the major research institutes.

A student member of the College Policy Council remarked:

> The administration dominates the operation of the CPC. They make the ultimate decisions. The administrators are the only ones who have the overall picture of what's happening.

An administrator commented on the strong role senior administrators play in policy decisions:

> My sense is the presidents [of Teachers College] were very, very powerful people. The presidents and deans were always very powerful people in this institution and essentially it was kind of a laissez faire faculty.

A senior faculty member concurred:

> Traditionally, from what I can tell, I think that Teachers College has operated in the past as a fairly closed corporation in terms of decision making. The president, Larry Cremin, was a strong person with strong preferences who liked to get his way. The place was pretty much administratively run.

Another administrator with a 20-year tenure at Teachers College agreed. He described the past president's relationship with the College Policy Council as follows:

> You appoint a committee only when you know what you want it to decide
> and you put people on the committee who you know will decide that. He
> did what was necessary to keep CPC at least symbolically thinking that it
> was doing something.

The Deans and Directors are characterized as a major influence in college
decision making. A veteran administrator remarked:

> Real power is held in the Deans and Directors and it wasn't so much in
> the group meeting as it was that's where the powerful people met, so the
> power tended to be localized there. . . . I've never seen a vote taken [in
> D&D] but it's a way you influence the president and the dean. . . . It's
> usually the last body consulted by the president and the dean.

He maintained that the CPC had no impact on the distribution of influence
or the decision-making processes at Teachers College. A senior faculty
member with 24 years' experience at TC agreed:

> Basic decisions were still made by the same people—the D&D and the
> senior administrators.

Planning

As described earlier, the College Policy Council, created as a direct result of
student unrest in the late 1960s and early 1970s, was launched to provide
broader representation in the decision-making processes of Teachers College.
It was not established for the purpose of furthering TC's planning efforts. The
broad responsibilities of the council, however, provide it with major opportunities to influence plans and planning. Those responsibilities include formulating resource allocation policies; considering institutional policies regarding programs, personnel, organization, operation, and finance; preparing the
annual budget; and establishing student academic discipline regulations.
Decisions in any of these areas directly affect programs and planning at
Teachers College.

As noted previously, the actual impact of the College Policy Council on
both academic and financial affairs appears to be negligible. Accordingly, the
CPC's inability to influence either academic or financial decisions results in a
corresponding inability to influence planning at Teachers College.

Impact on Campus Climate

The campus climate at Teachers College is profoundly shaped by its continuing financial problems. Concern over these problems exacerbates tension
between faculty and administrators. A senior administrator opined:

> There is a feeling that the administration is feathering its own nest at the
> expense of the faculty. It is a competition for scarce resources. The

number of administrators increases, yet the number of faculty decreases and faculty wonder why it takes so many people to run the show that used to be run by two people.

A staff member characterized the relationship between faculty and administrators as "often antagonistic" and reported that the faculty often made negative comments about the administration.

How has the College Policy Council influenced the relationship between faculty and administration? Five of the six individuals questioned about the impact of the College Policy Council reported that the CPC had no influence on that relationship. An administrator reported:

> I think there is a fairly great division at the moment between the faculty and the administration. . . . I think morale is pretty low at the moment. But it's not low because of the CPC.

Another administrator commented that the relationship between faculty and administration has endured periods of hostility and periods of tranquillity but that CPC had "no impact" on the relationship.

Expressing a minority view, a senior administrator suggested that the operation of the College Policy Council had a negative impact on the relationship:

> I think it has led to some mistrust. I think it's hurt the relationship. Its recent effect on the relationship has been negative because decision making is so diffused. . . . I think it has led to distrust.

Improving Communication

The College Policy Council serves as a source of communication among the various constituencies. A veteran Teachers College administrator contended that the CPC was "effective in communicating to the faculty an understanding of what the problems were and the seriousness of the problems." He commented further:

> CPC is a useful thing to have around providing you don't expect too much from it. It's useful precisely because it does to some degree facilitate communication across groups that otherwise might not be able to communicate with themselves that way.

A faculty member reported that "CPC membership provides a vehicle for wider interaction among faculty and between faculty and administrators" thereby serving to improve communication between the two groups.

A senior faculty member reported that prior to the existence of the CPC "the faculty and the community in general were hardly advised at all about what was happening" regarding the budget. He contended that the operation of the CPC forced administrators to "work harder about making their decisions public and palatable. They had to be more clever politically."

The College Policy Council, in providing an open forum for considering and discussing policies of the college, also afforded the community an opportunity to "let off steam" and to voice concerns. A senior administrator commented:

> The College Policy Council has been best as a sort of governor on a steam engine. When an issue becomes highly controversial, it's there and the issue can be aired and people can think they've had a role in it.

Another senior administrator added:

> Many of the social scientists on the faculty at the time thought [the CPC] was a rather bizarre structure but they saw it as a political symbol that probably was useful at that time to absorb the various constituency complaints. So that, I think from the point of view of CPC emerging at a specific time to do specific jobs, it did absorb the criticism.

EFFECTIVENESS OF THE COLLEGE POLICY COUNCIL

According to the Statutes of Teachers College, the Faculty Handbook, and the Bylaws of the College Policy Council, the CPC has great potential for influencing the major decisions that determine the institution's priorities and direction. Its potential, however, is essentially unrealized. As one faculty member of the College Policy Council contended:

> CPC in its current form has no teeth, as far as I can tell. If it does, it is invisible to me. Does CPC influence me? Not much. Does CPC influence my program? Not much. Does it influence my department? Not much. Does it influence my division? Not much. Those four statements I can make with certainty since I am both on CPC and am active in those other units. Does it have influence on larger issues in the college on policy? I have never seen any evidence of it.

Instead of playing a major role in college decision making, the College Policy Council functions mainly as a "rubber stamp" for administrative decisions. A senior faculty member commented:

> To my knowledge, nothing CPC has ever done . . . has influenced a decision that was ready to be made prior to the time it was brought to them for discussions. That is, they don't make decisions, they discuss very little. When they do discuss something, it's usually something for which a decision has already been made.

A senior administrator confirmed:

> [CPC] doesn't make any decisions that I can't actually make myself. CPC can't—doesn't—do much but give after-the-fact approval for things I've already decided to do.

The inability of the College Policy Council to realize its potential has led to widespread dissatisfaction within Teachers College. The overwhelming vote by the faculty to separate the Faculty Executive Committee from the CPC and to sharply reduce its membership on the CPC plainly demonstrates the faculty's dissatisfaction. An administrative staff member expressed her disappointment in the CPC's effectiveness and remarked that she would not run for CPC membership again. One faculty member summed up the College Policy Council's status: "irrelevant."

Factors Limiting the Effectiveness of the College Policy Council

Several factors at TC serve to constrain the CPC's effectiveness. One chronic problem at Teachers College is its difficulty in securing adequate faculty representation in various governance committees because of the size of the faculty (only 140 faculty members) and, according to some observers, the faculty's general disinterest combined with a disinclination to grapple with enrollment and financial realities. An administrator remarked that between the CPC and the faculty governance bodies, there is "not enough horsepower to do the job." Another administrator reported that adequately filling the various departmental, divisional, faculty, and CPC committees was extremely difficult because of the small size of the faculty.

In addition, many faculty are either too busy or simply not interested in serving on committees. An administrator commented that "one has to have the luxury of participating in faculty governance" and that the majority of the faculty at Teachers College were just too busy. A faculty member suggested that the core problem is faculty disinterest:

> Professors [at TC] are not good collective citizens. They want to be left alone. Faculty thinks of itself in a very individualistic, small way and have no feel for the needs of the institution.

An administrator agreed:

> This faculty is a long way from being concerned about having a voice. We have a lot of senior people who [the CPC is] not going to affect too much. They teach their classes, work with their doctoral students, and it's not going to affect their lives to any great extent.

The overlapping responsibilities of the College Policy Council and various other governance committees constitute a third limitation to the CPC's effectiveness. As a faculty member observed, "As long as the CPC is dealing with issues identical to other groups, there is no role for CPC." A senior administrator also pointed to the overlap between CPC and other governance bodies as undercutting CPC's effectiveness.

Fourth, the perceived lack of commitment and support of senior administrators also weakens CPC's effectiveness. A senior faculty member recalled situations in the late 1970s and early 1980s in which administrators "tended to be disingenuous with CPC." He described the operation of CPC as "becoming a sham." A senior administrator confessed to a lack of personal support for the council:

> If I could get input in different ways, I would be just as well pleased because I think in many decision-making terms, CPC is dispensable.

While discussing possible changes in the College Policy Council, a senior faculty member commented on the need for strong administrative support: "Change must be desired by the president. Without such a desire, it's meaningless."

The recent faculty decision to "withdraw" from CPC participation and faculty efforts to strengthen the faculty governance system backed the ailing CPC against the wall. Indeed, the unanimous agreement about the ineffectiveness of the College Policy Council in influencing decisions at Teachers College left in serious doubt, at the time of the site visit, the prospects for the CPC's very survival.

It came as no surprise that in 1988, not long after the visit, the CPC was disbanded. It had long outlived the primary purpose for which it had been created as the volatile conditions that once led to its birth receded from view. The surprise is that the CPC—an anachronism that was not revitalized with a post-60s mission—had endured as long as it did.

SUMMARY AND POSTSCRIPT

In sum, the College Policy Council's impact at Teachers College had been very small indeed. It was widely perceived to have had virtually no effect on the governance of academic affairs or on TC's finances and budget making. Nor did the CPC play a role in planning.

Whereas the CPC had been established to afford greater access to various campus constituencies, it is clear in retrospect that the intended primary beneficiaries of the CPC concept—the students—were provided seats at the table and an opportunity to express themselves, but they accrued no real power. The faculty, who in troubled times had traded off their hegemony in academic affairs in the interest of a more democratic structure, came to see themselves as net losers and rebelled for the restoration of their primacy in academic matters. And the administration, while nominally given over to sharing at least the semblance of authority, by all accounts gave up nothing of significance. An inner circle of senior administrators is "in control." The CPC's one accomplishment appears to have been to serve as a forum for interconstituency communication, but this escape valve function—the "governor on a steam engine"—should not be confused with a substantial purpose.

Created for one purpose, the College Policy Council outlasted its *raison d'être*. No one seems to have sought to infuse it with new purpose, new life. Its vital signs having barely registered for years, the CPC finally succumbed in its sixteenth year. No mourners were seen at the funeral.

Postscript

Dissatisfaction with the College Policy Council from all quarters, but especially from the faculty, triggered a review of the CPC by the president (in consultation with faculty, staff, and students). This led to its dissolution at the end of the 1988-89 academic year, and to the creation of a new college-wide entity, the College Policy Committee. The CPC reborn is half the size of its predecessor, is consultative in nature, and is more narrowly focused; it is now out of the business of reviewing budgets and formulating broad campus-wide policies.

Ohio University's University Planning Advisory Council

The now tranquil campus of Ohio University stands in stark contrast to the turbulence of the late 1960s and early 1970s when student unrest resulted in the campus closing early in May 1970. Established in 1804, Ohio University is the oldest higher education institution in the old Northwest Territory. The main campus of this state-supported institution is nestled in the Appalachian foothills surrounded by small farms, woodlands, and state parks.

The residential campus is bordered by the small college town of Athens and the Hocking River. Athens's brick streets and restored buildings reflect its heritage as the second oldest city in Ohio. The brick walkways and buildings of the university blend easily into the city. The university's three oldest buildings, red brick structures with wooden shutters, date from the early nineteenth century. One of them, Cutler Hall, erected in 1816, has been designated a National Historic Landmark.

During its early years, Ohio University remained small, graduating a trickle of 145 students over its first 50 years. It remained open during the Civil War when Athens and the surrounding communities provided stations on the Underground Railroad.

Today Ohio University offers more than 120 undergraduate programs through nine colleges: Arts and Sciences, Business Administration, Communication, Education, Engineering and Technology, Fine Arts, Health and Human Services, Honors Tutorial, and University College. Additionally, master's degree programs are offered in nearly all major academic areas and doctoral degrees can be earned from selected departments. The Ohio University College of Osteopathic Medicine opened in 1976. It is the only medical school in southeast Ohio and the first in the state devoted to the training of osteopathic physicians.

Ohio University enrolled some 16,000 students (13,800 undergraduate, 2,200 graduate) in 1987. Eighty-one percent of its undergraduate and 47 percent of its graduate students are from Ohio. Out-of-state students come from every state in the nation and include more than 1,500 students from nearly 70 countries.

The university employs approximately 900 faculty (700 full-time, 200 part-time) in its various programs. Approximately 76 percent of the faculty is tenured.

During the 1960s, the university, like many other higher education institutions, experienced dramatic growth. During the 1969-70 academic year, the enrollment on the Athens campus peaked at 19,000 and was projected to reach nearly 25,000 students by the 1980s. These enrollment expectations were never met. Beginning in the fall of 1971, enrollments began to decline, dipping to a low point of slightly over 12,500 students in 1975.

The 1969-70 academic year was especially traumatic for Ohio University. Following several days of student demonstrations and general turmoil, the university was closed in May 1970 prior to the end of the term. In response to expressed student and faculty concerns, then President Claude Sowle convened a task force of students, faculty, administrators, and local community leaders to examine the events of that turbulent spring and to plan for an orderly reopening in the fall. The task force formulated numerous proposals. Among the resulting institutional policies, reflecting the spirit of the times, were expanded visiting privileges, conversion of dormitories into co-educational residence halls, increased privileges regarding the consumption of alcohol on university property, funding for the office of university ombudsman, funding for a child care center, and an increased respect for the rights of students, particularly as these rights related to dormitory room searches.

In addition to the activities of the task force, a plan was developed for university budgeting and planning. Approved on October 15, 1970, the plan included three major changes. First, there was increased participation by students and faculty on various budget committees. Second, requests for funds were required to provide standards of measurement that would permit decision makers to judge the merits of the various expenditures. Third, the budget process was to be open to the public so that any individual could raise questions regarding the expenditure of university funds.

It was at this time, as noted, that enrollment declines began, resulting in a reduction in revenues. A 30 percent reduction in enrollment and income between 1971 and 1976 triggered intense competition for limited resources and a preoccupation with the need to make immediate expenditure reductions and staff terminations. Commitments resulting from tenure-based or contract obligations left some units mostly unaffected while units with untenured faculty or unobligated funds had to absorb significant budget reductions. Wide disparities quickly resulted in the staffing and funding levels among various units.

The open budget hearings, intended to bolster confidence in the budget process, ironically served mainly to exacerbate tensions. The hearings spawned pointed and often personal attacks on budget managers. Particularly aggressive questions were directed at politically weak units and units that could not clearly substantiate the need for particular expenditures. Some budget managers reportedly capitalized on the hearings by preparing their presentations to obscure important aspects of their budgets, thereby prompting prolonged discussions on trivial issues. Budget hearings were also seized upon by some audience members to expound on broad social issues that had little relevance to the university's internal budgeting. In sum, the open budget hearings, initiated ostensibly as a democratizing governance reform, resulted instead in hostility, resentment, and suspicion.

It was this environment that awaited Charles J. Ping as he began his presidency in 1975 following President Sowle's resignation. President Ping believed that a new planning process—comprehensive, long-range, and program based—would restore a sense of direction and shape to the university. The major thrust was to be the integration of the budgeting and resource allocation process with the goals and commitments of the university.

A flurry of activity ensued as the 1975-76 academic year was devoted to a year-long study by dozens of groups of faculty and staff to develop statements of goals for the various broad areas of university life. In the fall of 1976 two retreats took place to explore directions and opportunities for the university. Participants included campus leaders, faculty, students, and national education leaders. Two key documents resulted: a mission statement for the university and a description of the planning process. While these documents were being reviewed by the campus community, the dean's council prepared a series of environmental evaluation statements that described the context in which Ohio University would have to plan.

The elaborate process continued. In January 1977, nine teams were selected to prepare goal statements for the university. The goal statements consolidated the mission statement and the environmental statements into a description of desired results that would serve as standards for program planning and resource allocation decisions. The result was the university's *Educational Plan 1977-1987*, adopted by the board of trustees on October 1, 1977.

In September 1977, the three major components of the planning process at Ohio University were initiated: the University Planning Advisory Council, a staff planning process, and a space management study. The space management study provided a flow model for the reduction and reallocation of space needs that were anticipated over the next two decades. The major change recommended by the study involved the conversion of a number of dormitory buildings into academic facilities. Many of the recommended changes were implemented, and additional conversions were planned for the near future.

The staff planning process produces enrollment projections for a six-year period. These are revised annually. Enrollment projections are made on the bases of both optimistic and more conservative assumptions. Overall enrollment projections are refined to establish projections of likely course, department, and college enrollment patterns. These projections serve as guidelines on which to base staffing needs.

The two components, just described, are significant; however, it is the University Planning Advisory Council (UPAC) that lies at the heart of the new planning process and was the focus of the study. "UPAC" is composed of faculty, administrators (including deans), and students. Its major function is to review, evaluate, and advise the provost and president on budgetary, staff, space, and administrative issues. UPAC's specific tasks are extensive: to review planning unit objectives and priorities to assure conformity with the *Educational Plan*; to advise on integration of all planning unit program plans into the total university plan; to advise on budget development as well as capital planning and program planning; and to consider and evaluate proposals that recommend major changes in the scope and direction of the university.

Since the arrival of President Ping in 1975, enrollment at Ohio University has steadily increased from the low point of 12,500 to 16,000. In 1981, *The Wall Street Journal* (Prestbo 1981) published a laudatory article documenting the success of Ohio University's planning process:

> While some colleges and universities across the country are in such financial straits that they are lopping off whole courses of study, firing faculty members and otherwise yanking their belts painfully tight, Ohio University, while also pinching pennies, is doing so in carefully planned rather than panicky ways.

By all accounts, Ohio University had emerged from its turbulent experiences in the early 1970s as a stable, growing institution.

GOVERNANCE AT OHIO UNIVERSITY

The Ohio University, as a state-supported institution, works through the Ohio Board of Regents regarding most of the state-supported portion of its budget and is under the board of regents' purview for purposes of new program development. In all other matters of operation, the university is governed by a board of trustees whose members are appointed by the governor of Ohio to serve nine-year terms. The trustees operate independently of the board of regents.

The Faculty Senate, the Administrative Senate, the Student Senate, and the Graduate Student Senate comprise the network of campus governmental bodies at Ohio University. The Faculty Senate is an elected body with 48 members who represent proportionally all of the faculty. Administrators and others may participate in Faculty Senate meetings, but only elected faculty vote on senate issues.

The senate meets monthly with special meetings called by its chair when necessary. Recommendations by the senate are considered by the provost and the president and are transmitted to the board of trustees for approval. The president and the provost report regularly to the senate and respond to questions.

The Administrative Senate is a 33-member elected body representing the university's administrative staff. Its members are drawn from some 700 university employees who are neither faculty members nor Civil Service employees (employees who are unionized and represented by a bargaining agent).

THE UNIVERSITY PLANNING ADVISORY COUNCIL

The University Planning Advisory Council is integral to Ohio University's planning and budgeting processes. Its major responsibility is to advise the provost and president on major budgetary, staff, space, and administrative issues including recommending the budget for the succeeding year. The 18-member council is chaired by the provost. Its complex membership includes eight members of the faculty, five of whom include the chair and executive committee of the Faculty Senate plus three others appointed by the provost; three members of the Deans' Council, named by the provost; three administrators including the chair of the Administrative Senate and two other administrators appointed by the provost; two undergraduate students and one graduate student, including the president of the Student Senate. Additionally, four people representing the provost and other vice presidents are assigned as staff assistants to the council. Members typically serve three-year terms with one third of the membership changing each year.

During 1977-78, the first year of UPAC's existence, the council's major focus was on evaluating program objectives developed by the various planning units, identifying proposed changes that could not be accomplished within existing departmental resources, and establishing a program enhancement pool that would be used to fund special requests from the planning units. Since that time, UPAC discussions have extended to nearly all facets of university planning and budgeting.

Among its responsibilities, perhaps UPAC's most important function is the development of the annual budget. Each fall the provost presents UPAC with an estimated range of income based on projected enrollments, tuition levels, state subsidy, and other income, along with mandatory expenses such as utility costs, the continuing salary base, Title IX requirements, and so forth. The range of total expenditures—including the range of possible compensation increases, the size of the planning pool, equipment and supply cost increases, increases in graduate student stipends, and mandatory expenditures—are reviewed by UPAC. Once it has established the range of likely expenditures, UPAC considers changes in income chiefly by adjusting student tuition and fee levels. The final step in the budget-building process involves refining expenditure and income estimates until a balanced budget has been achieved.

In conjunction with developing the university budget, UPAC recommends the size of the university planning pool. Funds for the planning pool, which annually amount to approximately 1 percent of the general university base budget, are set aside prior to the allocation of any other resources. All 20 planning units are invited to submit proposals for support from this pool. Each unit is limited to a total dollar request of not more than 3 percent of its base budget. All proposals are submitted to UPAC for evaluation, and UPAC in turn presents a final rank ordering to the provost and president as part of the final university budget recommendations.

Additionally, UPAC is involved in the evaluation of staffing needs and priorities of the colleges and other planning units, as well as reviewing the staffing changes that take place as a result of discussions between the deans, vice presidents, and the provost's office. The changes that result from these discussions are taken into account by UPAC when individual units submit requests for additional staff or faculty as part of their request for planning pool funds.

UPAC stays busy throughout the academic year. It usually meets on a weekly basis, September through June. Periodic meetings during the summer are held as needed. Initial meetings involve a review of the previous year's Action Agenda (university priorities) and planning pool allocations. Program and staffing plans are evaluated early in the year with initial budget discussions typically beginning in December. Meetings during the spring are devoted to the review of planning pool proposals and development of the budget. A preliminary report is presented to the president and the board of trustees, usually in April. The final budget recommendations are forwarded to the trustees by the president in June.

While the deliberations of the UPAC are confidential, the final recommendations of the council are made available to the university community and are presented formally to the various senates by the president. Additionally, UPAC meets with the directors of each planning unit prior to consideration of planning pool requests and provides each planning unit with feedback regarding that unit's proposals. Further, prior to major budget decisions, the budget managers of the planning units are provided with a full briefing and explanation of anticipated UPAC actions by the provost's office.

Profile of Interview Subjects

To explore the effectiveness of the University Planning Advisory Council and its impact on governance and planning at Ohio University, a total of 14 semi-structured hour-long interviews were conducted during April 1987. The interviewees consisted of seven administrators (including the president and provost), three full professors, two associate professors, and two undergraduate students. In all, 12 of the 14 individuals interviewed were either current or past members of UPAC. Excluding the students, the interviewees' tenure at the university ranged from 6 to 25 years, averaging 17 years. All but one of the nonstudent interviewees had joined the university prior to UPAC's founding.

IMPACT OF THE UNIVERSITY PLANNING ADVISORY COUNCIL

How effective has the University Planning and Advisory Council been in the arenas of planning and governance? The following sections examine the UPAC's impact on the governance of academic affairs and of administrative and financial affairs, on planning, and on communication. The case study seeks also to assess the redistribution of influence among campus constituencies and UPAC's impact on campus climate and on the overall quality of decisions.

Governance of Academic Affairs

Like Princeton University, Ohio University has a long tradition of faculty control over academic affairs. Recommendations about the academic program are reviewed primarily by two university councils: the University Curriculum Council and the Graduate Council. The former is a statutory body established by the Faculty Senate to be responsible for curriculum matters. It is the culminating unit in a network of committees that includes departmental and college curriculum committees. Matters related to courses, academic programs, academic requirements, and review of programs come before the University Curriculum Council. More specifically, the function of the University Curriculum Council is to make recommendations concerning 1) addition and deletion of programs; 2) after formal review, the quality and priority of existing academic programs; 3) addition and deletion of courses; and 4) academic requirements for students.

The Graduate Council is advisory to the provost and makes policy recommendations relating to graduate programs. These matters include graduate faculty status, graduate admissions standards, and program monitoring. The composition of the council is representative of all departments granting advanced degrees and includes graduate student members.

All seven individuals questioned about academic decisions concurred that these decisions are controlled by the faculty. A professional school dean maintained that the faculty and the Faculty Senate possessed a "strong and healthy control over academic matters." A senior faculty member commented that, in comparison to colleagues at other institutions, faculty influence at Ohio University was "one of the strongest that exists" and argued that the curriculum was "controlled by the faculty."

Only one interviewee—a full professor with 20 years' experience at the university—questioned the extent of actual faculty control over academic affairs:

> The faculty think they control the curriculum. However, the administration is able to bring the faculty along. For instance, the general education requirement was reintroduced not through faculty initiative but by administrative initiative.

Even so, he conceded that faculty, through the University Curriculum Council and Faculty Senate review processes, do exert substantial influence over curriculum issues.

The University Planning Advisory Council's activities have little direct impact on academic decision-making processes and decisions at the university. While UPAC's resource allocation decisions and planning activities affect the academic affairs of the university, these decisions are made after the proposals have been reviewed by the Faculty Senate, the University Curriculum Council, and the Graduate Council. A senior administrator noted that initially UPAC's funding decisions had curricular implications that had not been reviewed by the Faculty Senate. He reported that the situation was very quickly corrected and procedures were implemented to ensure the appropriate review of any proposal with academic program implications prior to any UPAC action.

Governance of Administrative/Financial Affairs

The University Planning Advisory Council has a substantial impact on resource allocation and planning processes and decisions at Ohio University. The establishment and operation of the council provide an orderly, systematic, participatory process for the determination of budgetary and planning decisions. Prior to UPAC's creation, the open budget hearings conducted by former President Sowle were characterized by faculty members as a "zoo" and "very destructive" to the campus. In fact, several critics asserted that while the open hearings provided an appearance of total participation in budget decisions, the hearings were merely "window dressing," leaving decisions to be made in actuality by four or five senior administrators. A senior faculty member declared that, in spite of the open hearings, budget decisions prior to the establishment of UPAC were actually made by central administration and were heavily influenced by campus politics and individual "selling of proposals" by deans and senior faculty.

The UPAC process, according to a senior administrator and long-time faculty member is "a more orderly, systematic, consultative process that leads to the most important decisions the university makes." Another senior administrator noted that the establishment of UPAC provides a more systematic process for budget decisions, resulting in units assuming greater control over input into the process than the previous "system" of individual contacts.

The UPAC with its membership of administrators, faculty, and students provides for formal participation by these constituencies in the budget and planning processes. Indeed, one administrator contended that "the most important role of UPAC is providing a sense of participation in determining how . . . funds are spent." A senior administrator concurred that this involvement is one of UPAC's most important roles.

Governance: A Redistribution of Influence

The University Planning Advisory Council has a direct impact on the university's financial affairs. Additionally, while decisions about academic programs are made elsewhere, UPAC resource allocation decisions influence the funding of academic programs. How has UPAC affected the distribution of influence among the various participants in these resource and planning decisions?

A major consequence of UPAC's activity has been to expand faculty influence in budgetary decisions. A senior administrator commented that the successful operation of UPAC has in general "strengthened the credibility of faculty participation in governance." Prior to its establishment, no formal mechanism existed for systematic faculty input into budget decisions. The UPAC provides for formal faculty participation in the process. Of the 12 people questioned about faculty influence, all but one agreed that the UPAC process had increased faculty influence in financial decisions. One administrator reported his "amazement at how powerful faculty are in the UPAC process." A senior administrator and former faculty member remarked that the faculty had always exerted a strong influence over curricular issues but that the establishment of UPAC extended faculty influence into major budget decisions.

Four of the individuals interviewed argued that the inclusion of the five members of the Faculty Senate Executive Committee on UPAC increased the Faculty Senate's influence on financial affairs. A senior faculty member suggested that because the executive committee members are able to discuss UPAC concerns among themselves, they have a larger influence in "pushing their agenda" than do other UPAC members. The Faculty Senate chair agreed that this ability to "develop strategies" as a group within UPAC has, to a minor extent, increased Faculty Senate influence over budget decisions.

While UPAC may have strengthened the role of the Faculty Senate in budget decisions, one result has been the diminished role of the Faculty Senate's Finance Committee. The chair of the Faculty Senate commented: "UPAC has vitiated the ability of the Finance Committee to do anything of consequence as the Finance Committee is not privy to the information that UPAC has." A senior administrator agreed. He reported that in the "old days" the Finance Committee directly influenced compensation and other faculty-related budget issues. Now, although the Finance Committee continues to advise the Faculty Senate, its recommendations in actuality make very little difference.

Both the Faculty Senate chair and a senior faculty member, however, maintained that, on the whole, Faculty Senate and UPAC activities are not closely integrated. They contended that the Faculty Senate was never viewed as a budgetary entity but was primarily involved in academic matters and faculty rights and governance.

The establishment of UPAC not only created a formal mechanism for faculty input into budgetary decisions but also formalized student involvement in the process. Both undergraduate student members of UPAC agreed that student input is seriously considered by UPAC members. A senior administrator concurred that students are listened to seriously by all UPAC members and noted that other members actively solicited comments of student members during UPAC deliberations.

The administrative role in budgetary and planning decisions continues to be strong. Most of the interviewees described the UPAC process as being guided by the administration. However, none of the individuals believed that this guidance led to UPAC's "rubber stamping" administrative decisions. The Faculty Senate chair reported that during UPAC deliberations:

> . . . the cards are more in the Provost's Office because they have more information and spend more time and analysis on it. However, . . . decisions from UPAC have been different from what might have been made by the administration.

Two student members of the council reported that they had never felt pressured to make the "right" decisions by any administrator. As a senior administrator commented, the administration did a lot of talking and data producing for UPAC deliberations and certainly guided the process "with a firm hand." He insisted, however, that this was accomplished by information and persuasion rather than through administrative authority.

A senior faculty member recalled an initial concern of the deans that the establishment of UPAC would lessen their influence in the decision-making process since prior to the operation of UPAC "deans and senior administrators made the decisions about the university." This concern contrasts with the comment of one faculty member that the deans who were members of UPAC were much less forceful than he assumed they would be and indeed less vocal than the faculty members on the council. The deans, however, continue to have an impact on the process outside of their membership on UPAC. The Deans' Council regularly advises the provost on academic and budgetary issues. Moreover, operational budgets of the units are controlled by the deans. Additionally, planning pool proposals are reviewed and prioritized by each unit—that is, each dean's office—prior to submission to UPAC. Consequently, while UPAC may have decreased the influence of the deans in reaching final determinations for funding planning pool proposals, it has not substantially diminished their influence in the total decision-making process.

Planning

The activities of the University Planning Advisory Council have a large impact on planning processes and decisions at the university. Since its inception, UPAC has been significantly involved in planning activities. UPAC's major responsibility during its first year was the evaluation of program objectives that had been developed by the various planning units. Since that time, UPAC deliberations have included many facets of university planning and budgeting.

In addition to evaluating program objectives, UPAC reinforces the link between planning and resource allocation decisions at the university. It accomplishes this through its annual evaluation of staffing needs and priorities of the colleges and other planning units and its review of staffing changes that take place as a result of discussions between the deans, vice presidents, and the provost's office. UPAC decisions on planning pool requests for additional staff or faculty are then made in accordance with these staffing plans.

During the 1984-85 planning cycle, a renewed effort was mounted to expand UPAC's input into planning. Seven task force groups were appointed, each charged with studying and reporting on major issues that might face the campus in the next three to five years. Task force findings were used to develop a UPAC Action Agenda that now guides UPAC's work in focusing on a planning horizon beyond the annual budget. Similar task force groups are established each year to review and recommend revisions of the Action Agenda to reflect additional issues or conclusions raised during the course of the groups' deliberations.

In sum, the University Planning Advisory Council had been established in conjunction with the university's strategic planning efforts and is now considered integral to planning and budgeting activities. Its operation provides an important link between planning processes and resource allocation decisions. Through its responsibilities for determining the total university budget, for allocating special funds through the planning pool, and for ensuring that these decisions are made in conformity with institutional priorities, UPAC exerts a major influence on campus priorities and direction.

Impact on Campus Climate

The planning and financial decision-making processes at Ohio University, of which the University Planning Advisory Council, as has been shown, is a crucial element, appear to have had a positive impact on the university generally. There is a widespread perception that opportunities for meaningful participation in decision making exist. A senior administrator commented that this sense of participation changes the character of the decision-making process:

> The degree to which planning is done *to* people, even when they think it's right they're going to resist it. But the degree to which it's done *by* them, and they have some sense of ownership, changes the whole character of decision making.

Another senior administrator argued:

> This sense of sharing and authorship and belonging is necessary for faculty, staff, and students. They need to be part of the decision-making process. This sense of participation has turned this place around. People need to feel responsibility and ownership in what happens to the university.

It appears to be more than coincidental that since UPAC's establishment, morale at the university is said to have improved significantly. An administrator who had been at the university for 27 years argued that the UPAC process had substantially reduced the tension and anxiety resulting from the turbulent experiences in the early 1970s:

> A benefit of this broad participation and more knowledgeable faculty is that it reduces the fear and anxiety level. This was especially important during the financial difficulties of the mid-1970s.

Further, he maintained that

> UPAC decisions may be secondary to the process which creates a feeling
> of goodwill and good faith on the campus. . . . The UPAC process gives
> people confidence that the university is being run all right and thus the
> campus is at peace.

A senior faculty member reported that morale on campus was "as good as it's
ever been," and added, "That was saying quite a lot."

One advocate, an administrator, contended that the UPAC process served
to build

> a broad-based confidence in the process resulting in more confidence in the
> administration. University members are less zealous than they used to be.

Another administrator added that

> There is a measure of trust that was not there ten years ago. It's a rather
> dramatic difference and UPAC has fostered this trust and understanding.

A senior administrator reported that increasing confidence in the administration had led several faculty members to suggest that the administration should
make more decisions on their own since "they know what the university
needs." He commented that this would never have happened prior to UPAC
when there was general suspicion and disagreement about all decisions. A
senior faculty member agreed:

> My personal preference is for more centralized decision making by the
> administration. I would have the provost control more funds directly
> rather than routing these decisions through UPAC.

This improvement in campus morale is echoed in the improved relationship between the faculty and the administration. Only 2 of the 14 interviewees
characterized the relationship as anything less than positive: one senior
faculty member described the relationship as "distant" and an administrator
suggested that the relationship was "confrontal on some issues." The
remaining 12 interviewees, however, concurred that the relationship between the faculty and the administration was "better than it's ever been." A
faculty member reported that while the relationship in the past had been
confrontational with "open sniping" between faculty and administrators,
there was now a "solid working relationship" between the two groups.

Indeed, during the Sowle presidency, a serious effort was made to organize
the faculty into a collective bargaining unit. The vote, taken during the first
year of President Ping's administration (1975), was reportedly a close one
against unionization. A senior faculty member who had been actively involved
in the organizing campaign reported that the relationship between faculty

and administration had improved so significantly that no subsequent move to unionize had occurred. Another senior administrator reported that the most recent North Central States' accreditation report of Ohio University had commented, in 1983, on the "unusual climate of trust" and on the high levels of confidence in the decision-making process and in the administration. He concluded that the University Planning Advisory Council had made a "substantial contribution to the feelings of trust and to the good relationship between faculty and administration."

Improving Communication

As shown, the University Planning Advisory Council has improved communication at Ohio University regarding planning and budgetary decisions. UPAC recommendations are presented by the president to meetings of the Faculty Senate, the Administrative Senate, and the Student Senate. Additionally, planning units that have submitted proposals for planning pool funding are fully briefed about UPAC decisions and the rationale behind those decisions prior to UPAC's announcement to the university community.

This communication process among constituencies is credited with "building an understanding of the decisions" within the community and creating a better informed campus community. A senior administrator contended that UPAC facilitates an understanding of the decision-making process that is crucial to the acceptance of UPAC decisions:

> There's nothing particularly hard about planning. The really hard part is developing understanding and acceptance. I think the great failure [of the previous process] was not that . . . decisions were made [that were not as good as UPAC's] but [that] their decisions did not produce understanding and acceptance in a similar way.

A senior faculty member suggested that UPAC's major role is informational in that it "educates the faculty on general motivations for the allocation of resources." A senior administrator concurred, crediting the UPAC process with "producing well-educated people with a broader understanding of how decisions are made."

A faculty member argued that the UPAC informational process is a two-way process:

> Faculty . . . are more knowledgeable about the situation of the university and the constraints on the administration. The administration is more informed about faculty concerns.

A senior administrator put it another way, describing the UPAC process as an "early warning system" for the administration by making them more knowledgeable about the community.

EFFECTIVENESS OF THE UNIVERSITY PLANNING ADVISORY COUNCIL

All interviewees save one believed that the University Planning Advisory Council strongly influences budgetary and planning decisions at the university. As one senior administrator observed:

> The budget proposal . . . which we just took to the trustees comes out of UPAC. It is not the result of the deans getting together and bargaining or horse trading or the result of the Faculty Senate laying its demands on the table or that sort of thing. It comes from UPAC. From that standpoint, it's enormously powerful.

The chair of the Faculty Senate agreed, maintaining that with respect to larger general budget issues such as faculty and staff compensation and campus renovation, "UPAC certainly has influence and input and can push decisions in particular directions."

Indeed, since its establishment in 1977, all UPAC recommendations have been accepted by the president. One senior administrator commented that, in fact, the trustees usually meet with UPAC members to discuss the budget prior to final trustee action and that senior university administrators are excluded from this meeting. That such an extraordinary step may occur as a part of the normal budget process serves to demonstrate UPAC's substantial influence upon the budget.

On the other hand, one interviewee submitted that UPAC's influence over the budget is not very significant because it deals only with the "whipped cream," that is, a mere 1 percent of the total university budget. A senior administrator suggested a different perspective, conceding that UPAC's budgetary responsibilities

> may be more form than substance. But a university's form and substance are inseparable. If people [in the institution] believe things are true, they're true.

Quality of Decision Making

How has the University Planning Advisory Council affected the quality of decisions and decision-making at Ohio University? Eight of the nine individuals who commented on that point said that UPAC had improved the quality of decisions. The lone dissenter felt that UPAC had had no effect on decision quality.

The degree to which interviewees judged quality to have improved varied greatly. One senior faculty member contended that issues received a fairer hearing through the UPAC process because the personality of an individual spokesman did not unduly influence UPAC decisions; he believed that the quality of decisions had "probably improved." Another senior faculty member argued UPAC's impact on quality is "generally positive" and that the process is useful in "keeping the administration from making major errors."

A senior administrator suggested that UPAC had the effect of forcing UPAC members and administrators to "do their homework" in preparing for meetings. This resulted, she contended, in more and better data and more informed consideration of issues. A veteran senior administrator commented that the prevailing belief prior to the establishment of UPAC was that *all* decisions made by the university were wrong; he believed that the UPAC has created the perception on campus that good decisions were resulting from the process.

According to one faculty member, the perception now prevailed that campus life had improved significantly in the last 10 years—the university was well run, many programs had been cited for their quality, graduate programs were gaining in reputation. She argued that these attitudes were an outgrowth of the quality of UPAC's decisions.

Factors Contributing to the Effectiveness of the University Planning Advisory Council

The University Planning Advisory Council and the strategic planning process at Ohio University are essentially the creation of its president, Charles Ping. It has operated with his strong support and commitment since its inception. This support and commitment have been crucial factors in the continuing, effective operation of the council. As a senior administrator and former faculty member opined, the importance of "President Ping's leadership cannot be overestimated in this [UPAC] process." Another senior administrator concluded that "the real reason [UPAC] works is President Ping," citing his leadership commitment as one of the most essential factors in the effective operation of the council. His commitment to the process is reflected in the fact that UPAC recommendations have, with minor exceptions, been accepted by the president and transmitted by him to the board of trustees.

Committee membership is another factor crucial to UPAC's effective operation. A senior administrator cited the need to have the "best people involved—the best thinkers and leaders." Equally as important as having the "best people" on the council is the need for balanced representation. Membership, especially the nonelected portion of the council's membership, is chosen to achieve balance and representativeness. Two observers—one a senior administrator, the other a senior faculty member—testified that this balanced representation, drawn from different functional areas, minorities, and both sexes, contributes to increasing institutional confidence in UPAC's decisions.

The university's ability to provide the council with correct and accurate data, especially financial data, is also seen as being essential to UPAC's successful operation. As one senior administrator suggested, the ability to provide the council with good data builds continuing trust in the system and in the council. Another senior administrator declared that the UPAC process "would become unraveled with inaccurate financial data."

Finally, the acceptance of UPAC's decisions by the president and the trustees is essential. One senior administrator put it this way: decisions made by UPAC must be "real decisions; they must have real consequences and cash values." A senior faculty member echoed that a crucial key to UPAC's success is that it is seen as "a unit with the power to make things happen."

Governance Gone Right

The University Planning Advisory Council at Ohio University stands as a model of how to balance planning and governance. UPAC brings together a carefully considered structure (albeit quite complex) and process and a highly consequential mission. Above all, UPAC is an example of leadership at the presidential level that is committed to making the process of shared governance work. And, it appears evident—and crucial, too—that the governing board shares in the conviction that UPAC's role in university governance and planning activities is appropriate, competently discharged, and well balanced. This judgment presumably reflects the board's confidence in the president.

UPAC and Ohio University appear to have "gotten it right" and, so far as could be discerned, to a remarkable consensus-producing degree. UPAC is at once powerful (but respectful of its boundaries), expert, hard-working, and respected. In an era when strategic planning and governance tend to collide, creating muddled results and unhappy stakeholders (especially faculty), Ohio University stands out as a place where dedication, expertise, and extraordinary leadership have prevailed to yield a model of good practice.

PART
3

· · · · · · · · ·

Initiatives in the
1980s: Accent on
Planning and
Management

CHAPTER 7

· · · · · · · · ·

University of Montana's University Planning Council: Metamorphosis of the "Vision Quest"

The University of Montana is located at the hub of five high mountain valleys deep within the Rockies, west of the Continental Divide. The cultural center of the state, Missoula, population 68,000, is crisscrossed by the Clark Fork and Bitterroot rivers. Timber and livestock are the cornerstones of western Montana's economy, but "UM" constitutes a large part of the region's economy, and relations between town and campus have long been excellent.

The university was established in 1893, three years after Montana's statehood. It is one of 14 state-supported postsecondary institutions and the flagship of the state's two universities. Providing a regionally renowned liberal arts education, UM offers an extensive array of 128 degree programs, bachelor's through doctoral degrees. The College of Arts and Sciences is complemented by seven professional schools housed principally on the 200-acre campus adjacent to Mt. Sentinel. A number of field camps and forest and lakeside laboratories extend the university's academic work throughout western Montana. Slightly smaller than Montana State University in Bozeman, UM at the time of the visit enrolled approximately 9,000 students and employed about 460 full-time faculty members.

The university is governed by a board of regents vested with wide powers and authority to oversee the Montana University System. The board, appointed by the governor, itself appoints a commissioner as the chief administrative officer of the system. The management of UM is vested in its board-appointed president, the campus's chief administrator.

An elected and representative Faculty Senate historically has been the vehicle for faculty participation in governance. Its constitution provides for jurisdiction over academic matters, encompassing curricular and academic program changes, as well as admission, retention, and degree requirements.

Until the University Teachers' Union (UTU) was recognized in 1979 as the exclusive bargaining agent for the faculty, the senate also had represented the faculty in discussions to set salaries, benefits, and terms and conditions of employment. However, the UTU now fills that role.

An elected Staff Senate represented the university's 760 nonteaching employees. Most of these employees are also members of one of ten labor unions besides the UTU. UM's student government arm, the Associated Students of the University of Montana (ASUM), presents student opinion to the administration and faculty. Student representatives are often included on important campus committees.

UNIVERSITY PLANNING COUNCIL

During its brief lifetime, the University Planning Council, or UPC, was integral to planning efforts at the University of Montana. Convened by the president and chaired by the chief academic officer, the UPC consisted of a plurality of faculty representatives along with student, staff, and administrative members. While its deliberations were not particularly guarded, its final voting procedures relied on secret ballots. At the conclusion of its work cycles, the UPC would offer advice to the president in a final report on matters of institutional concern.

Profile of Interview Subjects

To examine the impact of the University Planning Council, 16 fifty-minute semi-structured interviews were held in August 1988, at the University of Montana. Twelve of these were with former members of the UPC: 5 faculty members, 2 staff, and 5 administrators (including the vice president for academic affairs who chaired the UPC). The remaining 4 interviews were with key individuals who were believed to have definite opinions to offer about the effects of the UPC on the university; these included the president (he had originally formed the UPC), faculty members representing senate and union concerns respectively, and one other nonmember administrator who had assisted the UPC with its logistical and data needs. Former student members were unavailable for interviews.

Historical Preconditions

Although many attribute the UPC's launching to the arrival of a new president in 1981, earlier events at UM laid the groundwork for the UPC's planning role. Under the previous president, massive program cuts in 1978 had necessitated 60 faculty layoffs and had left an indelible mark in the institution's memory. Forced to undergo a wrenching retrenchment, the campus community became disenchanted with its lot. Some perceived that decisions were being made for reasons of expediency. Others came to believe that the faculty's traditional resistance to being led made the campus barely manageable. One faculty member explained, "This was because there really was no plan for the place. We would expect the president to come forward with a plan, but then, if he did, we'd get angry with him for being authoritarian and dictating to us what the institution should be."

In the absence of commanding campus leadership, the Faculty Senate speculated about a planning committee that would be dominated by faculty but would also include administration and staff. This new entity was to engage in a five-year planning process and was to tackle tough, pragmatic issues, but it would also dream about where the university ought to be heading. The "blood bath" of '78 had driven home the fact that UM was attempting to do, in the words of one faculty member, "too much with too little, with no reasonable prospects for improved budgeting." The time had come for a change.

The Prime Mover

The arrival of the new president in 1981 was "a shot in the arm and morale boost," observed one dean. "People looked at him very positively when he came to this campus. He had lots of energy and dynamism," reported a faculty member. The new president was young, charismatic, energetic, and had a successful track record in institutional planning. Enthusiasm abounded in most quarters.

The president brought with him a model (complete with software) of resource allocations he had used successfully on another campus. His stated planning goals, however, were much more specific than what the Faculty Senate had been contemplating. He wanted to describe the environment in which the university was working and speculate about how that environment would change in the future. Out of this exercise were to come strategic planning recommendations. According to a faculty activist, the campus hoped that deliberations by a planning group would help protect the campus against the "buffeting of legislative winds [and enable them] to get a hold of the situation [themselves] and to do some reasonable thinking about it." One administrator observed, "UM was ready for this type of process. It was fertile ground."

What had motivated the president to move so rapidly and decisively in installing this planning model? To begin with, this president was committed to long-range planning. A senior administrator noted that it was the president's belief that "you can build on a sense of community that develops when you have participants in decision making." A dean believed that a broad cross-section of constituencies was invited "to the table" to assure diverse perspectives on planning.

Others were much more skeptical about the president's motives for using this planning model. A faculty member serving on the UPC commented that, "On the one hand, long-range planning was a goal; on the other hand, the *appearance* of involvement of the faculty was an objective. It's supposed to improve morale." "Going head to head with faculty over budget issues was not his mode of choice," offered another UPC faculty member, adding that he thought the president "assumed that the UPC would come to the same kind of reallocation decisions that he already had in mind." Still a third faculty person wondered: "I don't know that he was keeping us busy to keep us diverted. It was more like [he believed] this was the way things were done on campuses."

The UPC Model: Membership

The objectives and the membership of the University Planning Council were designed with some flexibility, for changes were anticipated in the introductory document, "Framework for Planning," dated February 1982. It provided that "once underway, the proposed process needs to be treated as a dynamic, evolving activity. Needed improvements will become evident, so flexibility will be necessary." In fact, the UPC did undergo annual changes.

The voting membership, intricately constructed to provide checks and balances among constituencies, was to range in number from 14 to 17 in any given year. There were seven UPC faculty representatives. The Faculty Senate elected three UPC delegates, the faculty union—the UTU—appointed two, and two more faculty members were appointed by the president. The Staff Senate named one staff person to the council while the president appointed another. The two administrative members were presidential appointments. The ASUM would appoint two to five student representatives (depending on the cycle). Terms ranged from one to three years.

In its fourth annual cycle the UPC's membership nearly doubled to 29 with the addition of 16 nonvoting members, primarily academic administrators. It was believed that they could illuminate discussions that preceded actual decision making.

The UPC Model: Purposes and Processes

Originally the UPC was charged with examining the long- and short-range plans submitted by the university's 19 planning units. Accompanying these plans were funding requests from a pool of money made available by the president to the UPC for the purpose of resource reallocation. The council was to judge each planning unit's proposals against a series of 14 "themes"— developed by the president and said to articulate the mission of the university for the 1980s—and then recommend funding priorities. Over time, the focus of these themes was to sharpen until one received predominant attention as a top UPC priority.

UM's planning cycle would begin in the fall. The UPC would meet for orientation sessions that occasionally included a workshop conducted by an off-campus planning expert. Each unit would compose its planning agenda and accompanying budget requests; these would be submitted to the UPC in January. The council would then divide the plans and proposals among four subcommittees whose task was to review and recommend funding action. After several weeks, the UPC would reconvene to discuss the subcommittees' analyses. Late in the spring the UPC would vote, and a final report on recommended funding priorities would be submitted to the president.

The UPC was provided with complete logistical support by the president's staff. Additionally, the offices of budget and institutional research provided data needed for group decision making. Further, a special assistant to the president was responsible for drafting the pair of annual planning documents: "Framework for Planning" at the beginning of the academic year, and "Planning Report," a late spring summary of the UPC's deliberations.

Evolution of the UPC

The University Planning Council got underway late in 1981. The timing appeared to be propitious. The University of Montana was basking in the best legislative treatment it had been accorded in years. The budget had increased 25 percent over the previous biennium. Faculty salary increases amounted to 11 to 12 percent per year. Enrollments were increasing. Thus the economic environment at the point of the UPC's inception was decidedly positive. Even though the stars seemed to be favorably aligned, there was some apprehension about the prospect of an administration-dominated process. This fear was attributable in part to the university's long-standing tradition of faculty governance. Its powerful, vocal Faculty Senate and faculty union were unaccustomed to keeping a low profile. As one dean observed, "It's more difficult at the University of Montana to make decisions out of a planning office or a president's office. Elsewhere such decisions can be routinely made by central administration." And the faculty did not know just what to expect. As the president recalled:

> The formation of the UPC was met [with] somewhere between hostility and fear by certain elements. The faculty senate was very concerned about it. The UTU never challenged it as directly. . . . I think I would have had extreme difficulty implementing it had I not been new and forceful. I think the fact that I moved it with some speed caused it to happen despite what some people really wanted to have happen.

And so, despite some misgivings, the campus entered into the new planning process with a mix of great expectations and considerable wariness.

In the UPC's first year—its first round of planning—units were invited to think about growth, expansion, and new projects. But in assessing their circumstances, many units realized they had to address basic maintenance needs before they could consider growth. In the second cycle, the president suggested that units think about reallocations; in the event the legislature would not appropriate new money, what would the units be willing to forgo? Apparently, few were willing to discontinue anything at that point, although some facetiously volunteered to cut "services," for example, student advising, office hours, and so on. The prospect of budget cuts via reallocations had a chilling effect on the enthusiasm originally generated by the new planning process.

By the end of the second cycle, the UPC reported to the president a need "to take a more global orientation in its deliberations." The group believed that too much of its time was consumed by reallocations, or "small grants" activities. The president responded at the beginning of the third cycle by naming five "goal authors," each to focus on a strategic area for institutional development. The subjects were student enrollment maintenance, general education, select program development, research agenda, and communications. It was assumed that these goal reports would help to define important future activities for the UPC. Yet, the council's small grants activities persisted. The UPC's third end-of-cycle report again entreated the president to utilize the council's acquired university-wide perspective in more consequential ways.

One of the five theme areas identified during the third cycle—"select program development"—was to become the focal point of UPC activity during the fourth cycle. A campus consultation with George Keller, an authority on strategic planning, inspired the inclusion of a new feature in that fourth cycle. Lengthy "strategy sessions"—three-to-four-hour joint meetings with the UPC and 16 of the planning unit heads (that is, the deans and vice presidents)—took place throughout that fourth cycle.

The UPC finally was addressing what it considered to be some very significant matters. But, alas, its foray into more substantial matters was derailed; 1984-85 was unexpectedly transformed into an extremely difficult year for the university—an abrupt return to bad economic times. Not only had the legislature cut the university's budget, but it subsequently sought to recall a portion of the funds it had already budgeted.

The result was a torpedoing of a more-or-less orderly process. "The president asked us to look at ways of cutting back UM budgets and recommend to him where to cut," recalled a UPC faculty member. A Faculty Senate representative reflected on those tension-filled days:

> We had some shortfalls [mandated by] the legislature—they were saving money, too. . . . For a couple years we were on the outs. We knew we would have to make cuts. We didn't want to do what we'd done in 1978 and cut all the young people, the nontenured people, out of here. The argument was that the UPC knew the university better than anybody and should advise on the cuts.

The UPC's overriding objective for that year became to consider specific program priorities for each planning unit. Its deliberations included adding, enhancing, and curtailing programs, noting opportunities and problems, and identifying unresolved issues. An academic administrator who served on the UPC recalled:

> One term we used quite a lot was "resource reallocation" which really referred to taking faculty lines away from areas that were not growing or developing and putting them into areas that were. There was some controversy in that, obviously. But the president was quite adamant about putting the resources where the growth or growth potential seemed to be.

By year's end the UPC had allocated planning pool money. But it stopped short of earmarking specific areas for cuts.

Whatever prospect the UPC may have had for success, the economic circumstances, having turned grim, put an end to enthusiasm for the new planning scheme. In an atmosphere of apprehension, academic departments were loathe to identify their own weak areas for fear that these programs would be lopped off and the money redirected into another department or program. The reluctance to comply was hardly without foundation. As one faculty senator explained, "Putting something in writing about reallocation was like writing a contingency plan in the event the legislature wouldn't fund us. That was like *inviting* the legislature to cut us back!" There was no guarantee of stable budgets from year to year. All too soon, faith in the planning process dissipated. A skeptical union leader reported that the infamous massacres of 1978 had left deep wounds:

> The hearings, the investigations, the reports, the committees, resulted in such bitterness. People are convinced that long-range planning will [not] come to fruition. . . . Any programmatic changes will be made under the gun, based on short-term financial problems, and on what can be done legally—who's not tenured!—rather than on academic planning.

Academic departmental support for the UPC process quickly evaporated.

In its fifth year—its final year as it happened—the UPC was asked to pinpoint specific budget cuts. It began the task by reviewing volumes of material at the beginning of its work cycle. The process was cut short, however, by the president's imminent resignation; he had accepted another campus presidency closer to his familial home. The end-of-year report was no more than a summary statement on the status of planning at the university and a recapitulation of outcomes during former planning cycles. The impending change in leadership had brought to a screeching halt the model of planning that the president had installed with high hopes just four years earlier.

THE UNIVERSITY PLANNING COUNCIL'S IMPACT

The University Planning Council affected a number of aspects of campus life at the University of Montana. These included governance, planning, communication, and campus climate.

The Impact on Governance

Of particular interest in studies of strategic planning councils is the extent to which such entities lead to a redistribution of power within the organization. After all, the introduction of new participants into institutional decision-making practices unavoidably affects existing interests. Had decision-making power shifted to the UPC from other entities?

Some believed that the UPC had siphoned power away from other "players." One view held that the faculty had lost ground during the UPC era. As a faculty senate representative recalled:

> When the UPC came, it was viewed with concern by some who saw it as a presidential group that served to further remove the faculty from the decision making. These people felt the decisions put to the UPC should have been put instead to the senate. Also, the UPC represented the whole campus, academic and non-, which put a further layer between the faculty and the president. Some felt there were too many layers of governance and that the faculty was reduced to a listening body.

"There's no question. The UPC did have a lot of authority," noted a dean who did not serve on the UPC.

The domain of the UPC, however, was different from that of the faculty union or senate. Accordingly, some thought the UPC was not in direct competition with traditional faculty governance. A union representative, for instance, commented that

> The attempt of the UPC was to fill a vacuum in the area of planning. Neither the senate nor the union has a committee to deal with that. There would have been a hue and cry if the UPC had overstepped territorial bounds of the Faculty Senate or union.

Most faculty members, it appears, held a less sanguine view of the UPC's reach. As one faculty member elected to the UPC commented, planning activities *did* constitute an intrusion into the faculty's proper jurisdiction, adding that "You can't get rid of eight [instructional] lines and not impact academic programs; you're making a curricular decision!" Indeed, throughout its life span, the UPC was looked upon by many faculty members as a group that had usurped faculty power. In fact, a former faculty representative to the UPC reported with pleasure following the UPC's disappearance that "The Faculty Senate had become an active forum again."

Although there were mixed perceptions about the extent of a power shift to the UPC from the Faculty Senate or union, there was less uncertainty about the consequences for the deans. The president recalled that the deans had indeed felt threatened by the UPC. Indeed, it was the consensus among others interviewed that during the UPC era the Council of Deans had been rendered an ineffective group. Previously, the deans, vice presidents, and president had handled decisions of the UPC type. A former dean lamented:

> The enhancement pool the UPC worked with came from money that [otherwise] would have gone into the vice presidents' budgets and on down to the deans. When I was a dean I spent a lot of time squeezing budgets for thousands of dollars. I would then go to the UPC and ask for it back—and get it back *if* I was lucky! The UPC was allocating money that the dean normally would allocate.

A faculty senator concurred:

> I think [the UPC] reduced the authority of the deans or at least contributed to their lack of authority. Deans were involved in prioritizing but were really just a conduit to the UPC. . . . As a result the University of Montana has suffered for many years with powerless deans. They don't have discretionary money. They just bear the bad news.

So, the deans clearly were being bypassed in the planning process.

Speaking more broadly of academic affairs—the domain of both deans *and* faculty—one faculty representative to the UPC expressed the resentment that surfaced when academic matters were channeled to a heterogeneous group of decision makers:

> Too many decisions were taken to the UPC where they could be treated with the whim of the group—faculty cuts, enrollment-driven stuff that would have been handled by the deans. I would prefer to have our dean—someone who knows the history of our college—making those decisions rather than the telephone operator!

Protests from the ranks continued that the UPC was not the appropriate group to be handling the planning concerns of the university. George Keller's 1984 visit to UM yielded a similar conclusion: the UPC, as constituted, did not have the proper composition. So, in 1984-85, during its fourth cycle, the deans and the vice presidents joined the planning council as nonvoting members to involve academic officers and heads of planning units in the decision-making process. But that effort to give greater voice to academic administrators came too late, for the UPC was, without knowing it, on the verge of extinction.

For students, the UPC proved to be inconsequential. Student government at the University of Montana is entitled—as provided by the faculty union contract—to name student members to important faculty committees. For the first two planning cycles, the student government appointed five students to the UPC, three students to the third, and two to the fourth. No former student members of the UPC were available for interviews; however, the consensus among other observers was that students neither contributed to nor were affected by the UPC decision-making process in a significant way. "Students would float in and out; some were responsible and some not," noted a faculty member. In its last two active cycles, the students who finished the year with the UPC were not even the same ones who began it. "Students could not be counted on to attend," confirmed the UPC chair.

The Staff Senate, on the other hand, was very pleased to participate in the UPC process. Such involvement in campus-wide matters was a welcome departure from their traditional role. As one staff member on the UPC observed, "To us it was *wonderful* to have a voice and feel staff were included in the process, to express a viewpoint and to look at where the university was going, and what some of the goals should have been." Understandably, the staff welcomed the opportunity to be seated at the head table. In all, they were the only constituency that saw themselves accruing power under the new regime.

Impact on Planning

To what extent did the University Planning Council engage in *strategic* planning and, if it did, how effectively? The UPC may have had the potential to renew a sense of vision for the campus, but were matters of strategic importance put before the UPC for its deliberations? Interviewees had mixed feelings about this question. Planning units could submit requests totaling no more than 3 percent of their annual budgets, thereby strictly limiting the potential for making substantial changes. Generally, it was agreed that during its first two cycles, the UPC had bogged down in preoccupation with "small grants." It was assumed that over time these small-scale reallocations would have an overall positive impact on the campus, but they were viewed mostly as "nickel-and-dime" changes.

"A planning council should be more of a policy-making group," complained one dean who did not serve on the UPC. "It was a stated parameter that [the UPC] would set some priorities that would affect the campus," noted one UPC faculty member. "The big decisions were made somewhere else." Observed another, "I don't think the council was empowered to deal with them." A third UPC faculty member agreed:

> Decisions of importance—the $400,000 per year upgrading of the law school; the football stadium—were all made *outside* the UPC. Meanwhile, here we are supposedly talking about the future of the university and we're deciding "should economics have secretary time cut back 0.5 FTE?"

In the third cycle, with the introduction of the five goal authors to the planning agenda, a sense arose that at last important issues would now be addressed. "The goal papers were presented to us, we had to respond to them, and recommend how to proceed with them," noted a UPC staff member. But, as one UPC faculty member observed, "It wasn't until things got really critical [with the legislature in the fourth cycle] that we were called on as an advisory group. Up until that point we didn't have critical things to deal with."

All who were interviewed, without exception, agreed that long-range planning was not one of the UPC's accomplishments. "It was really a money-doling process," said an administrator. "When Keller came to campus, I remember sitting over in the law library listening to him and thinking, 'that's not what we're doing.' " Although the UPC had some value, planning objectives were definitely upstaged by more immediate resource allocation requirements. "The president had not intended for it to be strictly a reallocation program," said a dean, "but the UPC was not making a major impact on the campus because so much of its time was spent on this reallocation [of 1 or 2 percent of the university's budget]." According to one faculty member:

> People would come to us with their problems to solve. We would give them a little bit of money to buy test tubes or computers. But long-range planning wasn't there.

Nonetheless, some significantly positive contributions can be attributed to the UPC. In fact, three large-scale programmatic changes can be traced to its decisions. Hailed as its "greatest achievement" by some (its "only achievement" by others), a general education plan became a part of the university's curricular requirements following UPC deliberations. (One faculty member, however, cautioned: "But if the senate and the president hadn't been in favor of it, it wouldn't have happened.")

Second, discussions on general education led to the establishment of University College as a means of addressing the needs of the "academic homeless," the nondeclared majors. The UPC is credited with bringing this matter to light. One dean described University College's significance:

> The importance of that issue to all of us in terms of recruitment and retention began to be recognized. Funds were reallocated through the planning process to deal with it, and something was created.

It was one of the few UPC outcomes that had such broad impact. "But that probably would have happened anyway," warned a staff member, "because there was so much support for it. It probably didn't need the UPC to kick it into gear."

A third contribution was the recognition of the need for a reorganization of the life sciences. This awareness is attributed to UPC deliberations, and a substantial reordering consequently took place.

In all, the UPC made a difference in several consequential aspects of campus academic life. But in terms of a larger scale impact on planning, the results were negligible. The UPC arguably had the potential to meet both "small grants" and more profound planning objectives. The evidence shows that it fell far short on the latter; the UPC simply failed to become a vehicle for consequential campus planning.

Improved Communication and Consciousness Raising

The quality of intracampus communications surfaced as a benefit attributable to the UPC. The opportunity to acquire an institutional overview prompted frequent testimonials. In the words of one faculty member, "After three years on the UPC, I had a pretty good idea of what was going on [on] the whole campus. In that sense I didn't figure my time on the UPC was a total loss." Another faculty member added, "I learned we all had a lot more things in common than I ever would have realized." A staff member concluded, "I learned a lot about human nature and the politics of the university. Participation got me out of my narrow perspective. It was a good reminder of the real purposes of the university." "I remember people would stand up in the senate and make pretty sophisticated statements that showed an understanding of the complex nature of the university," noted a senator. "It stretched all of us."

An administrator confirmed, "We all grew." Frustrations aside, there is no doubt that the process, however vexing, was enlightening and informative.

Thus, perhaps the UPC's most significant contribution to the campus was the fact that it drew attention to the university's overall circumstances. It caused the institution to put into writing what had previously been less well-articulated plans. Facts, attitudes, and ideas were assembled, digested, and promoted. Goal formalization became a focal point for the community. The UPC also provided the campus with a forum through which all its constituencies could air their desires and vent their concerns.

Unhappily, as noted previously, during this time the campus was forced to reckon with the appalling state of the economy. As noted by the UPC chair, one aim of the planning process "was to educate people. That objective certainly was met." One faculty member spoke to the importance, if not the satisfaction, of learning about hard realities:

> In the process of studying themselves, the departments noticed how short they were. They couldn't ask for new things as much as they needed to ask for replacement things, like turn-of-the-century microscopes. We knew we weren't going to fare well because just to replace broken stuff in the College [of Arts and Sciences] would amount to $1.5 million. The enhancement fund was only $400,000!

"[The UPC] must have felt overwhelmed when they saw the raw conditions everywhere," observed a faculty senator. And the situation only grew worse. With each year it became increasingly more difficult to create the enhancement fund. This depressing information was broadly shared with the campus community. If it did not help to improve campus morale, at least the campus's constituencies became more aware of the financial realities that hemmed in everyone's aspirations.

Impact on Organizational Climate

The inability of the UPC to effectively address long-range issues and to relieve economic hardships resulted in many disappointments throughout the campus. Frustrations mounted. In part, cynicism about the UPC arose from the feeling, evident among some faculty members, of being used. "I resent committees that are set up for show to keep the natives from getting too restless," objected one faculty member. "The president's attitude seemed more like it was aimed to keep us busy and make us feel like we were doing something important," said another. A third faculty member added:

> There is speculation that the goal authors were asked to write those papers to stall for time. The planning process was becoming an increasing source of frustration. Everything came to a halt while they waited for [those] papers. As the president was leaving, he told some people that it

had been [designed merely to provide] a break in intensity for the people involved in planning.

Such suspicions, warranted or not, are one legacy of the UPC.

Because the UPC's strategic planning objective was not achieved—"We could never get more strategic than to decide if chemistry should get more test tubes," a faculty member scoffed—there were exasperations about the poor use of people's time. "It became a chore, an albatross. A lot of us wished it would go away," an administrator complained. A faculty member concurred:

> In the end the faculty decided it was a waste of time. So even if the thing hadn't died out because of an incoming new president, it would have died because people were simply refusing to participate. It wore itself right out.

Another added:

> That's the shame [of it]. It was a group of people who had abilities to do things. If you're going to use their time, you should use it well.

An additional source of personal frustration can be attributed to unrealistically heightened anticipations that exceeded the UPC's potential. One faculty member believed the president's expectations for the UPC were pragmatic and that he intended the UPC to be a management vehicle to address hard realities. But, on the faculty side, initial aspirations may have been a great deal loftier—and all the more unrealistic:

> I think they saw it as a sort of "vision quest." That's where a lot of the pervasive disappointment for the faculty came from. The expectation that we could address larger issues—free ourselves up from day-to-day business and really think about the future—was the reason the faculty entered into the planning process.

"The expectation was really beyond what the process was able to deliver," summarized a dean. Then, when asked to participate in the distasteful exercise of apportioning cuts, greater frustrations were unleashed.

Initially, the UPC held the promise of improving the sense of community by educating and involving a broad representation of campus constituencies. Such potential, however, ultimately was overshadowed by the threatening economic conditions. In the long-run, morale deteriorated; the climate of the organization during the final throes of the UPC could only be described as gloomy.

EFFECTIVENESS OF THE UNIVERSITY PLANNING COUNCIL

One means of assessing the effectiveness of a strategic planning council is to examine the extent to which it makes decisions that lead the institution in promising directions. A threshold question arises: Was the UPC a genuine, decision-making body?

Most of the 10 UPC members who were interviewed realized from the outset that they were "an advisory group to the president." The president retained final decision-making authority on all matters the UPC recommended to him, and he, in fact, exercised this prerogative. He reported that at times the UPC would forward to him recommendations that caused him to go back to the UPC:

> I'd have to tell them, I'm really disappointed that "X" isn't on here. We did a little more negotiating. [Subsequently,] they would give [me recommendations] in draft form and ask me to comment on them.

For the most part, however, UPC members were granted considerable leeway in deciding how to allocate planning pool money. There was never enough money to do justice to the requests that came before them. But always their year-end reports included a prioritized list of proposals to be funded, a tangible result of their decision making.

Insofar as other matters were concerned, particularly recommending cuts, the UPC did not act as decisively as it might have. Recalling when the UPC was asked for advice about where to inflict cuts, a staff member said: "We never could come to a good consensus. We wouldn't resolve the matter, or we'd just end up wishy-washing around, just asking for more information." A faculty member concurred: "These [fourth cycle] mass meetings were designed to provide us with information we felt we needed to make recommendations on everything from program to staff to budget cuts. But after we had all that information, we still never made recommendations, really." A faculty senator not on the UPC agreed:

> When it came to making a hard decision like dropping an unaffordable school in order to support the university; they didn't make those kinds of decisions. They didn't cut that deep. They tried to make sure everybody survived.

So, at one level the UPC, when grappling with planning pool allocations, functioned as a decision-making body. When asked to make recommendations that entailed cutbacks, however, the UPC found its choices unsavory. It became stuck in what the psychological literature identifies as an avoidance mode of decision making. The outcomes of either choice were so unpalatable as to render UPC members essentially paralyzed as decision makers on the hard, consequential choices.

Given that the president retained final *de jure* decision-making authority, can it be said that the UPC engaged in *de facto* decision making? That is, did the UPC's recommendations become final decisions, deferred to by the president and the board of regents? The answer appears to be complex and issue dependent.

First, the president clearly did not rely exclusively on the UPC for advice. The president sought guidance from other advisors about UPC recommendations. "The president had his '8:30 Club' of trusted advisors [vice presidents] who were probably in on his decisions," commented a dean. "It was clear that the president was using a number of groups as advisory groups. He'd distill information from [them and then] inform them of his decision," a UPC faculty member observed.

Second, if a UPC recommendation had to be forwarded to another group to take action, the recommended action may or may not have been taken by it.

Third, if a UPC decision affected the curriculum, the issue would have to work its way through the Faculty Senate and its curriculum committee, or even through the board of regents.

Fourth, if a UPC decision pertained to the use of planning pool funds, the final decision was reserved for the president.

Commenting on the UPC's influence, a UPC faculty member concluded that "there was indeed group power, not [just] individual power." But it was of limited scope; for most of its short life span its business, in effect, was restricted to granting planning pool money. Moreover, the president, as noted, could always modify the UPC's recommendations—and sometimes did. Because planning money, though hardly plentiful, could be used to fund staff and faculty lines, the UPC was empowered to do what the deans were unable to do: facilitate the creation of new positions! In sum, within the scope of its limited charge and what it chose to take on, the UPC did exercise power.

The UPC's ultimate power was held in check by the president. Although the special assistant who served as staff to the UPC recalled that he could see "that the president's position changed many times as a result of the educated deliberations of the UPC," former council participants do not remember it quite that way. They perceive that the UPC's decisions influenced the president minimally, if at all. Following is a sample of comments, the first from an administrator, the last four from faculty members:

> [The president] was so persuasive that he would carry his position no matter what the discussion had been. Some of us got the feeling it didn't make a helluva lot of difference what we decided.

> When on occasion the UPC disagreed fairly strongly with the president, he would say, "You are just an advisory group." So when push came to shove [he would respond], "I'm going to do what I want to do. You guys are here to tell me *if* I want to listen, but I don't have to listen."

> The council had no real power save its ability to persuade the president. But the president was never there. We would have to speak to him through the chair.

> At times even when the UPC was in unanimous agreement about something, the president would ignore our recommendations, and we wouldn't know why. When this would happen, we would feel ineffectual, like we had wasted hours and hours of our time. We were strictly an advisory group, but when we'd advise in one direction, he would go in another without explanation, and it was frustrating.

> In my case and that of another goal author, our reports were just not accepted by him. He just wasn't willing to deal with our conclusions. I felt used.

Despite the evident frustration and skepticism embedded in the above appraisals, there was a sense that the president tended to respond favorably to the UPC's recommendations on funding reallocations. The UPC chair estimated a presidential acceptance rate "in the high 90s." But the president did not always agree with their rankings. "My guess is that he would respond favorably to the first two or three ranked items. After that, I think he had his own agenda," commented a faculty senator. A dean concluded that the UPC might have been witness to a clever administrative technique: "If the president really wanted C, D, and X out of A through Z, he could select those, and thereby get his own will without really doing violence to the UPC."

Despite such perceived machinations, the UPC did not see itself as "rubber-stamping" a set of predetermined priorities. It did, however, feel that its hands were tied when it came to making plans of significance for the university. For many, the deck appeared to be stacked with the president holding all the trump cards.

In summary, the UPC functioned as a decision-making group when it addressed the task of resource reallocations or making small grants. Some perceive that the UPC's decisions resulted in insignificant changes for the university. As one UPC member disparaged, "There is certainly no standing monument to what we went through." Yet others concede that when money was otherwise unavailable to departments, planning pool allocations were, in many cases, crucial. A UPC faculty member observed:

> When the chemistry department talked about wanting to improve their laboratory equipment, they were talking about safety—a refrigerator to store materials—not state-of-the-art laboratory! Basic needs!

When the UPC was asked to consider places to save money by cutting programs, budgets, or staff, its decision-making ability stalled. In a time of budgetary crisis, the task of downsizing the university simply overwhelmed the UPC.

Be that as it may, this "board of advisors" was asked to be responsible for decisions that formerly had been made elsewhere. In good faith and with high hopes, the UPC deliberated and came to closure on many issues that were put before it. However, it had no authority to assure that its recommendations would be accepted "on high." Over its lifetime, the UPC addressed many issues. But it was limited by circumstances—nightmarish economic circumstances—and by its uneven ability to persuade the president. In all, there was both an up side and a down side to the UPC.

Constraints

Seen in retrospect, the UPC's effectiveness was hampered by several limitations both inherent in its process and imposed by the environment. The first constraint, as previously described, was that long-range planning largely was not a part of the UPC's explicit mission. Not surprisingly, planning of a strategic nature was not among the UPC's achievements.

A second limitation: the UPC shied away from making big decisions. Despite the time and effort invested, very few substantial changes came about as a result of UPC deliberations. A faculty member suggested, "We chipped away at [issues] but have not resolved them. There are lots of improvements, but we have not tackled fundamental problems."

Third, recommendations were just that—recommendations. The perception was widespread that the UPC's decisions were not always adopted. Sometimes this was because the president would rearrange funding priorities. In other cases it was because the implementation of recommendations actually rested in the hands of another body, for example, the board of regents.

It was not always clear to the UPC why some of their recommendations came to naught. A faculty member attributes much of what happened—or what failed to happen—to the political and economic climate in the state, but also there was a lingering suspicion that the president was "using the campus as a launching pad to something else—that he used the faculty, that that's what the planning process was about."

A fourth constraint was the disagreeable nature of the task left to the UPC in an unforgiving economic environment. Personal frustrations abounded, growing out of the UPC's insufficiencies. Departments resented having to go through "the proposal writing process" to request money needed to maintain normal operations. The UPC symbolized a loss of decentralized budgeting autonomy. And, as the UPC's goals evolved, the rules of the small grants "game" changed for the proposal writers. One UPC faculty member recalled, "Every department would try to shoehorn their requests into one of these new categories. For example, math needed [teaching assistants], so they would [invoke] enrollment maintenance concerns, [while] the library [expressed its needs in terms of] communications technology." For many, it was an exasperating exercise. Indeed, some of the UPC members resented having to go on record with recommendations of cuts. A faculty senator complained, "You've got faculty colleagues publicly commenting on where to cut programs of their fellows. After all, the UPC members weren't paid to be public administrators, or executive decision makers. That's real tough."

Describing the UPC's noxious chores under the new economic conditions, one faculty member declared, "Every time we made a recommendation about cutting, someone from the program would have to come in and defend it. We'd be convinced that [the] cut wouldn't work and we'd have to look elsewhere." Another recalled that reducing programs was nearly impossible: "Anytime anyone tried to cut out anything, there were very complex questions of union contract, public support for a program, and all those mechanisms that go into effect immediately as soon as you start to reduce anything at a university." Basically, not very much resulted from the UPC's actions—or inactions—over proposed reductions.

Fifth, the UPC was the president's creation, and his leaving effectively abandoned the virtually friendless body. As the president prepared to leave the campus, the momentum of the UPC dissipated. A faculty union representative ruefully observed:

> Since [the UPC] is a presidential committee, it's back to square one if you change presidents. That's what happened here. Nobody had any commitment or inclination to follow through with the "Tarmac Report," so named because it was finished just in time for the president to toss it out the window as he boarded the plane.

Sixth, the timing of UPC decisions tended to be poor. With only a few exceptions for extraordinary matters, decisions were held to the end of the academic year. This would throw routine decision making at the deans' level out of kilter. Questions concerning the shifting of faculty or budgets that would normally have been resolved in January or February could not be finalized until April or May.

A final irritant was the involvement of nonacademic administrators in making academic decisions. Many academics believed that routine structuring and shifting of monies would have been better done through appropriate administrative channels rather than through such a heterogeneous group as the UPC. A faculty member reflected:

> Sometimes we bypassed basic academic issues. You could talk about retention and how it influenced funding and how [under enrollment] would affect the budget. But you couldn't talk about the crucial problem of not having a Shakespearean scholar because the intellectual concern

would often be overridden by a larger concern for the entire institution. So the smaller concern that would typically be handled by a dean would be moved into the whole cosmos, and money would go to larger, global projects instead of smaller, day-to-day replacement needs.

In these many ways, the UPC process, saddled with constraints internal and external, proved to be an aggravation to the campus community. It did not accomplish its long-range planning objective, nor did it result in much visible change for the campus. It did, however, fuel frustrations aplenty. This was the down side of the University Planning Council.

Positives

All was not grim or ill-fated. There was a brighter side. Three products of the UPC era, identified earlier, culminated in significant programmatic changes: a revised general education plan, the birth of University College, and the reorganization of the life sciences departments. Unfortunately, as previously noted, these three changes stand as isolated and atypical examples of UPC decision outcomes that had a broad impact.

Another positive outcome was that the UPC succeeded in broadly involving the campus in planning efforts. "Everyone participated at the department level," said one faculty senator. Not everyone agreed that the UPC was a genuine example of shared governance. "The president knew that the more people he could at least in a cursory way involve, the more support there would be," said an administrator. For all the UPC's liabilities, the opportunity to participate in decision making was one of the positive UPC outcomes.

Perspective suggests a further positive dimension—relatively speaking. When comparing the UPC process to the process that had preceded it at the university, the UPC could be viewed in a more favorable light. One dean (and former UPC member) concluded:

[The UPC] was genuinely a different kind of decision making than what had been. . . . [The UPC added] a significant dimension of information gathering, comment, discussion and recommendation from a broad set of constituencies. Aside from the Council of Deans and other interest groups making their views known to the president, there had been no predecessor to the group.

Perhaps, the most positive spin was suggested by one dean who thought the UPC to have been "a significant improvement. Not perfect—didn't print money!—but a healthy process that did generate some things that were in the long term useful." Whatever its shortcomings, the UPC was a step up over previous conditions.

As its chair noted, "Some major things got started under the planning process. It had its moments of glory!"

SUMMARY

Launched with high hopes, the euphoria for the University Planning Council was short-lived. Circumstances began to deteriorate in 1982-83. The campus community, slow to accept these conditions, continued with the planning process in a state of persistent denial about the new realities. As one faculty member recalled, "We were literally in a state of decline, but we thought we were in a state of growth—sort of schizoid! It was a schizophrenic environment." A union representative believed the UPC should have known what deliberations would come to:

> They just chose to pretend that they would invest this effort into rational decision making. Then, when the moment of truth came, they had to concede that's not how the world really works. The legislature didn't give us any time to "slide" into it. They said, "Here's your budget, live with it!"

Eventually the university's circumstances could no longer be denied. A faculty member recollected:

> It took a long time for people to think that planning could also mean downsizing instead of growing. In hindsight, if we had come to grips five years earlier with that notion, we would not have gone through as much trauma. Oddly enough, there were people on the UPC who kept saying we had to plan for cuts. It just wasn't computing. We could not get people to talk about cutting back.

As difficult and painful as the reversal of fortune proved to be for the University of Montana, there was no avoiding the truth. The planning process had raised hopes, hopes that were rapidly dashed. But the university was not responsible for the state's economic downturn. The larger environment would ultimately smother the UPC's early planning aspirations. To quote a union representative:

> To be fair, the basic situation is almost an insoluble dilemma. Do you downsize yourself hoping that you're going to be able to keep all your savings? Or do you say, that would be foolish when financial salvation is just around the corner in the form of finally a reasonable legislative appropriation. There is always that hope.

The UPC filled a vacuum; it constituted a heretofore absent effort to plan. Its chair pointed out that at least in the beginning the UPC worked reasonably well, despite some very questionable assumptions that underlay the process:

> Those assumptions were that there would be some enhancement pool money to allocate, that basic issues of faculty salaries and operations costs would be addressed in normal conventional budget terms, and that a

rational planning process could be developed. . . . As things got tighter in Montana, all of those assumptions turned out to be erroneous. There was no enhancement pool, normal budgetary processes could not and did not address the issue of routine operations and salaries, the regents and legislature were completely unresponsive to planning priorities, and the faculty union saw planning more and more as a threat to its interests.

Nonetheless, the UPC set a few very significant programs into motion. It mobilized the university community to focus on institutional goals. Participation across the campus became a reality. Planning activities compelled the university to address harsh, economic realities. This was the upside of the UPC. Yet, in the final analysis, the UPC disappointed everyone, for its potential seemed much greater than impinging realities allowed. As that dean had observed, the UPC didn't "print money."

Launched with enthusiasm, the UPC never hit its stride. Preoccupied in its first years with mostly mundane matters, by year three it had begun to raise its sights. But in its fourth year, the UPC's hopes were struck a savage blow by the legislature. Its fate was sealed by the president's departure the next year.

A flower that never fully blossomed, the UPC withered in youth and died before its time. It had not grown strong enough to resist the misfortunes visited upon it.

CHAPTER

Georgia Southern
College's Institutional
Planning Council:
Post Mortem on a Mismatch

G
eorgia Southern sits amidst pine-forested farmlands 50 miles north
west of historic Savannah and 200 miles southeast of Atlanta. Its
457-acre campus is a prominent feature of Statesboro, population
15,000. The college—now Georgia Southern University—is the hub of the
local economy.

The campus began as an agricultural and mechanical school in 1908,
offering only elementary and secondary studies. It became a teacher's college
in 1924, then joined Georgia's other state-supported colleges by merging into
the University System of Georgia in 1931. Enrollment grew by an unprecedented 72 percent in the second half of the 1980s making it the largest and
most comprehensive of the 15 senior colleges in that system. The institution's
six component schools offer a wide array of programs that span more than 150
fields of study at the graduate and undergraduate levels. When the visit took
place the campus served a student population of more than 11,000 with a
faculty of about 590. It became Georgia Southern University on July 1, 1990.

GSU is one of 34 public institutions that comprise the University System
of Georgia. The system is governed by a 15-member, governor-appointed
board of regents. A chancellor presides as chief executive officer of the board
and of the system. The president of Georgia Southern is elected by the board
upon recommendation of the chancellor and serves as the executive head of

the campus. The president's administrative team, the Executive Council, is made up of 15 academic officers, principally deans, directors, and vice presidents.

A Faculty Senate serves as the representative and legislative agency of the faculty and as the official advisory body to the president. The senate consists of 40 members drawn from the core of full-time teaching staff; they are elected to represent their various schools. Deans and the academic vice president are included, and the campus president presides as chair of the senate. The senate has had as many as 15 standing committees that address not only the campus's academic policies, but also conditions of faculty employment, campus safety issues, and the domain of student life. The senate, however, meets only quarterly; there are limits to what it can handle.

Nonacademic employees are classified either as professional/administrative or as staff. These employees are governed by personnel policies set forth by the university and the regents. Students at Georgia Southern elect a 25-member student senate and five executive officers to represent them in a Student Government Association. This body conveys student life concerns to administrators and faculty.

INSTITUTIONAL PLANNING COUNCIL

The strategic planning council studied at Georgia Southern was known as the Institutional Planning Council or "IPC." (Because the IPC had lived out its life during the campus's days as "Georgia Southern College," the campus is routinely referred to herein as GSC rather than GSU.) The IPC "qualified" as a strategic planning council in that it was a body that was convened by the president, was chaired by the chief academic officer, and consisted principally of faculty members. The IPC also had nonacademic representatives among its administrative membership; students and classified staff, however, were not IPC participants. The IPC's deliberations were not conducted in secret. In fact, its intent was to open communications between central administration and the faculty. It was to offer advice to the president and the Executive Planning Council (EPC) on those matters within its purview.

Profile of Interview Subjects

To discern the effects of the Institutional Planning Council, 17 fifty-minute semi-structured interviews were conducted in July 1988, at Georgia Southern College. Twelve of these were with former members of the IPC: 6 faculty, 4 staff, 1 middle-management administrator, and the chair of the IPC (the vice president for academic affairs). The remaining 5 interviews were with nonmembers: 3 key faculty senators, 1 support staff person representing the physical plant, and the current president who was living with the legacy of the IPC.

Historical Background: The IPC's Inception

GSC had begun to climb on the planning bandwagon as early as 1979. Some 20 months later a document entitled "Framework for a Five-Year Plan for Academic Affairs" was issued. It guided the institution for several years as the college expanded programs and assessed its role in the statewide system. By 1985 the college decided to expand the scope of its planning from a focus exclusively on academic affairs to planning that encompassed the entire institution. The resulting document, "Framework for Planning," described the overall philosophy of the college and identified general directions in which progress was desired. Concurrent with the drafting of this document, the president had commissioned a task force to design a structure through which formal planning could be implemented at Georgia Southern. The Institutional Planning Council and its administrative complement, the Executive Planning Council, were born in 1985 out of this task force's endeavors.

One individual was clearly the chief architect of the new structure. A former member of the faculty, he was appointed by the president to serve as the director of the new Office of Planning. He had an enormous impact on how the IPC would be structured: he detailed the scope of the IPC's activities, devised an elaborate timetable for it, and influenced the composition of its membership. The president himself was detail oriented, but, as noted by an IPC faculty member, he found in this planning director someone who would attend to details for him.

Why had the president chosen this particular approach to planning? Five reasons for instituting the IPC emerged from interviews. First, spectacular enrollment growth necessitated a carefully considered response. The student population had exploded from 5,600 to 10,000 in only five years. This growth has since been attributed to the introduction of intercollegiate athletic programs, an increased emphasis on recruiting, and improved retention efforts. Then in 1983-84, enrollments suddenly dropped. An IPC faculty member recalled, "We had no idea why students were enrolling here. Not knowing what triggered the decline and growth was unsettling." Rapid changes in enrollment necessitated planning that would justify budget increases and enable the campus to project facilities and personnel needs. Rapid growth was also impeding campus communication channels. A senate leader commented, "We had reached that point in our growth level where we simply needed another group level to communicate things."

A second reason for initiating the IPC was that lack of formal planning had been cited in an accreditation report as a problem for Georgia Southern. "Our regional accrediting association made it clear that formal planning needed to be more regular, continuous, systematic," said an IPC faculty member. "The president decided planning was the way of the future," a senate leader explained. The president had invited George Keller to visit the campus as a consultant. The IPC chair recalled:

> Keller came several times. His presence on our campus and his presenta-
> tions added to the excitement and the felt need for a strategic planning
> model. He is a great salesman of strategic planning and had a great impact
> on our proposal that came later.

In short, the community was primed for a more formal approach to planning.

A third reason for launching the IPC was that Georgia Southern's president was intent upon changing the institution's status from that of college to university. He was said to have made some "end runs" around the board of regents to accomplish that objective and appeared thereby to have alienated himself from the board. "Perhaps it was thought that the switch to university status would be more likely to happen if we planned," suggested a faculty senator.

A fourth reason is that GSC was moving, albeit cautiously, toward a more participatory governance model during the president's tenure. The IPC chair noted that prior to this administration, GSC, at least according to some, had been run by the "Benevolent Dictator approach." Decision making had been handled more centrally:

> But when the president came in the late 1970s, circumstances changed.
> In 1981 we revised institutional statutes, expanding the role of the faculty
> senate and creating a much more shared governance approach.

These changes encouraged the college to aspire to a more open approach to planning. As a task force reviewed various planning models, the campus realized GSC was not in the national mainstream of shared governance practices. "We knew we needed an updated approach to governance, and the president had that same kind of orientation," the IPC chair noted.

Many of those interviewed, however, doubted that the president was truly committed to shared governance. He possessed a very persuasive and outgoing personality. "He liked big ideas. He liked to 'wow' folks with his style," commented a faculty member. The president had independently decided to put money into major new programs. He had reintroduced intercollegiate football to GSC and built a stadium. He started a museum and a nursing program. A common conviction among faculty members was that money invested in those projects equated to money diverted from other areas. Equipment purchases, travel, and faculty development were some of the budgets adversely affected. Accordingly, some faculty members became keenly interested in exerting control over the president's spending patterns.

As one faculty member described the setting, the president "had upset enough people that he had trouble building a political base enabling him to do what he wanted to do." The senate wanted to curtail his spending, and the faculty had administrative allies, too, in seeking a more orderly process for planning. A vice president reported:

> There was a growing feeling among the administrators that we needed a more structured process to decide on these new initiatives. So we had some discussions with [the president] and he agreed to commission a task force to design a planning process, out of which came the IPC. The idea came from outside the president. It was brought to him, and he agreed to look into it via this task force.

The president seemed to believe it would be appropriate to pull others into the decision making. "The IPC was a political animal created to respond to those various [concerns]," observed a nonacademic administrator. "I think my predecessor had it in the back of his mind that it was a means of getting the faculty to feel they were involved," commented GSC's current president. One senate leader believed it had been the president's objective to work with a small group "that could handle things more easily than the senate." An administrator suspected that the IPC was, in fact, established to serve as a buffer between the president and the senate: "It was to help appease the faculty so that they could have some input."

A fifth and related reason for forming the IPC, then, was to overcome the objections raised by faculty and administrators to the president's predisposition to commit to costly initiatives, noted above, without adequate in-house consultation. Representativeness was desired to enlarge the perspective that went into decision making. It was thought that the IPC "would eliminate some of the administrative biases and hang-ups that would develop from the deans' council where you'd have people concerned for their own areas," explained a professor. The Faculty Senate originally sought to create two planning groups, one for academic concerns, one for business and finance matters. Eventually, the senate endorsed the IPC design. "The IPC was formed as a compromise," said a faculty member. Its chair recalled that "an overriding political consideration was that there be a balance of faculty and non-faculty IPC positions, with a working majority of faculty." Faculty members were nominated and elected by their schools; senate representatives were voted on by the membership at large. "It was the more senior, experienced people who were elected," observed a faculty member. It was assumed that the IPC would broaden the perspective that influenced presidential decision making.

To recapitulate, the IPC owed its creation at Georgia Southern to five reasons: a huge growth in enrollments, an identified need for campus-wide planning (underscored by accreditation visitors), a campaign to have the campus status upgraded from college to university, a move generally (if haltingly) toward more widely shared participation in governance, and a realization on the part of the president and others that it was desirable to broaden the base of decision making for planning. The task force sketched out the IPC structure, and the director of planning fleshed out the design. The IPC threw itself enthusiastically into its work.

Membership Composition and Selection

The IPC was initially envisioned to have 20 members, but it functioned with 17 voting and another three nonvoting members. Ten of its members were from the faculty, one from each of the six schools and the library, plus three senate representatives. All were elected to either two- or three-year terms. Six representatives from administrative services—institutional development, student affairs, auxiliary services, plant operations, the controller's office, and admissions—were appointed by their respective area heads (the vice president for business and finance or the dean of student affairs). A student senator was to have been an elected member of the IPC but that never came to pass. The vice president for academic affairs chaired the group. The campus's other two vice presidents and the director of planning served as nonvoting members.

The IPC's Purposes and Arrangements

The IPC was unusual for a strategic planning council in that it actually outlasted its president. The president who authorized it left GSC in 1986, after the IPC's first year of operation, yet it persisted through another two years as campus leadership changed. Although it spanned a three-year period, it did not complete even one planning cycle as originally envisioned. Its objectives changed markedly between the first and second year.

At its onset the IPC was given a specific and reasonably ambitious charge; it was to undertake an annual review and revision of institutional mission, construct institutional goals and objectives statements, perform an annual review and evaluation of the extent to which the college's budget supported its goals and objectives, as well as consider any ad hoc planning decisions that may have been necessary.

And so the IPC began as a very busy committee. It met year round, beginning in the summer of 1985, convening weekly for two- or three-hour sessions. The IPC did not have a subcommittee structure; the group met as a whole.

The IPC was provided with complete staff support. The Office of Planning provided the IPC's data needs, and support staff attended all IPC meetings. The president's office supplied clerical assistance to the council. Minutes of these meetings were distributed for review at the group's next gathering.

However, the array of tasks in the charge was never put into operation. As the campus began a search to replace its outgoing president, its interim leader, the academic affairs vice president, who had been chairing the IPC, determined that that body should refocus its energies. Rather than continue with its earlier efforts to articulate institutional plans, it would now serve as a forum through which the implications of ad hoc planning decisions could be discussed with the campus community. The more ambitious setting of institutional directions was to be placed on hold, awaiting the arrival of the incoming president. During the IPC's third and final year, and with a new CEO now at the helm, the campus undertook an extensive review of its planning model. In light of anticipated changes, the IPC was virtually inactive that year; it met only a few times.

No annual reports were submitted by the IPC to the president. In fact, very little of their conclusions or opinions was ever put in writing. The three nonvoting members of IPC (the vice presidents for academic affairs and for business and finance and the director of planning) along with one faculty representative and the college president were also members of the Executive Planning Council (EPC). IPC deliberations typically were informally passed to the president through the Executive Planning Council. Given the significant overlap between the IPC and EPC, the importance of formal records may have been less necessary.

IMPACT OF THE INSTITUTIONAL PLANNING COUNCIL

The Institutional Planning Council influenced a number of facets of campus life. These included governance, planning, communication, and organizational climate.

Governance

At the time of the campus visit, Georgia Southern was adopting a revised approach to planning. The IPC had just been disbanded, and the visit focused on analyzing what had happened during the IPC's brief and not notably productive existence. The evidence was spare. Nonetheless, the IPC's impact can be discerned, mainly through the interviews that were conducted.

The matters initially brought to the IPC for its consideration unquestionably were of great importance to the college. Its original concerns were with the purpose and mission of the institution. It was also to work with the budget. Questions raised by Georgia Southern's rapid growth were always on the agenda. "The IPC was supposed to consider and resolve several important issues," recalled a senate leader. An IPC administrator concurred:

It was intended to have a major impact on the campus. We were to review budgets and goals of each unit to see if goals could be accomplished with those budgets, and to look for measurable indicators.

"The issues were there," affirmed a senate activist, "but the IPC was not in a position to do anything about them."

"We never fulfilled our mission," declared a faculty member. The IPC did not become the hub of decision making it was intended to be. A vice president observed:

Instead of being consulted in advance of budget decisions, the committee was advised about what was being done after the decisions had been made elsewhere. We really had no impact on the budget.

"The decisions would be made elsewhere, and then the IPC would learn of it," another administrator recalled. While some expected that the IPC would address matters of significance, the extent to which the IPC was deprived of the opportunity to decide these matters for the campus was unanticipated.

Did it appear initially that the IPC would wield considerable authority? Had it been assigned responsibilities formerly held by other entities? Some of those interviewed believed that the IPC symbolized a change in the college's philosophy and structure of governance in which decision making was shifted away from a more central approach to one that more actively involved the faculty and their senate. Before the IPC model was introduced, "the running of the institution was in the hands of a very few people—the president, the vice presidents, and a few deans," the IPC's chair commented.

Apparently the IPC posed no threat to the authority of the Faculty Senate although there was initially a lack of senate support for the new approach. This seems attributable to the senate's general discomfort with the president at that point. Reflecting on the senate's position, one IPC faculty member exclaimed, "I don't think it was concerned over [a loss of authority to the IPC]—it was obstinacy!" "I did not get the impression that anybody felt power or authority was being usurped," said a faculty senator. However, another senate activist added that "had the IPC been an effective body, it would have represented a shift of authority away from the Faculty Senate." Under the circumstances, this point remains moot.

Another widely shared conclusion was that some kinds of decisions that came before the IPC had not been previously addressed by the campus. Therefore, it was not a shift in decision-making responsibility as much as it was a filling of a decision-making vacuum. A senate leader recalled:

My impression is that [IPC concerns] were relatively new [and dealt with] late-breaking issues rather than things that have come up before. It was not so much a transfer of responsibility as newly articulated responsibilities.

One administrator on the IPC described it as "a more organized approach"; matters were funneled to the president through the IPC rather than addressed directly to the president from various sources. An IPC faculty member pointed out that there were many other groups on campus simultaneously deciding issues of importance: "I saw us as [just] another agency that provided input."

The IPC model was seen as a vehicle for sharing decision making more broadly at GSC. It was intended to impart a strategic thrust to the concerns of the college, many of which were not previously addressed by the campus. A muted redistribution of influence seems to have resulted. On the one hand, the IPC in no way jeopardized the authority of the senate. On the other hand, the IPC model bypassed two echelons of academic administrators. As one IPC faculty member observed, "The deans and department heads were left out. Their exclusion made the planning process less real than it could have been."

Given the limited scope of the IPC, how did the various interested parties on the campus react to it? Although the framework document suggested the council would have considerable power to direct the campus, the presiding chief executive officer confirmed that "it certainly didn't work out that way." An administrator not on the IPC commented: "I don't believe people were threatened by the IPC. [It] didn't function." An IPC faculty member affirmed that "We had no authority, we were just a sounding board, reactive rather than proactive." And apparently the IPC was suspect from the beginning. "People really didn't believe it would do anything but support what the president wanted to do," added a senate leader.

What of the faculty? "In its early stages, the faculty had wanted to participate in this new process and were disappointed that so little came of it," recalled one academic. A senator noted that there was a recognized need among the faculty "to plan for growth rather than to react every fall to the problems presented by a bigger and bigger freshman class." But many believed that only the teaching faculty should be involved in the planning process. An IPC faculty member described the cleavage between academics and nonacademics:

> There was, and is, a consensus about the faculty's central responsibility towards academic questions. The issue breaks down when planning goes beyond academic issues. Are those also to be dominated by faculty? That's a delicate political issue that raised its head more than once—and continues to.

The faculty were never fully committed to the model.

As noted, the Faculty Senate did not appear to be ruffled by IPC activities. The IPC was not an isolated group. In fact, several of those interviewed suggested that in reality the IPC functioned like an arm of the senate. One senator's account of the IPC was that it "was a small group doing senate legwork." It certainly was not the final ruminating point before ideas were passed to the president. Typically, IPC concerns were reviewed and voted on at senate meetings. Because major IPC recommendations had to be discussed in the senate before they could be passed on to the president or his Executive Planning Council, "log jams" resulted because of the senate's infrequent meetings. This created a tremendous procedural snag. A faculty member reported that "the IPC would come to a standstill or do things that were meaningless" while it waited for other bodies to act on its recommendations. The senate also shared the conviction that in the final analysis the president would do things his way. A senator (an IPC member) offered the following:

> The president chairs the Faculty Senate and so can come in and say, "I want to do this"—and the Faculty Senate rolls over and plays dead and says, "That's fine."

In sum, the senate appeared to have preserved as much control over its affairs, the IPC, and the campus as was possible under that administration. But, on the whole its authority was quite circumscribed.

And what of the IPC's relationship to the Executive Planning Council? A nonacademic administrator on the IPC noted that the IPC potentially could have resolved some important matters for the campus; however, he concluded, "the EPC was where the decisions were made." Another such administrator concurred. He cited as an example the IPC's construction of a lengthy set of campus goal statements that were then forwarded to the EPC: "I don't think they were ever acted upon." The IPC chair offered this explanation:

> The basic charge of the IPC was to primarily react to directions, decisions, and recommendations of the EPC which was [composed] of central administrators. The EPC would say to the campus through the IPC, "All right, folks, this is what we intend to do." We would play that through the IPC. What proved frustrating for some people was that the EPC was not following the schedule that the original document called for. As a result, the IPC was often waiting for the EPC to move.

Clearly, the EPC had not relinquished any of its autonomy to the IPC. IPC decisions were subject to EPC actions—and inactions.

As opposed as the faculty was to including nonteaching personnel in campus planning, the staff and nonteaching administrators seemed to have been very pleased to have had a voice in this new planning model. One such representative reported that many staff people had been disgruntled by their previous exclusion from campus planning. Other nonacademic staff believed too much control had been left to the Faculty Senate: "I'm one of those staff members who believes that a Faculty Senate that excludes staff members should not govern the [entire] campus. I know as much about parking problems as any Ph.D.!" The nonacademic staff, then, despite the fact that the IPC never became an influential player, at least enjoyed the status of being admitted to the IPC club. Students, as noted previously, simply did not participate in these deliberations.

Impact on Planning

The IPC's planning responsibilities looked very good on paper, prior to its reconfigured mission following year one. In that first year the IPC was presented with an elaborate flow chart detailing a number of objectives. The establishment of an institutional planning process was to have been its first year's end-product. But it quickly became apparent that those flow chart objectives could not possibly be accomplished in so short a period of time. As interpreted by one faculty member, the IPC "was charged with a mission it could never accomplish—too much detailed, day-to-day planning in the bowels of the organization." The council never moved beyond the first significant "hurdle" on the flow chart—the revision of the institutional mission statement and accompanying goals and objectives statements. That task consumed a year of its time and resulted in a product that ultimately was not accepted by the president.

In the second year, administrative leadership changes sharply redirected the council's activities. The flow chart approach was abandoned. Initially overstructured, the IPC became a group without sufficient structure. Matters now before it were less abstract than the original and much loftier tasks of defining mission and articulating goals statements. Its mandate significantly altered, the IPC never fulfilled its early planning objectives.

The IPC, however, can be credited at the least with focusing attention on the need to plan. "There were a lot of good elements there," commented one administrator. The IPC had set the stage for planning and laid the basic foundation. In one sense it served as a "trial run" by pointing out weak areas in the initial planning design. The frustrations it caused "prompted a review which led to a new process, the SPC [Strategic Planning Council]," said a vice president. At the time of the campus visit, with the SPC yet to get underway, it appeared that the design adopted for the IPC's successor addressed some of the problems that had constrained the IPC's effectiveness: its size, representation, lack of expertise, and ambiguous charge. The SPC was to begin with a clear set of goals established by its new president and with a clear understanding that it was to adopt and support a global purview of the campus. Said the president:

> We don't know if the SPC is going to work. But if it does, it will be a genuinely collegial process and will force people to make decisions. It won't fool around.

The IPC had provided a foundation of experience, albeit not of successes but of lessons learned the hard way. Upon that base the SPC, Georgia Southern's next iteration in planning, was being erected. Hopes for an effective governance and planning process once more rose.

Improved Communication

The IPC involved and informed the community—particularly the faculty—in ways previously not attempted. In these ways it made a genuine contribution to Georgia Southern.

First, it was viewed as a more participatory style of governance than had existed before. It was the first time that a wider circle of members of the campus community was brought into the planning process. The staff, in particular, were pleased to have been given a voice. There was also approval among the faculty. "It was an opportunity for faculty to participate in campus governance; no doubt about that," claimed one professor. Others perceived that the former president was not genuinely interested in sharing. "He was a great one for *saying* he has shared governance," complained another faculty member, "but the reality was different." A staff member agreed that the IPC merely provided an "illusion of participation." The council served as a forum for faculty debate and discussion "even though the president had already made up his mind."

It can be said that the IPC may have enabled the faculty to be more vocal. And it did, in fact, improve the two-way flow of communication on the campus. A staff administrator credited the IPC as a means of forwarding information to the faculty. It brought them closer to where the decisions were being made even if it did not make them responsible for those decisions. The IPC became a conduit for information sharing. Central administration was credited with having provided them with access to information. Even privileged information of the sort not intended for general campus release was shared with the IPC. One faculty member described that period as "an educational process for the college." But it wasn't exactly graduate school!

Impact on Organizational Climate

As often happens when expectations run high at the inception, the IPC appeared to promise more than it ultimately delivered. It frustrated and disappointed those involved. A faculty member mused:

> It was a tragedy that it did not work out the way most of us thought it was supposed to. When it first started there was interest back at the depart-

ment level to regularly hear of what the IPC was discussing. I didn't want to tell them we weren't doing anything. Finally, I just stopped giving reports—it got too embarrassing.

Expectations were raised that were only to be dashed. Another faculty member lamented:

It just was not what the teaching faculty thought it was going to be. They thought they were going to be in on all the big decisions. It was very disappointing for many.

The current GSC president offered a devastatingly succinct summary: "It was nothing less than a prescription for disaster."

One reason the IPC had trouble getting off the ground was because it was not able to shake off partisan perspectives. Many IPC members were there specifically to represent the priorities of their own constituencies. "Goals of *parts* of the organization were more important [to the IPC] than overall goals of the institution," one administrator declared. IPC members who were interviewed unanimously reported that this parochialism was never overcome.

The corollary of such parochialism, however, is that divergent opinions contributed to the overall education of all IPC members. Openly expressed, conflicting viewpoints obliged everyone to consider other perspectives. "This was one of the biggest advantages of the IPC," one faculty member professed. The council's representative structure thus assured that differences of opinion would be voiced, and it prompted IPC members to seek to understand other points of view during council deliberations. This aided in the development of a sense of campus community. A senate leader believed that "there was learning or sensitizing on both [academic and nonacademic] parts." This enhanced awareness helped to counterbalance the frustrations attendant to the council's ineffectiveness.

OVERALL EFFECTIVENESS OF THE INSTITUTIONAL PLANNING COUNCIL

After three years of IPC activity, the consensus among participants held that it had largely failed as a decision-making body. In its first year, it was asked to wrestle with institutional goals and objectives and to issue recommendations. But once that task was completed, the purpose of the council changed drastically. "We made few decisions. It was more a matter of receiving information from the president and vice presidents," recalled an administrator. Information was brought to them "as if" they were a decision-making group, noted a faculty member. But, in the main, the IPC was asked to react to matters already decided by others. An administrative member concurred:

"We had opinions about whether things were best done that way or not, but it really didn't make any difference. The decision had already been made."

Several of those interviewed described the IPC as a "sounding board" or a "debating society." Its chair discussed the limits of its decision-making authority as follows:

> The [Executive Planning Council] was responsible for the overall decision making in regard to the direction of the institution and stating assumptions and making final decisions on goals. The IPC was designed to react to proposals of the EPC and to seek faculty and staff input regarding stated goals and assumptions of the EPC. . . . Primarily we discussed items and shared information as opposed to any decision making.

One IPC administrator scoffed that no conclusions were ever reached, nor decisions ever rendered: "The IPC never really, finally took a position on anything." A faculty senator (an IPC member) expressed widely shared feelings when reporting: "It was kind of silly to be brought up-to-date by the vice president on matters over which the IPC had no discretion. There were no choices to be made!" One IPC faculty member described the council's relationship to existing campus structures as strictly advisory: "We were not a true decision-making body in that our decisions would lead to action. [We just made] recommendations to other groups on campus." Another concurred: "I never sensed that the group felt empowered to move the institution."

In the final analysis, the response of other campus governance bodies to the IPC's activities was, at the worst, one of skepticism, and at the best, indifference. The council was not perceived as a threat to anyone's authority or autonomy.

In all, the IPC was given few specific matters to decide; its decisions were looked upon solely as recommendations; it was dependent on other bodies for endorsement. In light of these limitations, was the IPC able to influence decision outcomes?

The evidence suggests that it did not. Although the IPC's originating document lists as the first of its assumptions and basic principles that "the president must demonstrate his support for the planning process by working with and within that process," only a small minority believe the president took IPC recommendations seriously. The overwhelming conclusion of those interviewed is that the IPC simply did not influence presidential decision making. The following comments are representative of the majority view:

> The president did not reject our mission statement but modified it to such an extent [that] the IPC did not feel a great deal of ownership in it anymore. (an administrator)

The IPC had the idea it could make decisions and that the president [would support] these decisions. [But] it just wasn't his style to be led around by anybody. (a faculty member)

The president came to one or two IPC meetings at our request and talked to us and let us talk to him. He answered our questions, but he didn't change his mind. (a faculty member)

To the extent that [IPC recommendations] coincided with what the president had in mind anyway, yes, he acted favorably on their recommendations. [But] the decisions had already been made. (a staff member)

As one faculty member put it, the president went his own way: "He had his own agenda."

Was the EPC influenced by IPC reactions and recommendations? One faculty member who served on both bodies believed that the EPC paid attention to the IPC:

The year I was on the EPC there were very few decisions made that did not take into account the IPC recommendations. I think they took it seriously.

However, another IPC faculty member was doubtful, reporting that the EPC took no visible action on IPC recommendations:

We never got started. Not much really came to us for recommendations. We weren't given anything to react to.

This sentiment was echoed by a staff representative to the IPC who observed:

The committee never influenced decision making. It was "stillborn." Decisions continued to be made by the same people who made them prior to the IPC. It was always an awkward appendage to the organizational structure.

With the change in leadership following its first year, the IPC never did develop its own identity, nor did it form clearly understood relationships with other governance bodies. Rather, it lingered on for two years as a reminder that the campus still fell short of instituting a viable planning process.

SUMMARY

The IPC failed to accomplish its institutional planning objectives because of limitations inherent in its membership, a lack of clarity in its charge, and an absence of adequate institutional support for its endeavors. Initial campus leadership that did little to empower the council, compounded by a change in campus leadership before the ink was dry on the charter establishing it, also impaired its functioning.

First, the membership composition posed several difficulties. Some felt the council to be too large to be manageable. "Seventeen egos meant lots of discussion and points of view," recalled an administrator. Also, its broad base was expected to be beneficial, but this feature actually worked against the group's productivity. In the words of a faculty member, many came with "axes to grind from their constituencies." "The lines were drawn early in terms of taking positions," agreed an administrator. Another basic problem with the membership was that line officers—excepting the chair who was the chief academic affairs officer—were excluded. Deans and directors responsible for planning and budgeting activities were left out of IPC deliberations. As a consequence, many IPC members had not previously been involved in decision making beyond the department level. It would take time to acquire a campuswide perspective. Group opinions tended to be narrow and uninformed. Said a faculty member:

> You can't step in to make global recommendations about an organization without being fairly well-educated about that organization. It takes time—about a year—to get those folks educated. And then they would go off the IPC, and you'd be dealing with another group!

A staff member suggested that "an in-depth orientation should have been provided in advance to educate them. We [lost a lot of] time trying to bring them up-to-date as we discussed issues." Several interviewees suggested that including faculty at that level of decision making will always tend to slow down proceedings. "The nature of faculty is to widen, rather than to narrow, the funnel of options," proffered a staff member. In any event, it appeared that the constituency-oriented IPC membership, combined with a limited organizational perspective, led to endless difficulties for the IPC. The current president of Georgia Southern concluded that the IPC had, indeed, "denigrated the role of expertise in favor of participation."

Second, the IPC lacked a clearly defined mandate. It was neither given a clear set of goals in advance, nor did it articulate one for itself. Part of what it was asked to do was unrealistic. In one faculty member's assessment:

> It didn't have a charge it was capable of handling. For example, our guiding document says we will review everyone's budget. No one on campus does that!

Its ill-defined role and scope impaired its functioning. One professor sadly put it this way: the IPC "was never sure of its own personality."

Third, the council was further hampered by a lack of adequate technical support. In the IPC's third year and final year, an in-house institutional study of the planning process was undertaken at the request of the new president. High on the study's list of criticisms of the IPC process was the observation that "too much detailed analysis was expected from the committee." The campus was unable to provide the IPC with the basic information it needed in an already synthesized format. Instead, it was fed massive amounts of data it was expected somehow to digest. In its first year, the director of planning had largely provided this service to the IPC. Upon his departure, however, such support was no longer available. "The [IPC] members were not people who had time to do this properly," observed a faculty member. And the institution did not make release time available to IPC members for campus planning.

A fourth problem was the leadership factor. Even the executive officer who initiated the IPC was seen by some as hindering its activities. One administrator described the former president as not having been interested in sharing authority with the IPC:

> He *knew* what was best for Georgia Southern College. Under his presidency we couldn't have created a planning process because of his leadership style.

Nonetheless, when the president departed, so did support for the IPC's planning process. While it awaited guidance from new leadership, the IPC lapsed into a state of limbo. Thus the change in organizational leaders short-circuited IPC activities. Its chair commented:

> We never really got to monitoring or reviewing the budget. In practice it was more of a sharing of information from central administration to the IPC.

The absence of genuine support from leadership proved the death knell of this planning council.

All of those interviewed shared the strong belief that some combination of these factors combined to prevent the IPC from ever really getting off the ground. It never did function as intended. Largely confined to receiving and reviewing information, the IPC had few opportunities to inform actual decisions, and so it was in no position to provide direction for the campus. It left behind no persisting recommendations as a legacy for Georgia Southern. "The institution was not a great deal better off for having had that committee," was one administrator's understated appraisal.

"A Planning Process for Georgia Southern College" was the paper that had first proposed and described the IPC. Its introductory remarks cautioned: "A plan should not be the ultimate goal of planning, *nor should the process itself become a goal* [emphasis added]." Unfortunately, that is precisely what befell the IPC. Its chair observed:

> I think the whole rationale for this planning process stemmed back to the need for what the campus wanted—a more open process in terms of decision making. Of paramount importance to the people of the IPC was that we follow a logical process, and that they be allowed input before the whole thing was decided.

IPC members—its faculty members and middle managers alike—shared the conviction that they were not instrumental to the decision-making process but rather were informed of decisions after the fact. Its members apparently were briefed on these matters in advance of the campus at large, and they did have the opportunity to voice their opinions among themselves before others were informed. But it was a case of too little, too late.

At Georgia Southern, the IPC broke new ground for the campus—not in the area of planning, but of process. Its nourishment, however, was too thin to sustain it, and it succumbed of irrelevance.

CHAPTER

•••••••••

Shippensburg University's Forum: A Spirit of Consensus

S hippensburg University of Pennsylvania is nestled within the Cumberland Valley of the south central Pennsylvania Appalachians. About 50 miles southwest of Harrisburg, the borough of Shippensburg in Cumberland County has a population of approximately 5,300. Farming forms the basis for the local economy, although "SU" is the major employer in the area, generating more than 2,000 jobs in the county.

Situated on 200 acres of rolling land, the institution was founded as a private normal school during the era of Reconstruction in 1871, just six years after the conclusion of the Civil War. It was purchased by the commonwealth and became a public institution in 1917. Its mission evolved as the needs of the state's citizenry changed, and it is now one of 14 universities that make up the State System of Higher Education of Pennsylvania. Affectionately referred to as "Ship," the campus today consists of three colleges: Arts and Sciences, Business, and Education and Human Services. Together these colleges offer 46 baccalaureate degree programs in 29 departments of study and 29 master's degree programs in 19 fields. Student enrollment exceeds 6,400. Full- and part-time faculty number about 345.

The universities in the state system are overseen by a board of governors vested by law with authority for the control and management of the commonwealth's public institutions of higher education. (This system should not be confused with the 20, mostly small, scattered campuses that are extensions of Pennsylvania State University.) A chancellor serves as their executive officer. Each campus is governed by a council of trustees that appoints a president as each campus's chief executive officer. At SU the president presides over a 15-member cabinet consisting principally of deans and vice presidents. Additionally, the four vice presidents and the executive director of university relations compose the president's five-member executive management team.

In the early 1970s, on behalf of the state universities, the board of governors entered into an agreement with the Association of Pennsylvania State College and University Faculties (APSCUF) for the purposes of collective bargaining. Prior to that time, faculty interests had been represented at Shippensburg through their Faculty Senate. However, campus senates throughout the system were abolished when the union came into being at SU. The statewide union contract subsumed traditional senate roles related to conditions of employment and curricular review. About 70 percent of the SU faculty pay dues to APSCUF.

The nonacademic staff employees may also elect to be represented by labor unions. Additionally, the students on the campus have a self-government body, the Student Association, with both a graduate and an undergraduate division. Students join with faculty and administrators to serve on many of the university's policy-making committees.

SHIPPENSBURG'S "UNIVERSITY FORUM"

The council that was studied at Shippensburg University is commonly referred to as the Forum. It is a body convened by the president. Its chair is elected by the membership, which is composed largely of faculty. The chief academic officer is a presidential appointee to the Forum and, by tradition, has been elected by the Forum membership to serve as a member of its own executive committee. The Forum also has student and other administrative members. Its deliberations are quite open; in fact, its business is routinely advertised in campus publications. It offers advice to the president on nearly all matters that come before it for review and recommendation.

Profile of Interview Subjects

To investigate the effectiveness of the University Forum, 16 fifty-minute semi-structured interviews were conducted in July 1988, at Shippensburg University. Twelve of these were with former members of the Forum: 8 faculty members (one of whom had served as the elected Forum chair) and 4 administrators (all vice presidents). The remaining 4 interviews were with nonmembers. Two were faculty union activists. Another was the person responsible for providing staff support to the Forum. The final interview was with the campus president. Student members were unavailable for interviews.

History and Development of the Forum

The president is credited for the creation of the governance structure at Shippensburg. Prior to his arrival in the fall of 1981, "there was no specific governance structure," said the Forum chair. "We had the curriculum committee and the union's 'Meet and Discuss' committee that took on some aspects of a university senate, but it did not function well." The president himself had quickly observed that SU for years "had been living without any kind of governance structure that would assure a high level of participation from the various constituencies." There were some procedures to deal with curricular matters, but all other concerns were legislated more centrally. Questions of union versus administrative territoriality echoed about, and a 1979 Middle States Accreditation Report cited this dichotomy as an organizational weakness.

Determined to rectify the situation, the president worked to establish relationships and trust levels during his first two-and-a-half years in office before formally approaching the union about making changes. He then proposed that a sizable committee of faculty, administrators, and students should be formed to study various models of shared governance that were in place throughout the country. The union president appointed the faculty representatives to this committee. A joint charge was then issued by the president and the union to carve out a suitable shared governance model for SU. After lengthy deliberation over an 18-month period, a committee report was eventually filed with both the president and the union.

The proposed governance structure then went before the faculty for a vote. A two-thirds majority was required for passage. On first introduction, the measure was narrowly defeated. The president advised the campus that the status quo would persist. However, he was approached by some faculty who asked him to modify a few aspects of the original proposal and resubmit it to the faculty for their approval. This took place; the revised proposal contained specific provisions for faculty involvement in matters of planning and budget. These inclusions were "of great significance to the faculty," recalled a union leader. The proposal was passed on its second referendum. The students' graduate and undergraduate associations also approved the new governance structure.

The Forum, as defined in the governance structure document, was intended to serve as the authoritative committee under the president. It was to receive and act on the recommendations of four key subcommittees: Planning and Budget, Governance Review, Curriculum, and Student Affairs. "Most of the major decisions are made by the [sub]committees," a faculty member explained. "They do all their business, and their work is then brought to the Forum." An academic administrator described the Forum "as a place for debate of issues in an attempt to achieve consensus." If agreement cannot be reached, the Forum instructs a subcommittee to continue working with the issue and then to reintroduce it to the Forum. If eventually consensus can be reached, the Forum transmits its recommendations to the president.

A significant problem with the previous system, noted one faculty member, was that many committees had made independent recommendations to the president. For example, it was not uncommon for curricular recommendations to reach the president's desk through two different tracks. There was poor communication between the tracks. "It was a time-inefficient process and frustrating," said a faculty member. "Your proposal could get sent back to you for more information from both tracks." Also, the proposal that eventually reached the president could look quite different from what was originally intended, and the president would be unaware of the extent of the alterations. The Forum was viewed as a means of streamlining this reporting process. By channeling recommendations through one central body, issues could be refined and ambiguities resolved before the president was invited to act.

In addition to unclogging these reporting channels, the president's objective clearly was to create a structure that would invite faculty participation in institutional decision making. A union leader recalled that there had been faculty "concern over how to acquire a clear and available input to decision making, to provide a faculty voice" in the process. "The president thought that decisions affecting faculty and students could be shared together," reported another union activist. Indeed, as the president explained it:

> The faculty needed a participatory voice in developing final recommendations and directions for the institution['s] academic mission. We had high levels of mistrust, duplicity, misunderstanding, miscommunication. On the one hand, it was great for the president; I was accountable to nobody! On the other hand, the development and maturation of the organization was [stalled].

A very open system that invites participation has resulted. Interested parties are given floor privileges at both the Forum and the subcommittee meetings. "Participation opportunities are important. Faculty are not shut out at any level," noted an administrative member of the Forum. The Forum chair added: "We try to get people to know what we are doing; we certainly welcome their feedback. And my phone does ring!"

Among the four strategic planning councils initiated in the 1980s and reviewed in chapters 7 through 10, the Forum is unique in that the president introduced the concept of forming a new governance structure but left its design to those who would have to live with the end result. The president presented the idea, jointly involved the union in promoting it, and saw to it that the faculty played the key role in formulating a constitution assuring shared governance. A faculty member observed:

> We got to name more faculty than administrators to the [planning] committee. We had three or four subcommittees to explore various parts of the structure. There was a lot of congeniality, a lot of consensus. I'm not sure how much choice we really had in whether to create it or not, but in terms of its shape, we reviewed many models.

The president allowed for a bottom-up process for structuring campus governance. The faculty were the chief architects. And the end product met the president's needs. As he himself put it:

> The concept was to create a structure that would guarantee a process where we would have open and clear and frequent participation by all the academic constituencies in governance and management—particularly the faculty. I also wanted a group that would have the responsibility for analysis, synthesis, and consensus-building prior to fragmented or controversial issues reaching the president's office. The Forum has provided for that. It provides for orderly, public management of business on this campus.

Membership Composition and Selection

The Forum consists of 18 members serving two-year, staggered terms. Forum bylaws restrict faculty members from serving more than two such terms consecutively. The five administrative appointments are made by the president. The Student Association has either elected or appointed its three representatives. Of the ten faculty members, eight are elected by their constituents—one from each of the three colleges and five by the faculty at large—and two union representatives, the president of APSCUF and a member of its own executive committee. There are no staff representatives on the Forum.

Forum Purposes

The Forum has been charged with evaluating reports coming to it from its subcommittee on university planning and budget, its two standing committees on curriculum and student affairs, and from the governance review committee. Members of these four "under committees" are not necessarily also members of the Forum. When the need arises, the Forum may establish ad hoc committees. The purpose of the Forum is to review issues brought to it and recommend presidential action to be taken. It serves as the capstone of the campus's governance system. Matters pertaining to the curriculum, academic policies, co-curricular matters, and student life are funneled through the Forum before the president takes action.

At the time of the site visit, the Forum had just completed its fourth cycle. It meets during the academic year from September to May on the third Tuesday of each month at a prearranged time for three- or four-hour sessions. The Forum's Executive Committee meets twice a month, before and after the larger group meeting. The five-member Executive Committee consists of the Forum's chair and vice chair, its secretary, and two other Forum members, all of whom are elected by the membership at its first fall meeting. Although not specified in its constitution, tradition holds that the chair and vice chair will be faculty members, and the secretary a student Forum member. However, at least one representative of each of the three constituencies (faculty, students, administrators) must be included on the Executive Committee, as must the union president. The governance document requires that the Forum chair, by virtue of that role, also sit on the president's cabinet.

Rather than submitting an annual report, the Forum forwards recommendations to the president on an ongoing basis. Complete logistical and clerical support is provided to the Forum by the president's office. An executive secretary to the president provides staff support. She attends all meetings of the Forum and its Executive Committee, takes minutes, prepares the monthly agenda, and distributes all accompanying materials to the membership. And she supervises final preparation of reports and recommendations to the president from the Forum or from any one of its subcommittees.

IMPLEMENTING THE FORUM

Forum architects were aware that, over a period of time, some modifications of their new system would probably be in order. The Governance Review Committee was created to serve as a "watch dog" for the governance structure. It advises the Forum of needed changes. If a conflict of interest surfaces in committee work, or if there is duplication of effort among committees, or if reporting structures need modification, this committee brings it to the attention of the Forum.

Curriculum Committee contributions to the Forum agenda serve as one example of how Forum energies can be redirected over time. The Curriculum Committee had been generating more work for the Forum than the other subcommittees. The Curriculum Committee's primary objective is to address the academic mission of the institution. The president noted that this mission

> is quite broad. It involves everything from curriculum to admissions to counseling. In the first few years, the Curriculum Committee has been so busy with significant matters . . . that if you looked at the agenda you'd see that a large portion of Forum time has been taken by Curriculum Committee [issues].

Many of those interviewed expressed a concern that too much time had been spent on curriculum issues at the expense of other pursuits. "Seventy-five percent to 90 percent of our time has been spent on curriculum matters. I don't think that was the intent at all," protested one faculty member. "Curriculum is the lifeblood of the campus—along with students. So, yes, it's crucial; but I'm not sure if as a Forum we should spend that much time on curricular matters," added another.

In response, the Forum amended its constitution so that the chair of the Curriculum Committee now has Forum voting member status. It was expected that future Curriculum Committee reports would be presented and approved at Forum Executive Committee meetings, thereby "freeing up" more Forum time for other discussions. It was unclear at that time whether or not this change would entail a shift of responsibility from the Forum's full membership to its Executive Committee. Although the Forum's recording secretary indicated that the Executive Committee took no action on its own other than the approval of minutes, a Forum faculty member disagreed: "There are a number of cases when the Executive Committee gets involved with settling things that might more appropriately be done by the Forum as a whole." The Executive Committee may be evolving toward a more decisive role.

IMPACT OF THE UNIVERSITY FORUM

The Forum's influence has been widely felt on campus. Areas that have been affected include governance, planning, communication, and campus climate.

Governance

A campus committee that is asked to make decisions that will affect the entire organization potentially could have tremendous impact. Has the Forum, indeed, been addressing matters of significance to the campus? The answer is decidedly affirmative. The president can introduce issues to the Forum, and the membership can raise its own issues. Additionally, the scope of the subcommittees' activities covers a broad range of campus concerns. Policy and procedure in their respective areas—planning and budget, governance review, curriculum, and student affairs committees—definitely are influenced by Forum deliberations.

"[Forum members] do hear these large issues," observed a faculty member. In fact, in its four-year history, the Forum has dealt with a broad range of topics including general education revisions, program review and proposal, sexual harassment policy, plagiarism policy, honors program, class size, and awarding credit for activities courses, like band and chorale classes. An administrative member cited such Forum deliberations as "evidence of key issues of importance to the image and integrity of the institution." The Forum "is considered to be the most important committee on campus," noted a faculty member. "If [a concern] doesn't go to the Forum, it is probably a dead issue. I don't know where else it would go," said an administrator. The president added: "I shudder to think how we would have handled some of the controversial matters that have been before [the Forum] without it."

But not all issues of significance are sent to the Forum. One administrator acknowledged that many matters of importance to the campus are resolved through other channels. This may be changing: "I believe the president will try to see to it that more things are brought to the Forum." A faculty member added:

> I don't think a real heavy, big issue has hit them—a politically sensitive issue, with gut wrenching about how it's going to go. I haven't seen them address an issue like retrenchment or faculty cutbacks. I would like to see how we would work through that type of problem. If something threatened the school on a campus-wide basis, the president would take immediate action. But the policy questions it would raise would probably be put to the Forum.

Apparently it is within the scope of the Forum to address such matters.

Clearly, the Forum tackles major issues that can broadly affect the university. Was there a shift of decision-making responsibility on the campus that enabled this? Since the dissolution of the Faculty Senate, there had been no other standing body on campus asked to consider matters of the type brought to the Forum. The APSCUF contract authorized a curriculum committee, but this marked the extent to which the faculty recently had been formally involved in decision making at SU. A union representative noted that prior to the Forum, decision making "had either been ad hoc or had been handled at a more central level." Decision making is now described as a process more broadly shared than it had been.

"I think it was much more of a splintered effort before," concluded one faculty member. Recommendations to the president could be made through various routes, including the union route. In fact, the responsibility for curricular review, formerly a union venue, was shifted to the newly created Forum Curriculum Committee. Also, matters now handled by the Forum "for the most part would come out at 'Meet and Discuss,' the interface between the faculty union and the administration," observed a union leader. Now, however, "Meet and Discuss" handles contractual matters only. There has been a shift of decision-making responsibility to the Forum from both the faculty union and from central administration.

What reactions has this shift prompted from other bodies of campus governance? It might seem that APSCUF, as the principal voice of faculty concerns, had the most to lose with the introduction of the Forum. "Some people worried that there would be a conflict of interests between the union and the Forum," recalled a union leader, "but that hasn't happened." Before this governance structure was put into place, "joint committees" were management-heavy by union reckoning. The management viewpoint was thought consistently to prevail. There was skepticism that union prerogatives would be usurped by the new entity. However, the union president has an automatic seat on the Forum: "If something seems to intrude, we refer it to Meet and Discuss." While the Forum now handles curricular and academic matters, the union is responsible for working conditions. "I don't think the union has been co-opted; it's more like a co-equalness," said a former union president.

The action, however, seems to have shifted to the Forum. Said another union representative: "Before the Forum, the union was the place where things happened." Despite the collective bargaining agreement, the Forum has become "a major voice in campus governance," a faculty member maintained. Another professor elaborated:

> The new governance process has somewhat circumvented, maybe even weakened, the APSCUF organization on campus. It's taken some of the power they had in the past on these committees and has created another policy-making body. Whether that's good or bad is a value judgment. You'll probably find parties on either side. APSCUF still makes appointments to committees of the Forum—it's represented. But the power it wielded once before is not there now.

In contrast, a faculty member refuted: "I don't think its powers have been eroded, but its visibility is less. The Forum gets more publicity than the union." In general agreement with this perspective, still another faculty representative believed the union has not been disenfranchised, but rather enhanced, because there are now more occasions for union members to participate in committee decision making. Indeed, there have been some faculty contests for elected seats on the Forum. One union leader issued a favorable endorsement: "The Forum seems to be working. People are not too upset with it."

Administrators do not appear to be upset with the Forum governance structure either. That may be because frequently there are administrative policy decisions that are not moved through the Forum. A faculty member mused:

> We get reports back on what's going on in the president's cabinet. But we've never had any debate on administrative issues in the Forum. Attempts to debate these matters cause defensive behavior on the part of Forum administrators. It has been rare for the Forum to take action on administrative decisions.

Interviewed administrators voiced only approval of the Forum process.

It was reported that as members of the Forum, students were frequently absent. (Student representatives to the Forum, as noted earlier, were unavailable for interviews during the summertime campus visit.) A faculty member commented, "One of the real problems with this structure is making sure you get adequate student participation." Another observed that "students don't say much" in Forum meetings. An administrator believed this may be because in the past students have not played a role in the design of policies that affect them. The governance structure provides them with an opportunity to express their opinions. However, this vice president observed, "usually [students] will respond as they sense the rest of the group is doing."

Because a curriculum committee preceded the Forum, the relationship of the Forum's Curriculum Committee bears scrutiny. Forum members *may* also be Curriculum Committee members, but Curriculum Committee members are not necessarily Forum members. A union representative reports that there have been periodic power struggles, claiming that the head of the Curriculum Committee "has tried to exercise power beyond the committee's jurisdiction at times, as if that office had more power than that of the Forum president." Shippensburg's president has seen evidence of the Forum's deference to recommendations, though the degree of deference may be waning:

> There has been a kind of ritualistic dancing that goes on within the Forum against the Curriculum Committee's recommendations. I think that will change in time. I think the Forum will be more assertive in its role and function in the long run.

A faculty member who has served on both committees recalled that the Curriculum Committee debated the nature of its role:

> We decided to take a curricular approach. The Forum would always raise the issue of affordability. We did not want to take a resources viewpoint. To me, the Forum ought to be a higher authority. Curriculum Committee reports to the Forum. The Forum should take additional information into consideration.

In the final analysis, both committees have their roles to play. The Forum does not have to approve absolutely everything that the Curriculum Committee addresses. As a minor example, course number changes are sent directly to the president without Forum involvement.

Another significant contribution of the Forum is that it has unquestionably increased the opportunities for faculty participation in institutional decision making. The faculty feel like they have a say in directing outcomes. There was an early concern that management would be reluctant to relinquish control. But, in one faculty member's view, "to their credit, [they] have accepted the 'evenness approach' to decision making—everybody counts." Anyone can provide advice—one need not be a Forum member to formally contribute opinion. And, exclaimed another faculty member, "there certainly are more positions within the governance power structure of the university that are open to faculty! People who never participated before can do so now." With a greater number involved in the decision making, "we have a broader base of representation than before," noted a union leader.

Impact on Planning

In designing the Forum, its architects believed that special attention should be paid to institutional planning. The Planning and Budget Committee was created to review the annually published institutional goals and objectives that begin as planning statements at the department level and work their way up through the organization. Said a faculty member:

> To us "review" means to make suggestions for change, not to just stamp and approve. This past year we probably made the most extensive review we ever had. The list of goals was considerably revamped. A new mission statement was written.

Another charge to this committee has been to consider three- to five-year long-range plans. Members brainstorm faculty needs. "We raise a lot of planning questions. Much is presented to us about policy and institutional space utilization," reported a faculty member. A third charge is reviewing annual budget figures, "something we didn't use to have access to," noted another faculty member:

> We are updated on budget and funding processes—whether [or not] we're under a crisis. Faculty input can be obtained; faculty can be notified. We don't understand it a lot—we don't have the CPA background. But we no longer complain that we don't see the figures.

The Forum has put faculty in a position for the first time to better understand the intricacies of the planning and budgeting process.

Improved Communication

The Forum indisputably has opened the channels of communication on the Shippensburg campus. Prior to its inception, decisions were typically made without any constituency consultation. "It used to be that things were handled administratively and then the faculty were informed," commented a professor. An administrator described the previous situation as having been more secretive: "Little was known about what went on. Now the [Forum] agenda and minutes are widely distributed." Secrecy was particularly evident in the area of budget: "Before this president came, budget matters were not publicly known. 'Who' got 'what' was administratively decided," recalled a vice president. "At least now [faculty] *know* what's happening; they understand the budget process as much as anybody can," said a faculty member.

It is the establishment of a "process" that really has energized the campus community. This process is credited with assuring participation in governance and with opening communication channels. Faculty believe they now have access to administrators and information that used to be unavailable to them. As one faculty member found, "Around here as long as people are in the stream of decision making, they will tend to agree with [the outcome]." A union leader echoed that sentiment:

> Giving people their say is sometimes more important than what comes out the other end. Given the fragile ego of the faculty (and even some of the administrators), if they have the opportunity to have their "day in court," whatever the outcome, they are going to be more satisfied.

The Forum process has yielded two more tangible benefits. First, it has created another level of review that is removed from the initiating department or committee or individual. This has resulted in greater objectivity in final decision making and has enabled the Forum to identify problem areas that were understated in preliminary subcommittee reviews. For example, a Forum appraisal raised what proved to be warranted concerns about changes in the grading system proposed by faculty. Similarly, reservations about a music department proposal caused that department to rethink its position and to make changes in its plans.

A second benefit of the Forum process is that it has established a mechanism arguably capable of handling any critical issues that may one day surface. One vice president declared:

> I think we haven't seen its best days yet. Down the road something is going to come up that will take the ingenuity of that group to make some decisions to take to this president. As long as he is here, I think they will work things out.

Reflecting on that possibility, a faculty member concurred: "It will be great to have this public organization—the Forum—to work on new policy issues that will arise." The Forum has lifted the veil off decision-making practices at SU and has established machinery that more objectively addresses current issues. It is a mechanism widely believed capable of handling unforeseen crises.

Impact on Organizational Climate

The Forum has contributed significantly to a sense of community at Shippensburg University. "Before the Forum, decision making was disjointed. Now it's a more integrated, unified process," a union representative declared. As the capstone of the governance structure, it advises other committees when decisions are not in keeping with the established mission and goals of the university. The consensus-building aspect of its deliberations assures that an issue is filtered sufficiently enough to answer all questions it may have raised. This contributes to a collective mentality in decision outcomes. As a faculty member explained:

> The things we refer to the president represent faculty opinion, faculty sentiment. What you have is proof of management and faculty in a joint discussion process. Ultimately, the president has the final decision. But because we hash things out as a team of faculty and management, it's a much more powerful opinion, policy, or position that gets passed on to the president.

Another faculty member commented on this opportunity to work in a collaborative endeavor:

> Instead of *hearing* that a dean has handed down a decision [that might kindle all kinds of animosity for this administrator], you're *talking* to the dean. You discover his real intentions are the best interests of a quality program. When administrators and faculty have access to each other's thoughts, it deflates a lot of issues early on, rather than letting them fester.

The president is credited with helping this spirit of common interest to develop. His personality and style, according to the Forum's chair, "is not to be confrontational, but to seek consensus. I think that helps to make this process work."

EFFECTIVENESS OF THE UNIVERSITY FORUM

Has the Forum been authorized on its own to move the university in strategic directions? There was complete agreement among the 16 people interviewed that the decision-making powers of the Forum are strictly recommendatory. "I think it's very clear to everyone that our line of authority is to the president, and he can say 'no,'" observed one faculty member. "I agree with that," said a Forum administrative member. "You've got to have some *one* with decision-making power."

Given that parameter, however, the Forum is definitely a decision-making body that sees itself as capable of making independent judgments on matters that come before it. An administrative member of the group recalled an issue that generated much debate on the Forum floor:

> Part of that discussion was: "If the Curriculum Committee endorses, are we bound as the Forum to endorse it?" The decision on that was "no." When it comes time to vote, we may vote it down! If we do that, it simply becomes a dead issue for us. We just remand it back to the originating source for further review and evaluation.

Process is not everything. A faculty member believed that the recommendations the Forum put forth to the president had to reflect good decision making: "You can have a good process and a lousy decision. Ultimately, [good] recommendations are more important than process."

Is the Forum autonomous in reaching its decisions? Is it empowered to move the campus in various directions? The Forum does have autonomy in decision making. "It's what the president and the faculty see as the top of our governance structure. Everything feeds into that," commented an administrator. Some of their recommendations by law will require trustee or board of governors approval. "But other matters are implemented once I sign them," explained the campus president.

The Forum can receive issues from any source. It is responsible for managing the activities of its subcommittees. It expects those committees to attend properly to tasks assigned to them and to report back their findings. It can and will exercise veto power over subcommittee recommendations. According to one administrator:

> We don't "bury" issues, and we don't blindly accept their recommendations. If a committee says there is no merit to the issue, the Forum will still discuss it to see if *we* think there is merit to it.

A faculty member described an occasion when the Forum overturned a committee recommendation judged to be premature:

> When a grading system change was proposed, the Forum thought a faculty referendum was in order. Curriculum Committee was upset; they thought they had taken into account faculty opinion. In fact, faculty *did* turn it down.

Also, the Forum can vote to "accept a report" yet take no action on it. An example was the credit-for-activities issue. A faculty member explained:

> I think that was because the Forum saw it as a resource issue, and they know we are in a real bind with resources and can't create any new positions. At that point it just died. It didn't get passed on to the president at all. No action was taken. It does happen that things just become squelched at that point.

In sum, the Forum, despite its status as a recommending body, has demonstrated repeatedly that it can act with finality.

The Forum also is empowered to make some strategic decisions that influence the campus's direction. Its chair conceded, though, that the Forum was not especially active in that regard—"perhaps not to the extent that we thought [it] would be when we began the process." A union leader expressed greater reservations: "There was a feeling that the Forum was going to have some real power and input and be able to accomplish some things. I think people are not so sure that's really the case." It is possible that the Forum has yet to meet—maybe even approach—the expectations of some observers in terms of its ability to lead the university. But it clearly is not merely a rubber stamp operation. "The forum is definitely empowered to move the campus in directions that will affect its future," noted a faculty member. "Of course, the president can still say 'no.' "

How often does the president say "no"? The fact is that the president rarely vetoes the Forum's recommendations. He is credited with accepting their decisions almost all—"95 to 99 percent"—of the time. "He does not reject out of hand," said a union official. And from the Forum chair: "He has remanded a few things to us with suggestions which we have thus far seen to be reasonable. His suggestions are incorporated and given back to him." The governance constitution requires the president to respond to recommendations within 30 days, providing a written explanation for any reservations he may have. One faculty member observed the following:

> He will always respond to things he doesn't like either with suggestions or with a request to push the issue back to the appropriate committee for further work. This may happen for legal or budgetary reasons because something is not technically workable or is not in line with the mission and goals of Shippensburg University.

Reasons for Success

The high "success rate" of Forum recommendations can be credited to several features of structure and process. First, the membership is well constituted. Administrative appointments are high powered. The president said:

> That was deliberate, and they will continue to be principally the vice presidents. . . . It's hoped with such people at the table, the best policies are developed and forged so that the recommendations that come to me may be approved without radical surgery.

A faculty member agreed that the group was properly composed: "You've got the appropriate administrators. You don't have faculty naively designing something that can't be done."

Second, the governance process itself builds consensus. The recording secretary noted that "everything has been hashed out from the ground up, so that by the time issues get to the Forum, there's not a lot of controversy." This perception was echoed by others, as well. "People just wait for things to get to the Forum level," commented a faculty chair. "Once something gets by that level, it's usually a *fait accompli*."

Third, there is a close match between presidential and faculty priorities on this campus. Said an administrator:

Our president sees the academic component of the university as "Number One." It's not that way on all campuses. Because of that, most of the faculty have a respect for the president. Also, he works at having a lot of dialogue with the faculty. He and the provost meet with the departments. He knows them personally. I think each pretty much agrees with the other's thinking.

He is described by others as very supportive and very humanistic. His support has been facilitated by faculty priorities not at sharp odds with his own. In the view of one Forum faculty member, "I think we were a pragmatic group in that we took into account what was going to happen at the president's office." Another faculty member agreed that "it's hard for the Forum to do something one hundred percent different [from what] the president might want; but it has not been co-opted." At Shippensburg, the president's objectives appear to be closely aligned with faculty interests.

Fourth, the president himself—his agenda and leadership style—comprise a key reason for the Forum's achievements. Accolades for the president are not uncommon. Many acknowledged that it was the president who has enabled wider participation in decision making. Although he has the authority to do whatever he pleases, he seems to prefer to let the Forum select from among alternatives available to the campus. High praise was voiced by one faculty activist:

I don't think there has ever been a president who has been truly collegial, who has ever given up the last word. Some would argue that structures like this are just smoke screens. My opinion is that there is a genuine desire on the part of the president and some of the administrators to give the community a voice.

Another faculty member described the president as considerate, even to a fault:

He will bend over backwards to do what he can do to solve any kind of situation in a humanistic way. That's his best characteristic: he's humanistic, he's right down there with you. I guess that's why a lot of people like him so well. His reputation is well known throughout the system. His style of management is participatory. His revamping of the governance structure is evidence of that.

There appeared to be little, if any, skepticism on the part of the academic community that the president was indeed committed to a shared governance approach.

Clearly, significant and positive contributions are seen as flowing from the Forum. Support for it among all constituencies is high.

Limitations

The Forum's structure and process, despite the laudable accomplishments, are hardly flawless. Five shortcomings surfaced.

First, although the Forum had expanded opportunities for faculty involvement in governance, participation was still limited to the committed few: the cadre who were routinely and intensively involved in committee work. The Forum chair observed that

> We have all been union president at one time or another. Those who get active, stay active. It involves a lot of time. Most faculty don't want to give that much time outside of their discipline.

Another member of the faculty compared current participation rates to the "olden days" when the senate was active: "It looks better and sounds better today, but overall I don't see much of a change in participation. The [potential] players aren't playing." New participants would be welcome.

Second, as noted earlier, many believed the Forum had expended an excessive amount of time with curricular details at the expense of other policy and planning matters. "Curricular matters get top priority because there is nothing else put on the agenda by the Executive Committee," complained one faculty member. This condition was also acknowledged by an administrator: "The nature of the Forum is not to address pressing problems, per se, other than those that are curricular." It was hoped that the inclusion of the Curriculum Committee chair on the Forum's Executive Committee would streamline the Forum's workload, enabling it to tackle other meaty problems.

A third limitation of the Forum was that it had thus far restricted itself to what some described as an overly reactive posture. It had not yet realized its potential as a strategic planning mechanism, as a means of shaping a vision for the campus. In other words, the Forum had not yet become a body comfortable with initiating bold, direction-setting policy. One faculty critic maintained, "It doesn't sit down and talk about what kind of curriculum we should have ten years from now. In my opinion, it certainly could happen, but it doesn't." Another offered this perspective:

> In the last four years the "process" has meant more to the system than the "generation of outcomes." Real shared governance means a system where recommendations to the president reflect decision making that goes beyond the "process of reviewing the process." When we get beyond that, the Forum will be where I'd like to see it.

A third faculty member expressed dissatisfaction that the Forum's potential has not yet been realized:

> If you're not assigned to do so, you don't tend to think of these matters in an organizational way. Concerns become diffused. They don't wind up in some kind of policy process. I think [the Forum] has been underutilized by faculty. We have tended to go to APSCUF when we had a problem. I don't think we've utilized the Forum and its subcommittees to the extent of what they can accomplish.

While the establishment of new directions for the university was seen to be a Forum potential, it had not yet functioned in that way. The president commented that within the context of its mission, the Forum had been empowered to offer such assistance. "It does not within itself generate the visions for the university, but it helps create them," he said. A union leader commented:

> The Forum could play a role shaping the mission of the institution, but that has been pretty well set in the past. The governance system probably *reflects* more than *sets* mission.

Perhaps this more restrained role was because not all important campus matters were being submitted to the Forum. A faculty member commented: "I sometimes find myself wondering, 'Are the important decisions made at the Forum, or are they made at the cabinet?' I don't know where the real directions are established."

There are still unanswered questions about the extent to which the Forum can direct the campus. Musing over this point, a union leader suggested:

> This may be because it's a change from what everyone was used to. Issues that would have moved the campus in one direction or another usually came down from up above. It can take a little while to get used to [a different mode].

A fourth area of concern targeted the role of one Forum subcommittee, Planning and Budget. One subcommittee member raised this question:

> I'm still struggling to establish our real role. Are we an auxiliary committee to the president? And to what extent are we a subcommittee to the Forum? It seems as though we operate both ways, yet we get more direction, assignments, and requests from the president's office than from the Forum.

Many expressed concern that this committee had not been operating as was intended. "We are disappointed in [Planning and Budget]," a faculty member decried:

> It was supposed to be a body through which both administration and faculty could make some hard recommendations about portions of the

budget where flexibility exists. [Instead, its] task has been to try to find *where* the planning is done, not to make actual plans. It's ludicrous!

At the time of the campus visit, the committee was still struggling to define the budgeting process rather than examining policies. Anticipated changes in the budget process had been expected by some to make Planning and Budget more active, noted a vice president. But, given the budgetary situation, at least one observer was skeptical that the committee's work would ever meet faculty expectations.

A final limiting factor of the Forum, in the view of some, was that as a shared governance model, no room had been made for staff representation. "I thought at the outset there was going to be staff on there. They are part of the university community and are affected by some of these decisions," said a faculty member. Another professor expressed a contrary opinion: "The kinds of things the Forum basically has to deal with, the staff certainly does not have much to say about." An administrator acknowledged that

> It's difficult to include staff on matters that often pertain to curriculum, academic policy and procedure. There's a sense of isolation among the 300 staff. They haven't made an issue of this. But I'm a little concerned about [their exclusion].

No plans appeared to be afoot to include staff among the Forum's membership.

SUMMARY

In summary, Shippensburg's University Forum has functioned as a successful, decision-making planning council. Despite its limitations, most would agree that it has impressive achievements to its credit—a campus vehicle applauded for significant advances in both planning and governance. The Forum was asked to address consequential matters that had broad impact, though its contributions at a purely strategic level have been muted.

In its first years, much of the Forum's agenda had been devoted to curricular concerns, although its purview was clearly more extensive. The Forum accrued decision-making responsibilities from both the faculty union and central administration. General harmony prevailed among the campus's various governance groups; the Forum was perceived to be doing its job without infringing on others' territories. The process of issue refinement was such that campus consensus was generally (although not always) achieved before recommendations were forwarded to the president. Barring technical, legal, or budgetary restrictions, the president typically acted favorably on the Forum's advice. In all cases he communicated his decisions and their bases to the various constituents. Overall, it can be said that the Forum was enjoying considerable critical acclaim at Shippensburg University.

Some shortcomings, as noted, were evident, but these imperfections should not overshadow the significant contributions the Forum has made to the university. For a campus that described its pre-Forum history as its "days before governance," this strategic planning council was acknowledged by the campus community as a genuine example of shared governance. The close match of interests between the president and the faculty may largely account for this harmony. There was good rapport between the president and the faculty union, as well. The president described the Forum as "progressively maturing" and as generally having met his expectations. "It's been a positive experience for us," he noted. Most others would agree.

The University Forum stands out as a model that has worked well. Presidential leadership has been a key ingredient. The Forum's potential as a *strategic* planning body has not yet come to fruition, but a solid foundation has been laid. In sum, the Forum is an effective mechanism that has the potential for greater achievements in wedding shared governance to planning needs.

CHAPTER 10

West Virginia University's Planning Council: A Collegial Success Story

W est Virginia University, founded in 1867, is situated on rugged terrain in the Appalachian highlands. Greater Morgantown has a population of about 45,000; Monongalia County, 75,000. Monongalia is one of the largest deep-mine, coal-producing counties in the nation. "WVU" is the largest single employer in the county.

WVU is the state's land-grant university and its flagship campus. Comprehensive in its academic scope, it offers more than 170 degree programs, bachelor's to doctoral level, through a decentralized group of 15 colleges and schools. Its two expansive campuses are conveniently connected to each other via a computer-directed, electric-powered, rapid transit system. The institution enrolled more than 18,700 students at the time of the visit and employed more than 1,500 full-time faculty.

The university is governed by a 17-member board of trustees vested by law with the authority for the control and management of the University of West Virginia system. The board-appointed president is the chief executive officer of the university and presides over a 15-member cabinet consisting principally of vice presidents, associate vice presidents, special assistants, and representatives of the Faculty Senate, Staff Council, and student government.

In addition to the cabinet, an 11-member board of advisors is composed of seven lay members from across the state, three campus representatives appointed by virtue of their elected offices (the chair of the Faculty Senate, the president of the student body, and the president of the Staff Council), and one appointed administrator. This board reviews all proposals involving the campus's mission, academic programs, budget, capital facilities, institution-wide personnel policies, and other matters as requested by the president.

A 100-member Faculty Senate has been the principal vehicle for faculty participation in university governance. It is a legislative body with original jurisdiction over matters of academic pertinence and educational policy that concern the entire institution or affect more than one school or college. Its decisions are subject to review and approval by both the president and, in some instances, the board of trustees. Senators are elected by their colleagues to represent their school or college constituencies.

In addition to these decision-making bodies, there is a 12-member Staff Council that represents nonteaching employees of the university. They are elected by their constituents from six different occupational groups. A labor union represents some of these employees. Also, WVU has a tradition of strong student government that presents student opinion to the administration and faculty.

WVU'S UNIVERSITY PLANNING COUNCIL

Established in 1986, the strategic planning council on the West Virginia campus is commonly referred to simply as the Planning Council or "PC." It fits the Keller description of a "Joint Big Decisions Committee" in that it is convened by the president and chaired by the chief academic officer, consists mainly of faculty members, and also has student, staff, and administrative representation. While the PC's agenda matters are more openly shared throughout the year, its actual end-of-the-year deliberations are private. At the conclusion of its work cycle, it offers advice to the president via a final report on matters related to institutional directions.

Profile of Interview Subjects

To determine the effects of the University Planning Council, 16 fifty-minute semi-structured interviews were conducted in July 1988, at West Virginia University. Eight of these were with members of the PC: 3 faculty members, 2 staff, 2 administrators, and the PC chair (the provost). The remaining 8 interviews were with nonmembers. Two of these interviewees were Faculty Senate activists, 2 were persons responsible for providing staff support to the Forum, and another was an individual acquainted with the history of planning at the university. In addition, a dean, a vice president, and the president were interviewed. Student members were unavailable for interviews.

Historical Background

Although this particular planning council had very recent beginnings, WVU itself has a two-decade history of planning. The nature and character of planning at the university, however, have changed remarkably over time. The effort to plan began in 1970 when WVU undertook systematic, institution-wide planning that involved faculty, staff, and students. The process continued without significant change until 1981. By the mid-1970s the campus's "integrated approach" to planning was well established. Budget allocations were tied to plan making, an administrator observed, to ensure that "fiscal judgments were made in keeping with academic decisions."

As the institution entered the 1980s, however, it became apparent that the existing process was unsuitable for the reallocation of resources, an unhappy reality of the economic environment facing the state of West Virginia and the nation as a whole at that time. Reporting on the institution's planning history, one administrator noted that the university's goals and planning assumptions, which were intended to serve as the decision criteria for the development of plans, appeared to reflect an intention to continue with the status quo. It was generally recognized that a revised vision of the future was needed, a critical strategy that would better serve an institution confronting change.

Strategic planning at WVU took hold with the appointment in 1981 of the university's nineteenth president. Disbanding the earlier process, this president established two major institutional review/planning efforts. The first was an internal review by an Academic Planning Committee composed of 13 members of the WVU faculty. Through 17 subcommittees, this group reviewed programs and curricula and made a series of recommendations for the future. His second strategic planning thrust was an external consultants' grant-funded review. Known as the Benedum Study (it was supported generously by the Benedum Foundation and carried out by the Academy for Educational Development), it combined the efforts of 42 educators and administrators from across the nation to measure WVU's programs and activities against national norms. Both the internal and external reviews were completed at about the same time in 1984. However, the president who had initiated them was himself preparing to step down from office. Consequently, little resulted from these reviews.

An interim president was appointed for a period of 10 months while the board of regents undertook the search for a new president. During that time no structured "planning activities" were undertaken.

The Prime Mover

Then, in spring of 1986, the twenty-first president took the helm. He was known as a "planner"; members of the selection committee who had interviewed him reportedly had been particularly impressed with that. The planning model he had put into place at a western university during his short tenure there as president had been widely reviewed and discussed among WVU's faculty and administrators. As one administrator recalled, "There were great expectations about this new president. People believed [his planning model] worked [for him before] and figured he would consider installing it here."

The new president was familiar with the planning model that had been in place at WVU in the 1970s and reviewed the reports and recommendations generated for and by the campus in the early 1980s. He wanted to avoid a cumbersome process and to pursue a streamlined model of planning. The "Planning Council" vehicle had proven to be workable for him before; some modifications were made, but the architectural design of West Virginia's Planning Council looks quite similar to his earlier model.

To the West Virginia campus, however, this president's design brought three new dimensions to planning and to decision making for the university. First, it signaled a conceptual shift in the planning process away from a focus on "operations" (that is, administration and finance) to one in favor of "academics." One source recalled that prior to initiating the PC, many believed that administration and finance, rather than goals and objectives, had been driving the university. Full responsibility for the planning process has now been lodged in the provost's office; planning has come to be viewed primarily as an academic affairs activity.

A second dimension of this president's plan is that now planning is conceived of as an ongoing process. In consultation with the board of regents and advisors and the Faculty Senate, a series of "strategic themes" was articulated by the president to serve as planning initiatives, namely: economic development; liberal studies; enrollment development; education reform and public schools; and international development.

The original list had contained some 14 strategic themes. But ultimately, the above five were seen as a more manageable number. These five, however, are not fixed indefinitely. "By definition," one administrator commented, " 'strategic' is something with a finite life. Other strategic themes will emerge." It was expected that the PC would annually review proposals against a backdrop of changing, strategic themes.

When asked about the relationship of institutional mission to strategic themes, the president responded:

> Mission is broad and reasonably static. The themes accept that mission
> and look for ways to establish priorities for development, growth, and
> change that will allow us to be effective within our mission over a
> reasonable length of time (say five years). Themes are priority goals that
> will help us change, grow, and develop, but within [the scope of] our
> mission.

A faculty member suggested that the president's themes were helping the
university redefine its purposes: "Mission has been out there, but there has
not been a lot of identification with it."

Third, the new addition of strategic themes to the planning agenda helped
to overcome the widely shared sentiment among the various campus cohorts
that planning efforts were merely an exercise with few tangible results. An
administrator said that the identification of the themes "was key to [the
president's model] being seen as something that would result in some plans,
and, in fact, it has!"

As noted, West Virginia University had been involved in the "planning
business" for many years. But the campus did not believe that goals and
objectives were responsible for the directions in which it was moving. Harsh
economic realities seemed at odds with notions of growth and development.
Institutional mission, *per se*, gave no clue as to how best to proceed. The
faculty was skeptical but full of hope that new leadership would light a way. A
tried president and an already tested procedure—decision making through a
Planning Council—arrived on the scene. Some innovations—the strategic
themes—were designed expressly to meet the needs of this university and the
state of West Virginia. And thus a new strategic planning council was
launched.

Membership Composition and Selection

The university's Planning Council consisted of 13 members, all of whom were
appointed by the campus president. The provost chaired the council. Six
faculty members were selected from a panel of names submitted to the
president by the Executive Committee of the Faculty Senate. Two classified
staff members were chosen from a list of names submitted by the Staff
Council. Two administrators were appointed by the president after consultation with his cabinet. Two students were included from a list of prospects
provided by student government. With the exception of the student members, who it was anticipated generally would serve only one-year terms,
membership was for a two- or three-year term, with only a portion of the
council rotating off at any time so that continuity would be assured.

Purposes of the Planning Council

The stated objective of the Planning Council was to assess the strategic directions the university might take and to support specific plans of action as suggested by the various academic and support units of the institution. Each of these 20 planning units would submit an end-of-calendar-year report to the PC. These reports were to address each unit's primary mission and how it would plan to enhance or reduce programs and activities in the future to serve its own mission better. Each unit was also to comment on how its current operations benefited those "strategic themes" the university was to pursue, and to propose ways by which it might become more responsive in supporting those themes.

At the time this campus visit took place, the PC had just completed its second annual cycle. The council began its deliberations in January and concluded its decision-making processes in May. The entire group met initially for an "orientation" and then broke into three work groups that met as needed over the next several weeks to complete an in-depth analysis of assigned planning reports. The PC as a whole then reconvened on a weekly basis to review and analyze work group results, to evaluate the planning process and the extent to which the university was able to fully participate in that process, and to edit and approve its final report.

The PC was provided with staff assistance to arrange for all required logistical support. This support extended well beyond the organizing of meetings to include provision of information, as well as any analyses that may be needed at all stages of their deliberations. In particular, a special assistant to the provost was charged with overseeing all the details of Planning Council activities, including the drafting of the final report and the arrangement of necessary clerical support for that body. This person attended all general sessions of the PC.

THE PLANNING COUNCIL'S IMPACT

The University Planning Council, in its brief existence, has affected governance, planning, and the campus's organizational climate.

Governance

The Planning Council was widely seen as having been responsible for a redistribution of influence within the university. When interviewees were asked if there had been a shift of decision-making responsibility to the PC, the answer was always affirmative. It was agreed that matters of the type brought to the PC previously had been handled by deans, by a team of vice presidents, by the provost, by the cabinet, or even by the president. Occasionally, the PC was debating concerns that had not previously been raised on campus. A staff representative to the PC observed that the council was not so much "a replacement of what had been, as much as it was an addition to decision-making practices at the university."

Clearly, previous decisions about which units would get dollars for activities had been made more centrally. This council viewed itself—and is viewed by others—as being a more representative and participative mechanism for reaching these decisions.

One administrative representative to the PC cautioned: "Keep in mind we are only working in the strategic planning area. Other persons on campus are responsible for other types of planning." The president himself has a very clear notion of how to best utilize the decision-making energies of such planning councils:

> Their strengths are the abilities to create [strategic] priorities against certain standards and goals. They are less effective in matters of retrenchment or of reallocation of resources—how to reduce, how to scale back. Those decisions should be made by the management team who come up with a program that is administratively designed and then present it to [the council] as a test of where management's plan has strayed from strategic directions. This is because [the council knows] the institution, they have read all the materials, they know where the institution is trying to go. But if you give them the task of down-sizing, you've asked them to do something they are not good at and something that politically is difficult for them. It has taken me some time to learn that, but I am more and more convinced of that.

Some administrators (deans and others) who oversee matters of finance and operations expressed a preference for limiting the PC's decision-making responsibilities. But what was the general response of other campus governance bodies to the responsibilities of the PC? How did the Faculty Senate, the Staff Council, and student government respond?

Faculty

As the president noted, when he arrived at WVU, his plans were accepted very readily, nothing was challenged: the Faculty Senate did not seem to have any serious reservations. That conclusion was borne out in conversations with senate representatives. Until about 1983 the university president had always chaired the senate. Then it developed its own constitution and became its own entity. Although the senate does not have veto power over policy formulation at WVU, senators have found this administration to be very receptive and supportive of what the faculty is trying to do. "There is no sense of conflict of interest between endeavors of the PC and objectives of the senate," assured one senate leader. Another concluded that "a PC that looks at individual reports, gets an overview, and makes recommendations [will fare] better than a series of colleges working independently of each other and coming up with plans that may be at odds with each other."

The personal leadership qualities of the chief executive officer himself had much to do with the positive response to the council by the senate and its faculty constituents. The president opens all senate meetings with a comprehensive address on the state of the planning process. Past presidents have not taken pains to assure that the faculty was kept abreast of such matters. In addition to these monthly presentations, this president has added the chairperson of the Faculty Senate to his cabinet and has organized the PC to have more faculty than staff or student representatives.

One senate leader did report some rumblings from the ranks: "You always wonder 'Where did they find the money to do things like fund the libraries and provide adequate math TAs to meet new liberal education expectations?' But so far, we haven't heard anyone complaining too loudly." Another leading senator acknowledged that because council-allocated funds were not new but were drawn from existing budgets, "some faculty are upset that money has been taken out of their hides, diverted away from ongoing programs to fund new ones." This apparently was a minority opinion, however. All in all, the faculty reported positive attitudes toward the council. In fact, the "senate expects to put forward the PC as a university accomplishment in the upcoming Carnegie study," said one faculty leader.

The council is credited with increasing faculty participation in decision making. Prior to its inception, "faculty participation tended to be [funneled] through chairs and deans," commented a non-PC administrator. There had been no direct involvement. A senate leader felt this was a positive change:

> Things used to be done and faculty were informed after the fact. Now faculty are part of the decision-making process. Previously, if faculty were involved, it was only to the extent they were requested to provide input to central administration. Now there is a formal avenue for such input— input is routine.

This observer also added that although some faculty "could care less about participation," for those for whom it mattered, the council marked an important change.

The president, too, viewed the PC as a participatory mechanism for the faculty:

> In most situations, faculty involvement is at the department, maybe at the college, level. It's almost never at the strategic judgment level of the institution. Faculty like to say "they are the institution." I think a good planning process makes them more a part of it than they are in any traditional mode.

He described the PC as a much more representative system. It is believed to be less personality oriented, less reliant on management discussions, and less dependent on squeaky-wheel tactics. The group is faculty-dominated rather than management-dominated and assures that those who submit proposals for change are not also those who determine whether or not such changes will be advanced.

Although faculty dominated, the PC model also has provided other constituencies the opportunity to participate in campus decision making. A council staff member noted that the PC process has evoked a sense of participation for staff: "We now feel represented in the decision-making process." "It *is* a representative group," an administrative member acknowledged, "but one of the problems with that is that not everyone has the necessary overview of the institution to make decisions initially." Despite the potential drawbacks of a lengthier startup time, the PC model was effective at WVU. "It is representative of a participatory model of governance," a PC faculty member observed. "Under this administration the participative structure is workable because it is also getting results." Additionally, several members commented that the experience of participation was a personally rewarding one.

However, the notion that the PC is a genuinely participative form of governance was not universally accepted. Some critics felt otherwise. One faculty member of the PC commented:

> One of the things that has bothered me is that many of the colleges have not moved the planning process back to the departments and the faculty and staff. What's coming to this committee is coming from deans; it's not reflective of directions the faculty would take. It may be a factor of the infancy of the process. It is evolving and people are feeling their way. The academic units have been the primary beneficiaries and the focus of the process. Support units have not felt embedded.

This impression was shared by a staff member of the PC who concluded that "in the proposal writing stage there is not enough trickling down to the ground level." This may be because the president had left it to planning unit heads to determine how to submit their plans. In a memo to the community, the president wrote: "Vice Presidents, deans or administrators are free to organize their internal planning processes as they deem appropriate." Elsewhere in the memo he indicated that "at every stage of the process the intent is to be concise and decisive *but* to assure the fullest range of consultation." Clearly, some unit heads involved their constituents in the process much less than did others. A non-PC academic administrator believed that those faculty members who were not directly involved with the PC were not as enthusiastic about it as were others. "I work closely with the chairs in this college and expect that the chairs will share these discussions with the faculty. But I think something is lost between presidential commitment to participation and actual bottom-up activity." The impression persisted that the desired ground swell of faculty involvement was lacking at that point.

Classified Staff

The Staff Council initially had some concerns about the Planning Council. It feared that staff members might suffer as a result of PC recommendations—for example, that layoffs might result from recommended program cuts. On the other hand, the nonacademic employees were glad to have a voice in influencing the university's directions. It was comforting to the Staff Council to know there would be members of the PC who were cognizant of staff concerns and would be vigilant in assuring that staff opportunities would be considered.

A major difficulty for the classified staff units of the campus was to put together proposals that flowed logically from the five strategic themes. Because council planning has an academic focus, it is difficult for support personnel to relate to the strategic themes from other than a "second string" perspective. As explained by one staff member, "the setting of major directions comes from the academic sphere, *then* support areas attempt to respond as best they may." The addition of a sixth strategic theme that would highlight efficiency and effectiveness of operations was under consideration; this was seen as one means of drawing support staff more meaningfully into council deliberations.

Students

Although no student members of the PC were available for interviewing, a common theme emerged in dialogues with other members: the students contributed the least. Some felt students *could* have done more. It was recognized that their knowledge of the campus and their contacts with campus personnel are so limited that the extent to which they can actively contribute is circumscribed. But as one member noted, "As representatives of the largest group on campus, it seemed that they should be a part of the PC." Another felt less generous, "If asked, I'd recommend they not be included on the committee." The general consensus was that perhaps because they generally serve only one-year terms, students are passive participants and have little impact on PC decision making.

Impact on Planning

Some strategic planning councils get bogged down with less important campus concerns and, subsequently, have little significant impact on institutional planning. Of the eight members of the Planning Council who were interviewed, seven believed that issues that came before the council were to varying degrees crucial to campus life. The exception, a faculty member, argued that during the second year of council activities the PC chair had pressed an agenda:

> The issues he supported were self-serving and not critical to the life of the campus. I don't think many matters of importance to the campus ever come to this committee. What comes to this committee is what the deans think will please the president and gain his support.

The perspective of those interviewed who were not PC members was positive. "The 'issues' [that PC members] address are the 'themes,' and the themes are very significant to the university," commented one administrator. "I believe they are profound matters" noted another.

The council has made three very significant contributions to institutional planning at WVU. First, some base budget changes have resulted from their deliberations. These changes have included line item recommendations for new positions and significant additions to the university's seven libraries. "The PC became a 'dutch uncle' to the libraries; the PC definitely had bite to it!" an administrative member rejoiced. Later, the provost used the group's library budget arguments to secure additional money to renew various journal subscriptions. Even though this particular request was not directed to the PC, its commitment to the libraries is seen as having persuaded others to show similar support for library holdings.

At the end of their first cycle, significant budget changes had been made. "We did affect a half million dollars worth of [base budget] allocations," observed the provost. This supplemented over $400,000 in strategic planning allocations. While, as suggested by one faculty representative to the council, "some of the changes were inconsequential," on the whole, council members felt good about their efforts. Why? "Because we could see how our work had resulted in monetary shifts that would affect the campus," a PC staff representative explained.

The PC has influenced the campus in a second way by showing that strategic planning cannot take place in a vacuum. The campus is endeavoring to integrate its strategic and budget planning activities to some degree. One administrator observed that the PC's composition was not designed to make informed budget decisions for the campus: "As it is now constituted, it is an inappropriate group to be making such decisions—it is not representative [and not] knowledgeable enough." The president commented: "They are not a resource for every issue that comes up. I have a cabinet for that and established governance avenues for many matters." The PC chair noted that given the nature of the five themes to which the council is to address itself, "their decision-making horizon was rather limited—[they had] a big impact, but a limited horizon." The PC's deliberations have demonstrated that its ability to influence budgetary decisions is, in fact, limited to matters of strategic development. This objective, in turn, underscores the desirability of greater interaction between the council and others who decide budget matters.

As a result, some changes were anticipated that would help to better integrate both the strategic planning and the budgeting processes. At the time of this campus visit, the University Budget Planning Committee (consisting of the provost, vice presidents, and several associate vice presidents) was making the major budgetary decisions for the campus. Their plan was to dovetail the two processes so that the PC would have the authority to review the budget and make recommendations and, conversely, the University Budget Planning Committee would be able to review the recommendations of the PC. It was expected that there would be much interaction between the two groups in large measure because the provost would chair both of them. He saw the effective coordination of the two bodies as a challenge: "What may be difficult is to keep PC members active, productive, and useful in the strategic area, but not have them involved in the base budget area. Deans are very concerned that the PC not get into that business."

From another corner there was concern that the PC confine itself to the tasks of developing ideas and making recommendations and that it should resist the temptation to get involved with the operational end of things. The PC should not move beyond making recommendations pertinent to the actual administering and reviewing of programs. "You need some pretty clear understanding of just how far follow-up should go," a non-PC administrator cautioned. "You need to revolve membership and take care that members don't get too involved in pet projects."

As a third—and what may be its most powerful—contribution, the PC can be credited with bringing discussions of university mission to the fore. Within the council, debates over proposals have inspired PC members to inquire as to how specific programs either mesh or do not mesh with the university's mission. And, according to a faculty member, thanks to the machinations of the PC, the five themes were themselves modified to fit the spirit of the university mission more closely.

Impact on Organizational Climate

Discussions of mission and purpose have had a very cohesive effect on the campus community. "It has been cementing," a faculty member of the PC maintained. When asked if the council's planning process was compelling the university to focus on the overarching mission and set of priorities of the institution, rather than just the mission of individual units, a non-PC administrator answered: "Yes, units are redirecting their resources to focus on institutional priorities. The workings of the PC represent one of the rare activities in the life of the university where everybody is pointed in the same direction." A senate leader confirmed that the PC utilized an institutional overview and looked for opportunities to "benefit the entire campus or the state."

The efforts of the PC seem to be helping the campus develop "organizational" perspective, one that considers the good of the institution as a whole. The effect has been unifying. Bridge-building qualities also have been attributed to the process. A PC faculty member noted that

> There is now a link between the administration and the vast majority of the faculty and staff. This is a very good thing to have. People believe this should exist in a college or university, but it rarely does.

OVERALL EFFECTIVENESS OF THE PLANNING COUNCIL

Was the Planning Council making autonomous decisions that gave direction to the university? When pressed, each person interviewed clearly understood that the PC was "an advisory group to the president," for the president retains ultimate approval on all the recommendations the council generates. Within the context of advice giving, however, the PC was definitely viewed as a significant decision-making body. The council must make judgments about the quality of unit proposals in light of strategic themes—the five identified primarily by the president—and then support a prioritized list of proposals for institutional funding.

Just how autonomous are the judgments of the PC? Is that group's work subject to the approval of other governing bodies? There was initial skepticism that little-to-nothing would come of WVU's latest round of "planning." Additionally, in the view of one professor (a member of the PC), "in the first year there was a concern by everybody that we were a rubber stamp committee to the president. We were concerned about that ourselves. Once [our final] report came out there was decreased skepticism, many people took the process more seriously." Even with visible outcomes, though, some skepticism remained "because we knew that decisions of importance were still being made elsewhere." A staff member serving on the PC believed that the group "was a tool the president used for decision making, that ultimately the decision was his."

Yet, the council perceived itself as a group of independent thinkers who diligently sought to follow presidential guidelines. The group agreed that the president consistently accepted their final report recommendations. "We struggle to make sure the proposals fit those themes," noted a faculty member. A staff member added, "We worked very hard to acquire a shared understanding of our purpose and [a shared] interpretation of the five themes." A non-PC administrator also reported the president's favorable response to the group's decisions and attributed that to the presence of the provost and his assistant: "There has been a lot of academic influence along the way to keep things from getting too far out in left field."

The council's conclusions were published in a final report that did *not* go before any other group for endorsement prior to the president's action. However, as one dean noted:

> [The president] appears to be very sensitive to the needs of other groups and tries ideas out on other bodies like the Deans' Council and the Faculty Senate. . . . The PC, indeed, represents a cross section of the campus, but it still makes sense to double-check [their work] with other groups on campus. He does this.

This same dean believed that presidential action *was* influenced by comments passed by others to the president after the release of the PC's final report but before the president issued his formal response to PC recommendations.

Whether other governing bodies are actually influencing the final decisions of the PC may well be known only to the president. It would seem to be politically astute on his part, however, to permit that perception to stand. It was the provost's understanding that while the president would discuss the PC recommendations with him, they were not submitted to any other entity for approval. The president "has taken [the recommendations] very seriously. This group is empowered to move the campus in specific directions within the confines of the strategic themes."

It appeared that this strategic planning council was definitely empowered to deliberate and judge matters of crucial importance to the campus. The jurisdiction of its decision making, however, had been deliberately limited to the strategic development dimensions of the campus as defined by the president. The group had been given decision-making responsibility that was formerly housed elsewhere, constituting what was probably less a shift of power than it was a sharing of power more broadly. Other governing bodies on the campus did not appear to be at all threatened by the appearance of this PC. Nonetheless, one sensed that vigilance was being exercised, particularly at the deans' and vice presidential levels, to assure that territorial bounds were not violated.

Despite initial doubts expressed by uncertain campus constituencies, the Planning Council appeared to be winning over the skeptics with evidence of legitimate changes resulting from its deliberations. But, speaking of his fellow PC members, a faculty member claimed that the group still had some reservations as to its ability to direct the institution: "We feel a certain sense of satisfaction because our recommendations were accepted, but we're not sure if those outcomes wouldn't have happened anyway."

Contributions

The council appeared to have affected positive changes for WVU in five distinct areas, one of them statewide and the other four on the home front. First, it had been ascribed by Faculty Senate leaders as introducing the concept of strategic planning to the state legislature. According to one faculty senator:

> There has been no history of strategic planning in the state of West Virginia, [not] in government, business, education, etc. [But, since the president's arrival, we] have taken discussions of strategic planning to the legislature which puts the university on the cutting edge of strategic planning in the state. This has been very important for the university.

This particular contribution affected the larger, external environment within which the university operates.

Additionally, there were four identifiable internal contributions of the PC to the campus that have already been noted: the ability to affect base budget changes, the move toward integrating strategic and budget-planning activities, the increase in faculty participation in decision making, and the articulation of institutional mission. Despite the positive results of the council's work, however, its impact nevertheless was limited in some specific respects.

Limitations

For example, as was intended, the academic units had been the primary beneficiaries of the PC's decision making. As a consequence, support units across campus had experienced some difficulty in identifying with the five strategic themes. But the support units were not alone in their struggle to relate to the themes. For one thing, "there has not been consensus on the priority of the five themes," one administrator noted. Further, there was some confusion over how to link the themes to unit missions. Another administrator, a unit head, elaborated:

> We have had some difficulty plugging into the five goals and have thus attempted, in specific and disciplined ways, to expand the traditional definitions of these goals in order to fit within the category defined by each goal. . . . We have juggled creatively—broadly—to redefine the five initiatives in order to make them applicable.

This individual went on to point out another difficulty the units encountered when writing proposals that addressed the themes. Money for many years had been so scarce at WVU that it was not only challenging but frustrating to think "globally":

> We are so caught up with some basic bread-and-butter issues that the initiatives do not always directly lend themselves to what we do. Another thing is these initiatives are designed to *enhance* what we do—"frosting on the cake." But you need to make sure you've got the cake before you start thinking about the frosting! We have bent the intent of the way we have used some of the resources because it makes sense to do so. For example, library money has been used to replace basic holdings rather than to purchase esoteric additions. But for us, this *is* enhancement.

For some of the recipients of PC-funded proposals, then, the so-called enhancement money was merely being used to "beef up" basic programmatic needs.

These realities combined with other factors at WVU to create a lingering skepticism in some quarters as to the council's effectiveness. An academic administrator ticked off several reasons for dubiety:

> One, there is a lack of economic stability that has resulted in low morale of faculty and staff.

> Two, there is a lack of trust, very much a we/they mentality—we the faculty, they the administrators.

> Three, there is a lack of stable leadership, a turnover in the president and provost, and even the deans and chairs, that has engendered a skepticism, a lack of stable anchor. "Can we trust these people? Can we trust them to be here long enough to do anything? Can we trust them to represent our interests?" This is part of the context within which the PC is set, and it cannot be ignored.

> Four, there is a tendency to spread the money around rather than use it in just one area because you can't be certain there will be more of it next year.

The Planning Council's demonstrable successes seemed likely to assuage such feelings of skepticism. Yet, it appeared that "the jury was still out" for many people on the campus, and it would likely take time for that to change. "My impression," offered an administrative member of the PC, "was that the proposals were not likely to have immediate, major impact; that the proposals were 'seed' proposals that would eventually grow into something bigger. We were laying the groundwork for things that would happen down the road." This seemed a fair judgment to render in the council's second year of being.

SUMMARY

The University Planning Council at West Virginia University, though still practically embryonic, was affecting the campus and the state in positive ways. The introduction of strategic planning was believed to have put the university into a stronger position with the legislature. The decision-making activities of the PC resulted in noticeable budget shifts and brought into sharp focus the importance of integrating budget and strategic planning practices.

This strategic planning council was representative in its membership and had enabled some faculty members to have a "hands on" experience in guiding the institution down its long-range course. In that sense, it operated as a participative governance mechanism. However, the institution was bypassing the opportunity to more fully include the faculty in the grassroots deliberations that precede unit proposal writing. The PC process envisioned a much greater potential for faculty involvement than yet was being utilized.

It may well be that this university community had never before contemplated its mission so thoroughly. The charge to the campus community had been to interpret the five strategic themes—carefully selected longer-range goals and objectives—in light of its mission. This task caused each planning unit to consider the "big picture" and to determine what part it would play in meeting institutional objectives, providing, en route, a common ground on which to unite the campus. Many had come to believe that all campus constituencies could work together to achieve mutually beneficial ends.

For others, a more guarded attitude prevailed. Years of economic hardships, instability of leadership, and resultant mistrust of "the others" had kept some from clambering onto the PC bandwagon. Signs of skepticism had begun to diminish, however. With the subsequent, successful completion of consecutive planning council cycles, more conversions seemed likely.

In all, the Planning Council at WVU appeared to be heading in a direction that few counterpart bodies on other campuses actually attempted—strategic planning—and fewer still had mastered. Once more, the qualities of leadership at the top seem to be the critical variable. Barring economic adversity and yet another change in leadership, the outlook for the Planning Council's contributions is very positive.

PART
4

··········

Lessons for Governance, Planning, and Leadership

CHAPTER

Making Strategic Governance Work

E ach of the eight case studies tells a distinctive story. Now we turn to synthesizing and integrating, pointing up the generalizations derived from our empirical evidence and fitting these "truths" into a larger pattern. Our purpose now becomes to identify the correlates of effective strategic governance—or, put simply and boldly, how campuses can make big decisions better. Toward this end the chapter first examines four crucial elements that bear on effective strategic governance, namely, governance, planning, communication, and leadership. Then we move to the more specific lessons that we draw from the cases and from our more general understanding of how planning and governance can be prompted to work in concert.

THE FOUR CRUCIAL ELEMENTS OF STRATEGIC GOVERNANCE

The eight institutions we visited each had established what we have called generically a strategic planning council. These "SPCs" were created to serve a crucial role: to bring together key constituencies to chart institutional direction and to make decisions, albeit advisory, about how to move their campuses toward the future. Or so we supposed.

As explained in chapter 1, each of the SPCs was selected because it appeared, on the basis of our initial inquiry, to meet the criteria for being a strategic planning council (or, as George Keller had dubbed it, a "Joint Big Decisions Committee"). By way of review, these criteria emphasized joint membership (mainly senior faculty members and key administrators), selected by the president, and chaired by the chief academic officer. The committee's "deliberations are kept secret" (Keller 1983, 61).

179

However, we discovered, not surprisingly, that the scope of responsibilities and functions served by the councils varied widely. They ranged from Northwestern's Budget and Resources Advisory Committee (BRAC), which focused primarily on relatively narrow budget questions, to Shippensburg's Forum, which engaged a wide array of large institutional issues. Indeed, in the end, even the most successful of these bodies did not perform fully the function theoretically described in Keller's *Academic Strategy*. We had anticipated that a strategic planning council would be a catalyst for boldly shaping an institution's future and would undertake the necessary reprioritizing of commitments. And we anticipated further that these SPCs would be able to act expeditiously (at least compared to the slowly paced norms of academic organizations). But we were disappointed to discover that none of the eight entities we examined actually played such a role fully—and several did not at all.

Each case tells a different story. Together they highlight the diversity of results that emerge from varied attempts to create a single body that is designed, explicitly or implicitly, to bridge the campus's governance and planning functions. While there was great variation in context, institutional characteristics, and the approaches used on each campus, some important observations nevertheless can be drawn from the empirical evidence. We turn now to the four crucial elements we found to be associated with effective strategic governance: governance, planning, communication, and leadership.

Governance

The successful SPCs functioned as enhancements to the normal governance process rather than as secretive, elite groups that circumvented traditional governance. Four of the institutions—Princeton, Northwestern, Teachers College, and Ohio University—had created their planning councils primarily as a result of the need to rethink and reform governance in the late 1960s and 1970s. During that period, many institutions—including our four—discovered that their existing governance arrangements had not adequately involved students in decision making; these campuses found that they had no appropriate means for discussing campus-wide issues concerning student interests, discipline (when the occasion arose), or other significant matters. Accordingly, it was during that volatile era that campuses commonly formed committees whose membership was drawn from all the major campus constituencies and whose mandate was to recommend policy on issues that cut across campus sectors. On many campuses, however, these new governance entities, products of an era of heightened sensitivity to student concerns, eventually ceased to function. This was in part because the salient issues on campus changed as financial and enrollment pressures required refocused attention. And the change occurred in part because, as the wave of student activism—

more or less corresponding to civil rights and anti-war movements—receded after 1971, the promotion of robust student participation (by students and their on-campus sponsors alike) also waned. This was indeed the experience on the four campuses examined in part 2.

In addition, the mandates of each of these four SPCs tended to be vague; there were few concrete multi-constituency issues to sustain interest and involvement. By the mid 1980s, however, concerns for revitalizing governance and planning had reemerged and each of these four councils, having survived where others had lapsed into disuse, were extant and available—at least in theory—to address the emerging needs for more effective institutional planning and decision making.

But an important shift had occurred. It is clear that the thrust for participation in governance had moved from student participation to faculty efforts to expand their own participation in institutional decision making. As we have seen in these case studies, student and staff participation were not significant issues except in those institutions where this had been an important part of the culture or where such participation had historically been part of the governance mechanism (as in the case of Princeton and Teachers College). All four institutions where SPCs had been created during the 1970s (we include here Princeton's Priorities Committee though it had been established in 1969) redefined their agendas to respond to changing conditions.

The remaining four institutions—Montana, Georgia Southern, Shippensburg, and West Virginia—created new entities in the 1980s to serve institutional needs particularly related to planning and strategic questions. As of 1990, five of the eight councils have survived (Princeton, Northwestern, Ohio, Shippensburg, and West Virginia) while three have ceased to exist (Teachers College, Montana, and Georgia Southern). (At two of the three—Montana and Georgia Southern—the SPC folded when the president departed, but the successor administration replaced it with another entity; at Teachers College, the College Policy Council was disbanded and replaced by a body—the College Policy Committee—with a different composition and scaled-back mission.)

In theory, none of the eight councils was intended to displace other governance mechanisms, and in general it appeared that they did not undermine regular governance structures or processes. The successful SPCs became, as intended, a more focused, more centralized structure for bringing together a variety of perspectives for addressing the needs of the institution as a whole. Indeed, it appeared that those bodies that had attempted to ignore well-established faculty or administrative decision centers (as in the cases of Georgia Southern and Teachers College) lost their base of support and could not function effectively.

In the case of faculty, it appears that the new structures served to increase faculty participation in broad institutional matters while preserving faculty autonomy in academic decision making. To the degree that the campus had been addressing matters that had an impact on academic programs and personnel, normal governance channels continued to function alongside the SPC. Virtually all academic program matters continued to flow through normal faculty channels either before or after an SPC had discussed it. As a result, the new entities often made for increased complexity (by supplementing existing structures and processes) rather than greater efficiency. (Shippensburg was an exception; its overall effect appears to have streamlined processes.)

While this "inefficiency" could be criticized as a serious shortcoming, it is probably true that any effort to delegate "pure" academic decisions to a very small number of faculty, whether elected or appointed, would not be possible (or desirable) under prevailing notions of governance, at least in most institutions of higher education. Thus any governance-planning structure that might attempt to harness academic issues to larger institutional objectives must respect the traditional role of academic units—schools, departments, and programs—as well as serve overarching institutional needs. In short, whatever their advantages, planning councils tend to add complexity, even messiness, to the decision process rather than streamlining it.

Since relatively few administrators were (or could be) participants on these councils, each institution had to grapple with ways in which normal venues for administrative decision making—for instance, a council of deans or a president's cabinet of vice presidents—would be accommodated in the process. Where deans and directors were bypassed, the process quickly broke down. At Teachers College and Georgia Southern the SPC never achieved significant influence in part because the roles of deans and directors remained intact, virtually unaffected by these new mechanisms. More successful SPCs were created with interlocking membership, that is, council membership overlapped with key offices (for instance, a vice president for finance) or committees (a faculty senate executive committee). These integrating links were important in keeping the components of campus governance operating in concert.

The SPC's role in institutional budgeting varied widely, from serious involvement in the establishment of budget parameters, as at Princeton, to merely symbolic approval of the final budget just prior to its adoption at the governing board level, as at Teachers College. The evidence suggests that those councils that became involved in budgetary deliberations—without getting bogged down in the details of operational budgets—were more likely to be successful and more likely to actually shape larger institutional issues.

In general, the successful SPCs had had the opportunity, because of the participation of important faculty and administrators, to create support on campus for difficult decisions and to stimulate an institutional climate for change. Thus, a successful SPC was likely to be one that achieved a balance between insulation and interaction. Insulation meant being buffered from the normal routines and political pitfalls, avoiding preoccupation with detailed tactical (rather than strategic) decisions, keeping a distance from turf struggles, and so on. It meant not exposing the consideration of controversial issues prematurely to attack. Yet near-total isolation, whereby an SPC met in secrecy until firm decisions (that is, recommendations to the president) were reached, proved to be politically unsustainable and ineffective as a practical matter. Such exclusionary approaches failed to generate adequate campus support. It is thus demonstrably important not to sever connections to normal governance mechanisms. Interaction, on at least a limited scale, was important to build political support. Accordingly, the implications of Keller's prescription that such groups would need to operate on a confidential basis in reporting to the president appears from our cases not to work.

Planning

The more successful strategic planning councils avoided preoccupation with detail, particularly routine budgeting, enabling them to address larger, strategic issues. A measure of luck was important; deteriorating economic conditions constituted a barrier that SPCs could not readily negotiate.

The challenge of effective institutional planning is to evaluate the strengths and weaknesses of an organization in light of external threats and opportunities and to position the organization not just to survive but to thrive. Given the complex nature of higher education and academic governance, such a process needs the significant involvement of key constituencies. At the same time, the planning process requires the ability to respond to changing circumstances or emerging opportunities with reasonable speed. The opposing desiderata of broad-scale involvement and decision-making efficiency can theoretically be resolved through the creation of a single body. For instance, a committee that includes key constituencies in its deliberations and that can make decisions (or recommendations directly to the president) may be able to achieve the requisite balance. Were the SPCs we examined able to function as *strategic* planning entities? Few were successful in this regard.

It might be argued that several of the SPCs had not even been charged with the responsibility of engaging in strategic planning. Northwestern's Budget and Resources Advisory Committee, in particular, had been created to broaden participation in the *budgeting* process. The other SPCs, in general, were not successful in performing serious institutional planning because of the ways in which their charge was implemented. If planning was on the agenda, most began their processes with a discussion of institutional mission and goals. In the case of Georgia Southern's Institutional Planning Council, grappling with these large and amorphous issues consumed a full year—and with little to show for the effort. By way of contrast, those SPCs that engaged in concrete functions such as budget deliberations or even fund allocations were generally more successful. Both Princeton and Ohio used budget deliberations as platforms for discussing larger institutional issues. But there is a danger in becoming too preoccupied with detail. This danger is evidenced in the case of the University of Montana where the process became so routine and bureaucratic that the University Planning Council, having become absorbed with more discrete, more readily manageable matters, in effect opted out of engaging larger institutional issues.

There is a tension, then, between the need to create an agenda to address big questions and the danger of focusing on concrete, relatively routine tasks. Such tasks that become bureaucratized tend to displace the larger, inherently nonroutine strategic issues.

Another dimension where SPCs faced a challenge in formalized planning is related to academic decisions, where efficiency does not seem possible. Decisions about academic matters were either left to traditional forms of faculty governance or were funneled through the normal governance processes either before or after consideration by the SPC. Thus SPCs can serve the role of helping to integrate academic planning with other elements, but they may not add much to the details of academic planning.

An important factor in resolving these tensions appeared to be the degree to which regular decision-making channels and the planning functions were well integrated through overlapping membership and systematic communication. Ohio and Princeton had histories of integrating budgeting (a normal governance process) and planning, and West Virginia was moving in that direction. Where governance was kept separate, planning efforts tended to be less effective.

It was also clear that economic conditions had an effect on the success of the group and its ability to deal with larger and potentially very difficult institutional issues. While growth and economic prosperity was no guarantee of success (as evidenced at Georgia Southern), retrenchment and financial stress clearly strained the processes at Montana and Teachers College. In times of retrenchment, many SPCs found it impossible to set priorities or to make the hard choices among ongoing activities. Even discussions about the criteria for such decisions often proved to be very difficult. These cases suggest that such discussions were particularly hard for newly formed groups where the kind of trust and communication that had been created among older, established SPCs were yet to be developed.

The more successful SPCs, in sum, tended to be those that had struck a proper balance between lofty abstraction and preoccupation with detail. If their mandate or practice kept them on an ethereal plane, immersed in highly abstracted principles and divorced from more tangible issues, the evidence shows that such an activity could not sustain itself. Conversely, if the SPC let itself get sucked into operational details, however important it may have been for *someone* to take them on, then the SPC in effect could not get to the business of thinking strategically, and the primary purpose for establishing an SPC went unfulfilled.

Communication

Better intracampus communication was an invariable product of the councils. And for the well-functioning councils, improved campus morale appeared to be a byproduct.

Regardless of their effectiveness in making decisions and contributing to institutional direction, in virtually all cases the SPCs opened up decision making and created opportunities to educate more members of the community. In contrast to the contention of critics of SPCs that they had created a more "closed elite," SPCs in all of these cases actually appeared to move decision making and communication out beyond an inner circle of senior administrators. Moreover, a sense of shared information and communication appeared to extend beyond the members of the SPC. Knowledge of the institution and its condition became more widespread. Knowledge about institutional budgets also increased.

The value of openness in communications—despite the risks of premature disclosures—is crucial. As Keller noted, in a reappraisal five years after publishing *Academic Strategy*, "I've come to see the urgency of good, timely communication. When you start planning everyone gets nervous. . . . The strategic planning process will be hurt if fear and apprehensions build, if those planning do not keep their colleagues abreast of what is being considered for the future" (Keller 1988, 4).

It would also be reasonable to suggest that as perceptions of improved communication and broader participation increased, the councils generally had a positive effect on campus morale. While this would be difficult to measure, the sense obtained from scores of interviews was that the councils had a salutary impact on faculty morale on those campuses where the councils were generally successful, including Princeton, Ohio, West Virginia, and Shippensburg. In cases where the SPC itself became ineffective, however, there was the danger of heightened frustration because of raised expectations. This was particularly apparent at Georgia Southern and Montana where high expectations led to frustration when the SPC's efforts failed.

Leadership

Perhaps no other factor was more salient to the success of the strategic planning councils than skillful leadership. It was especially indispensable at the presidential level, but leadership qualities were crucial, too, in those playing key supporting roles.

While strategic planning councils are meant to facilitate leadership by providing an efficient and expert group to thrash out important institutional questions and to advise the president, it is also apparent that astute leadership is required at a number of levels on campus if the SPC is to function effectively—a finding consistent with John Gardner's thesis in *On Leadership* (1990).

We found that the role of the president was critical in determining the success of the SPC. In several of the cases, it became apparent that the SPC turned out to be more symbolic than truly consequential in terms of institutional decision making. SPCs whose advice was rarely taken or whose advice was sought just prior to a deadline with little or no opportunity for deliberation were quickly judged by campus observers to be merely symbolic and therefore meaningless or, even worse, diversionary "rubber stamping" activities. Moreover, where there had not been sufficient time to establish the SPC as part of the decision-making tradition of the institution and where the president who had been instrumental in its creation had left, the SPC had no staying power—and soon dissolved. This was the fate of the councils at Georgia Southern and the University of Montana.

Presidential leadership, supported by other administrative leadership, was also critical in guiding the process and creating and supporting tangible frameworks within which consequential deliberations could occur. Leadership also provided resources to staff and support the work of the SPC itself. A crucial factor was the president's willingness to take the group's recommendations seriously. At Princeton, Ohio, Shippensburg, and West Virginia, presidential support was very much in evidence. When such leadership was not evident, such as at Northwestern and Georgia Southern, the SPC often ceased functioning or retreated to a diminished role.

Chairing such bodies also required leadership skill to ensure that information overload would not occur. Adept leadership proved to be necessary to guide discussions and to maintain focus on "the good of the institution."

Faculty leadership both outside the SPC and in the SPC determined whether the faculty and others would be empowered to participate actively in deliberations. The support of Princeton's faculty made possible the Priorities Committee's long-running success. The support of the Faculty Senate at Montana facilitated whatever success the University Planning Council enjoyed. By contrast, when the faculty at Teachers College reduced their support of the College Policy Council, that SPC ceased to function effec-tively. More often than not, however, where it was clear that the president was intent on empowering the SPC, other constituencies as well took their roles seriously—even if only to serve as watchdogs.

As important as presidential leadership can be, it is clear that such leadership is necessary but not sufficient in creating a successful group. In two of our cases, the president was the same person. In one instance (West Virginia University) the effort succeeded; in the other case (the University of Montana), it did not. At the University of Montana, grim economic condi-tions made the initiation of a planning process very difficult and also undoubtedly contributed to the president's decision to accept the offer of a presidency elsewhere. At the second institution, West Virginia University, the economic climate was better, his support of the Planning Council over time contributed to its success, and there may have been a better fit between the president and the institution.

THE LESSONS FOR MAKING BIG DECISIONS

Eight basic lessons appear to derive from the experiences of the diverse institutions we studied. These lessons each bear on the adequacy of their governance and planning structures and processes. Each lesson is highly relevant to institutional efforts to synchronize governance and planning.

1. Institutional Context

We found that the success of a strategic planning council was dependent, in part, on the institutional context and the campus's readiness to accommodate such a group. Many factors in turn shape that institutional context and predispose a campus to be either amenable or resistive to a major new governance/planning initiative. A number of factors came into play; these include:

- *What is the past history and sophistication in participatory governance, particu-larly among the faculty?*

  Where there is less experience with participatory governance, more guidance may be needed so that complex discussions are fruitful and not directionless. Moreover, in such settings, sustained and active leadership will be required to ensure that the effort does not lose focus and substance. Where there is a change in leadership, the effort may well not survive unless the new leadership continues the effort vigorously. In contrast, in institutions where vigorous faculty participation is the norm, the injection into the governance process of a new body whose activities prove to be merely symbolic can be very damaging to communication and morale.

■ *What has been the campus's history with strategic planning?*

Suppose that a new president is appointed and announces the beginning of a major strategic planning process and the creation of a strategic planning council. If this is the third time in 10 or 15 years that a new entity has been created, a large segment of the faculty and staff is apt to become both skeptical and apathetic, particularly if such processes had in the past been announced with great fanfare and then abandoned when they proved cumbersome and ineffective.

■ *What has been the turnover in leadership at the institution?*

Some of the effective SPCs had had the benefit of long-standing administrative leadership; this facilitated communication and the development of trust. This in turn gave the council time to develop a strong niche in the institution's decision-making processes. Such bodies would appear to be less likely to atrophy when a leadership change occurred.

■ *What are the economic and political conditions facing the institution?*

Planning and decision making is much easier, not to mention a lot more fun, in a time of growth than in a time of significant financial constraints, especially retrenchment. While the literature is replete with exhortations about the importance of creating opportunities out of adversity, this can be very challenging if not impossible for a planning council saddled with the chore of making nasty decisions concerning programs and colleagues. Consequently, the role and structure for giving advice must be considered carefully. Ironically, in such circumstances careful consultation with major constituencies and campus leaders may be critical to ensuring support for whatever difficult decisions need to be made. Creating consensus for the proposition that retrenchment or significant reallocations will be required is often a first critical step for such groups. The jury is still out on whether faculty can or will join administrators in grappling with perplexing—not to say politically explosive—retrenchment issues.

■ *What is the status and maturity of collective bargaining?*

In one of the cases investigated (Shippensburg University), a mature collective bargaining unit played a strong and positive role in decision making. Without maturity, the appropriate lines between decisions appropriate for collective bargaining and "normal" governance decisions may not be sufficiently clear to allow for an effective strategic governance process to emerge.

■ *What is the level of trust on campus, trust particularly between faculty and administration?*

The presence of trusting relationships among constituencies can be understood to be a result of an effective SPC as well as a precondition for one. If the SPC process is used, for example, to demonstrate the sincerity of a president's desire to broaden participation, great care will be needed in establishing the process and the role given to others. At Shippensburg, the president allowed the major participants to design the specifics of the process while supporting the central idea. In other cases, the community was invited to respond to specific plans for structuring the SPC.

These, therefore, are among the factors that influence the context—the institutional environment—in which strategic planning attempts to take root and grow. The institutional setting may be propitious or toxic to a strategic planning committee, that is, the preconditions that exist will either ease the way or seriously impede the work to be done.

2. Framing the Questions

Individuals come to governance/planning bodies with different knowledge levels and different understandings of the issues. As a result, the charge to the group and the questions to be asked and answered need to be carefully framed to be appropriate to the membership present. While it is conceptually important to understand the basic mission of an institution to make recommendations about priorities and directions, it is also the case that abstract discussions about mission and goals are often unproductive unless such activity leads to identifying tangible issues to which the institution must respond. Alternatively, questions can be framed in ways that center on problems, opportunities, and their implications for the institution and its future. In cases where the process is trusted, these questions can effectively be framed by the president or chief academic officer to set parameters for discussion.

3. Skillful Leadership

Chairing a strategic planning council or providing the staff to such a group is hardly just a matter of setting agendas and providing relevant materials. It is fundamentally a matter of understanding the issues to be examined, the goal of the deliberations, and the skill to keep discussion open and focused at the same time. Interpersonal skills and a thorough understanding of planning and decision making is required yet not often articulated as a needed characteristic of the person chairing the group. All too often such persons are chosen based on their institutional role rather than on their skills. This is understandable, probably largely unavoidable in some circumstances, but it is risky to the point that the entire process might be endangered. This unhappy prospect militates in favor of the president making clear at the outset that the chair is not to be chosen solely on the basis of rank, whether the president appoints the chair or charges the council to select its own.

4. Support of the President and Senior Administration

Often the results of planning/governance initiatives, as previously suggested, are seen as symbolic rather than real. When this occurs, the integrity of the entire activity and that of the persons involved is called into question. In such cases, where opinions are advisory and where the president does not agree with the advice, the importance of explaining to the group the reasons for rejecting the proffered advice is critical. If recommendations are more often ignored than agreed to, then the council simply is not likely to survive.

5. Selection of Membership

Some observers, including George Keller, have urged that membership on the council should be appointed so that members are more likely to take on an institutional perspective rather than a political, constituency-bounded perspective. Selection by appointment may indeed increase the likelihood that members will embrace an institutional perspective. On the other hand, in cases where the credibility of the group is subject to question, or where serious issues of trust are present, election of faculty participants may serve to enhance their credibility and the ability of the group to "speak for" others. (A variation of election is ex officio representation. For instance, where the chair of the faculty senate serves on the council by virtue of office, that person has the credibility of having been chosen by the faculty though possibly in a several-step process.) A clear risk with election (or with ex officio membership) is that elected "representatives" may well find it difficult to resist functioning merely as a voice for other governance bodies (a senate, for instance). Some combination of elected and appointed members may work on some campuses. At West Virginia University, a variation appears to have worked well: the president requested key groups to give him lists of approved names from which he selected members for the Planning Council. In any event, balancing these perspectives is important in any institutional setting, and the selection process will contribute to an effective or ineffective body.

6. Integration of Planning and Decision Making

Separate bodies, like strategic planning councils, can broaden the decision-making process to bring new perspectives and representation to important institutional decisions. However, the more separate the SPC's membership from ongoing, "routine" decision-making structures and processes, the more likely its advice will be seen as irrelevant or uninformed. On the other hand, size limitations require that not all deans and vice presidents, for example, can be included, otherwise there will be little room for other participants. The challenge of integrating these two considerations must be taken into account and may come to rest on the degree to which the SPC is connected to the ordinary decision-making processes through alternative means of communication. That is, if there are effective links between the SPC and other decision makers and decision-making bodies, not everyone will need to sit on the SPC. To be effective, these links need to be intentional and ongoing. The connections can be enhanced via periodic reports from group members serving on the SPC, written information, and open forums.

7. Appropriate Use of Data

A critical element of the perceived success of the strategic planning councils is the ability to enhance informed decision making and knowledge about the institution. All too often, however, we observed SPCs being inundated with undistilled data (Georgia Southern was an example), leaving them with no choice but to take the word of the expert in the group or to ignore the data altogether. Careful development of data that is focused and responsive to well-articulated questions is a key to developing an informed body, and an adequately informed body is in turn a prerequisite for effectiveness.

8. Communicating Outcomes to Interested Parties

One of the great challenges to a strategic planning council is to keep interested parties informed of the disposition of ideas that come before it. Whether proposals originate as formal initiatives from outside the SPC or as new initiatives created by the SPC itself, there likely will be many others on the campus who will be affected by strategic planning council decisions. Some good ideas cannot be adopted because of limited resources or for other reasons. Nevertheless, those who contributed ideas are entitled to know whether their ideas have been taken seriously. They should be informed of the disposition and the reasons. They need to develop confidence in the process if they are to continue to support the strategic governance vehicle. Thus, in designing a model for strategic governance, campus leaders should take care to build in "feedback loops." In sum, regular communication between the SPC and other campus entities is critical to the development and nurturance of those "effective links" described earlier that lend credence to the strategic governance process.

STRATEGIC GOVERNANCE IN PERSPECTIVE

In theory, strategic planning councils have significant potential to bolster a campus's governance and planning functions. Such councils afford the possibility for in-depth discussion among participants who have important but differing perspectives, but to succeed the discussions must be carried out in a way that is relatively efficient and focused on the welfare of the institution as a whole. Our cases clearly demonstrate that simply creating such a group does not provide the necessary ingredients to make it successful. Indeed, such bodies bring with them inherent liabilities—vulnerabilities that militate against their prospects for success. The hazards surrounding these councils are many. Their mission and charge can be amorphous; their members may bring to the table narrow, constituency-bounded agendas; there may not be sufficient leadership skill to orchestrate diverse perspectives into fruitful dialogue; the new body may be perceived as a distraction from the real decision-making structures and processes, leaving the council with no important function left to serve; and the president and senior administrative leadership may demonstrate a fundamental lack of support by routinely rejecting the council's advice. As a result the practical effectiveness of such groups—the reality—can be minimal, particularly in matters related to strategic planning.

Leadership, clear focus, and institutional readiness are the critical factors necessary to contribute to the viability and effectiveness of strategic planning bodies. If these factors exist, these bodies can enhance a campus's ability to anticipate and plan strategically for the challenges that lie ahead. Moreover, such entities present the possibility, when linked appropriately to other decision bodies, to help ease some of the tensions between planning and governance evident throughout the study.

Planning and governance protocols too often exist in parallel, disconnected worlds or in each other's face. Neither condition is acceptable. A well-designed, adequately nurtured, ably led strategic planning council can bridge the worlds and help make a significant contribution in shaping an institution's future.

CHAPTER 12

The Opportunity for Strategic Governance: A Summing Up

The argument of the preceding chapters has been that an inadequately understood reality of campus life hinders the ability of colleges and universities to make appropriate strategic decisions, or as we have put it, to make big decisions better. The problem, simply stated, is that two spheres of activity that are crucial to strategic decision making—planning and governance—most of the time are out of sync with each other. They are asynchronous because those two domains or subsystems engender different orientations and perspectives and typically feature different prime actors who, with different priorities, drive the respective planning and governance processes. On top of this internal friction, the contemporary campus must accommodate to the forces or "imperatives" that press upon it from all sides. This reality is all the more problematic for institutional leaders because, we have argued, the forces are commonly pitted against one another.

The result is often excessive internal tensions within the organization, tensions that hamper effective strategic decision making. Planning and governance are indispensable components of strategic decision making, and the differences between them must be reconciled to take advantage of their respective strengths. The contradictory nature of the two domains can be described succinctly.

Strategic planning tends to be administratively driven and externally responsive. The planning process may draw on a variety of campus-based sources (from facilities planners to academic planners), but the decisions tend to be handed down from on high and/or are heavily influenced by forces external to the campus. Governance, on the other hand, tends to be faculty driven and internally oriented. Even though the requirements of a "shared governance" system are predicated on balanced, complementary contributions by academic administrators and faculty, the governance process is characterized by slow-paced deliberation, routed through an often complex network of committees, susceptible to delays, and tending to favor maintenance of the status quo. More fundamentally, the planning process tends to be the venue for anticipating and envisioning the future for the entire campus, for positioning the campus, for taking the larger, more comprehensive, more externally responsive view. Conversely, the governance process tends to be absorbed by the requirement of operational, here-and-now, day-to-day decision making; it is largely preoccupied with solving current issues and resolving disputes over resources.

Without a planning process that does what it can do best—compile data, project trends (resources, demographics, and so on), scan for opportunities, and identify options and niches—strategic decision making would not be adequately anchored in reality nor could it systematically assess and prioritize options for shaping a future. Correspondingly, without a governance process that is open to the contributions of stakeholders—particularly on-campus academics with different experiences, perspectives, and priorities—strategic decisions would be shortchanged of expert opinion crucial to the institution's core academic activities. And more critically, without a governance process that promotes legitimacy and acceptability through involvement, even the deftest strategic decisions are likely to run aground on the jagged shoals of skepticism and resistance. A viable partnership between planning and governance, in other words, is a prerequisite for effective strategic decision making. The typically inadequate linkage between the two domains is depicted by Figure 12.1.

There is nothing easy about establishing such a partnership. Inherent tensions can make for uneasy alliances. The problem is exacerbated, as noted above, because the entire campus, with its component planning and governance subsystems, increasingly is pushed and pulled by forces that act powerfully on decision making. We have described four such primary forces or demands—involvement, efficiency, responsiveness, and leadership—that in recent decades have sent colleges and universities scurrying to embrace new "technologies" (from Management-by-Objectives to Total Quality Management) to enable them to cope better. We have labeled these forces "imperatives" because each value is legitimate (within limits) and politically potent; none can be ignored. (We use "political" here in the sense that stakeholders inside and outside the organization vigorously pursue their respective agendas with the effect of magnifying the various forces.)

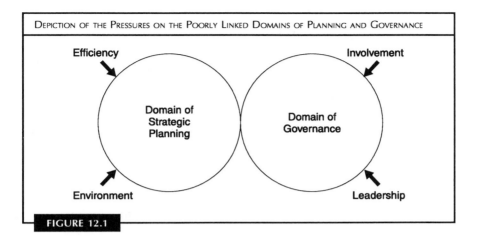

DEPICTION OF THE PRESSURES ON THE POORLY LINKED DOMAINS OF PLANNING AND GOVERNANCE

Efficiency

Involvement

Domain of
Strategic
Planning

Domain of
Governance

Environment

Leadership

FIGURE 12.1

The Swirl of the Imperatives

Thus, by way of review, we have posited that the principal forces that act upon strategic decision making—that is, the four imperatives—are:

- Involvement—the value of inclusiveness, of reaching out to internal and external stakeholders, of involving them as participants in the processes that yield strategic decisions.
- Efficiency—the value, all the more compelling under conditions of financial constraint, of obtaining greater outputs (results) with fewer inputs (resources) and doing so with dispatch, avoiding the delays and quagmire of endless committees and meetings that are often viewed as the curse of participatory governance.
- Environmental responsiveness—the value of identifying elements in the environment, primarily external to the campus, and accommodating those elements that have a legitimate role (in varying degrees) in postsecondary education.
- Leadership—the value of having proactive, vigorous, decisive leadership to shape an institutional vision, to orchestrate efforts, and to deploy resources astutely to realize institutional goals.

Alas, the four prime forces or vectors do not act upon the organization in the same way, that is to say, do not press it in the same direction. As we discussed in chapter 2, the forces sometimes converge, complementing one another. Sometimes, perhaps more often than not, they pull in divergent directions. Recalling Figure 2.2 in chapter 2, it is quite clear how often these forces in fact do collide. For instance:

- The value of involvement, which tends to be cumbersome and time-consuming, militates against the value of crisp, relatively efficient decision making.
- Similarly, the value of leadership—take-charge, decisive leadership—tends to clash with the value of being responsive to the campus's environment, that is, to forces that emanate from outside the campus. Such external pressures—political, economic, and demographic—often do limit the degress of freedom that a leader possesses (but may, at the same time, be congruent with the leader's goals).
- Or consider an example where the tendency is toward the convergence of forces rather than divergence. The demands for salient leadership and for efficiency tend to be convergent, to reinforce one another. Thus the take-charge leader is apt to seek to move the organization efficiently (though, as suggested previously, such assertiveness can run afoul of the value of involvement).

Where does this leave the contemporary college or university as the organization struggles to engage an uncertain future? Generally it leaves it without a process or a structure adequately suited to the complex task of making effective big decisions. And it would appear to be a situation in which neither the administration nor the faculty can take much solace—because the process does not work smoothly and in fact very frequently triggers unpleasant clashes between contending parties. The faculty frequently views the administration as keen to usurp authority and to act autocratically to impose decisions insufficiently respectful of academic prerogative. The evidence of such faculty viewpoints is widespread (as noted in chapter 2). The administration, in turn, undoubtedly is strongly displeased with perceived foot dragging by faculty, the seemingly interminable process for making decisions (or recommendations), and the faculty's indisputable distaste for making hard choices. (Of course, one does not find in "the literature" a great deal of blunt administrative criticism of faculty; prudence dictates a milder public stance.)

Moreover, the pressure and tensions are not confined to the interstices *between* the two domains; they are ever present *within* each domain. Although the planning and governance realms are tilted in the direction, respectively, of administrative and faculty orientations, each is complex in its own right, involves both "parties," and must take into account—albeit in different degrees—the forces or imperatives. In all, the strategic planning and governance subsystems have different valences. They exist parallel to one another yet with constant interactions—often marked by friction—between and within them.

Spanning the Domains

Efforts to bridge the two parallel but interconnected worlds through various approaches to strategic planning seem largely not to have been successful. The reasons cited earlier, grounded in divergent values and processes, provide an explanation. The campuses we visited for the most part attest to these difficulties—and, it is sobering to note, all eight were campuses that were said (not very authoritatively, as it turns out) to have created a process and structure well suited to make effective strategic decisions.

Our argument is that "strategic governance" is an approach that can help colleges and universities to bridge the divide more effectively, to "make big decisions better." To reiterate, by strategic governance we mean a process that is well attuned to the different values and practices that characterize the planning and governance domains. It does not suffice that these differences in organizational culture are merely recognized or comprehended; more is necessary. The process must be designed to forge a better connection between the planning and governance domains and, by recognizing and drawing on the strengths of each, provide a basis for synchronizing the two.

We think that the model we have labeled as a "strategic planning council" provides a sound basis for facilitating "strategic governance." This SPC model, derived from our eight cases, is similar to, but in important ways different from, the "Joint Big Decisions Committee" espoused by George Keller as a "new kind of cabinet government" (Keller 1983, 61) and which served as a stimulus for our own investigation.

It may be useful to recall the essential properties of the "JBDC" model. It was envisioned as a small, joint, elite (senior faculty and key administrators) committee, sometimes augmented by junior faculty members, students, and trustees. In its pure form, its members are selected (and, presumably, trusted) by the president. Its deliberations are conducted essentially in secrecy—that is, insulated from regular governance entities (deans' councils, academic senates, etc.)—in order that its recommendations can be formulated without being prematurely attacked and derailed. The JBDC's recommendations, thus formulated, would be submitted to the president for his or her disposal.

The evidence from our site visits suggests that the JBDC model has important virtues, but that several refinements in its conception would be helpful. In the first place, it is worth noting that despite our best efforts to identify (and to visit) a "real live JBDC," none of the eight campuses that had been recommended to us turned out to be a "pure" JBDC. Thus we were not successful in locating a strategic planning entity that fully conformed to the model's characteristics. Perhaps none exists. Or perhaps existing entities will evolve toward that ideal. That possibility aside, we concluded, on the basis of our site visits, that two aspects of the JBDC model do not appear to work well.

First, shrouding the JBDC process in secrecy, we believe, turns out to be counterproductive. The second problem lies in its circumventing the "normal" governance entities, as imperfect and as "inefficient" as they may be. By bypassing the regular governance bodies, the JBDC is deprived of input from a broader range of sources. And, more important in our view, circumventing traditional campus governance (and thereby downplaying the legitimacy of representative government) inevitably triggers suspicion and a predisposition of those left on the outside to reject the process as being autocratic and illegitimate.

The Strategic Planning Council

We think that the strategic planning council (SPC) model, a variation on the JBDC, has qualities that, while hardly assuring success, nevertheless recommend it to campuses engaging in strategic planning. The generic SPC remains a relatively small—some would say "elite"—group. Its membership is still drawn primarily from the ranks of senior faculty and key administrators. But the SPC does not place a premium on confidentiality. In fact, its strength—the antidote to the JBDC's most serious flaw—is that it is purposefully connected to the normal governance subsystem. That is, the SPC's composition does not seek to exclude but rather to develop links to the key governance entities. This also serves to broaden the base for informing the planning process and, accordingly, for developing planning priorities.

This can be a risky business; there are trade-offs. But the advantages, we believe our evidence establishes, outweigh the disadvantages. The primary disadvantage is that the communication links to, say, the faculty senate could lead to premature exposure of deliberations. Especially if the SPC is contemplating bold initiatives that likely will be perceived as creating winners and losers (at least in the short run), adamant opposition may well develop, and such initiatives may fall victim to vigorous counterattacks before they have been fully formed and before an opportunity has been afforded to "sell" them to the campus community.

On the other hand, if ties with key governance entities have been cultivated, a significant advantage is evident. Provided that the SPC and its leadership are seen as being trustworthy in the main, then the opportunity will be present both to draw on a broader range of opinions and, more to the point, to build campus support. The key is to compose the SPC in such a way that the faculty's "own" leaders—not just appointees of the president—are deeply immersed in the SPC's work. That approach addresses the legitimacy, the credibility factor. That is what the JBDC model appears to take too lightly.

Does such an approach assure success in strategic decision making? Of course not. We have taken pains in chapter 11, following the presentation of our eight cases, to identify the variables that we believe contribute to successful strategic planning.

Strategic Governance

By way of summary, we believe that successful strategic governance has four principal attributes, as developed in our case material and synthesized in the previous chapter:

- A *governance* system that is inclusive. The strategic planning council builds upon rather than bypasses existing governance mechanisms.

   The challenge is to balance the need to connect to regular governance entities with the SPC's need not to become enmeshed with normal governance processes and thereby lose a necessary measure of autonomy.

- A *planning* system that protects and promotes a strategic outlook. Planning proceeds necessarily at many levels and in differing time frames, but the strategic planning council must maintain a focus on its *strategic* mission. Correspondingly, the strategic planning council must avoid the temptation to be drawn into operational, annual budget firefights—except as those issues may be basic to the longer, larger strategic view.

   The challenge is to balance the visionary focus on truly "big decisions" with the need to stay in touch with operational realities that are important and that energize—and constrain—the campus.

- A *communication* system that emphasizes the importance of informing campus constituencies. The strategic planning council becomes a vehicle for receiving information, acting on it, explaining the reasons for its decisions and recommendations, and dispelling rumors and misperceptions.

   The challenge is to balance the need for openness with the need to avoid premature disclosures that would jeopardize the SPC's basic responsibilities.

- *Leadership* that is alert to the complexities and nuances of the campus's different organizational cultures and is astute in establishing conditions most likely to forge links between planning and governance. Leadership—and here we mean primarily the campus's chief executive officer—must be committed to the strategic planning process and the strategic planning council and must be sensitive to the composition of such a council.

   The challenge is to balance the need to be deferential to the council and its recommendations (and thereby bolster its credibility) without surrendering the heavy responsibilities of independent judgment indispensable to wise stewardship.

Leadership, we find, is perhaps the most crucial of the four elements just outlined. The other elements can be in place, but inattentive or, worse, devious leadership will surely scuttle it all. Astute leadership is necessary to launch strategic governance, to cultivate it, to provide the conditions in which it can succeed. It is *the* indispensable ingredient.

In contrast to our depiction (in Fig. 12.1) of the inadequate connection between strategic planning and governance processes—a "design defect" that ordinarily impairs a campus's decision making for big decisions—we show in Figure 12.2 our vision of the domains of strategic planning and campus governance when they are properly linked. The linking mechanism is an appropriately designed strategic planning council. And the result, we have maintained, is that effective "strategic governance"—adequately respectful of the requirements of both the planning and governance domains—can emerge.

• • • • •

If, as Clemenceau professed, war is too important to be entrusted to the generals, so too is planning too important to be left to the planners. Nor is it fruitful to entrust planning solely to the faculty lions. Both spheres of influence must be accommodated if strategic planning is to have a fair chance of success. Nothing is easy about making strategic governance work; there are certainly no guarantees. A strong dose of good fortune is advisable, for a brutal

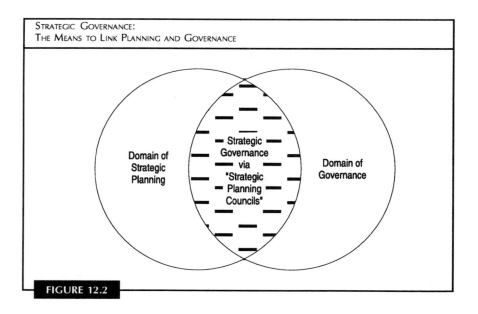

STRATEGIC GOVERNANCE:
THE MEANS TO LINK PLANNING AND GOVERNANCE

Domain of Strategic Planning

Strategic Governance via "Strategic Planning Councils"

Domain of Governance

FIGURE 12.2

economic environment can only undermine the likelihood for successful strategic planning—if all of the realistic options are conduits for pain.

If, however, the proper elements of strategic governance are embraced and nurtured, the prospects for success will be enhanced. There is much to learn from the successes and failures of those who have blazed this trail. And the stakes are very high.

APPENDIXES

. . . .

APPENDIX A

CHARACTERISTICS OF INSTITUTIONS IN THE SAMPLE[a]

Institution	Founding Date	Approximate Enrollment	No. of Faculty[b]	Control	Carnegie Classification[c]
Georgia Southern Coll. (now Univ.)	1908	11,000	590	pub.	Comprehensive I
Northwestern Univ.	1850	15,000	1,350 FT 350 PT	pvt.	Res. Univ. I
Ohio Univ.	1804	16,000	700 FT 200 PT	pub.	Doctorate I
Princeton Univ.	1746	6,000	600 FT 200 PT	pvt.	Res. Univ. I
Shippensburg Univ. of Pennsylvania	1871	6,400	345	pub.	Comprehensive I
Teachers Coll. (Columbia Univ.)	1887	4,000	140 FT	pvt.	Doctorate I
Univ. of Montana	1893	9,000	460	pub.	Doctorate I
West Virginia Univ.	1867	18,700	1,500	pub.	Res. Univ. II

a   At time of site visits
b   FT = full time; PT = part time
c   Based on the Carnegie classifications in effect at the time of the site visits: See Carnegie Foundation for the Advancement of Teaching, *A Classification of Institutions of Higher Education*, Princeton, NJ, 1987.

APPENDIX B

CHARACTERISTICS OF STRATEGIC PLANNING COUNCILS IN SAMPLE

Institution		Estab-lished	MEMBERS				
			Total Members	Voting	Non-Voting	Faculty	Admini-stration
Georgia Southern Coll. (now Univ.)	Institutional Planning Council (IPC)	1985	19	16	3	10	9
Northwestern Univ.	Budget & Resources Advisory Committee (BRAC)	1970	12	7	5	7	5
Ohio Univ.	University Planning Advisory Council (UPAC)	1977	18	18	0	8	4
Princeton Univ.	Priorities Committee	1969	16	all	0	6	3
Shippensburg Univ.	University Forum	1985	18	all	0	10	5
Teachers Coll. (Columbia Univ.)	College Policy Committee (CPC)	1972	40	30	10	18	10
Univ. of Montana	University Planning Council (UPC)	1982	17–29	14–17	5–15	6–11	4–18
West Virginia Univ.	University Planning Council (UPC)	1986	13	all	0	6	3

CHARACTERISTICS OF STRATEGIC PLANNING COUNCILS
IN SAMPLE *(continued)*

Institution	Members		Terms for Faculty	SPC Chair
	Staff	Students[a]		
Ga. Southern	0	0	2-3 yrs.	Chief Academic Officer
Northwestern Univ.	0	0	3 yrs.	A Faculty Member
Ohio Univ.	3	2UG 1G	3 yrs.	Chief Academic Officer
Princeton Univ.	1	4UG 2G	3 yrs.	Chief Academic Officer
Shippensburg Univ.	0	3	2 yrs.	Elected Member of Forum
Teachers Coll.	3	9G	2 yrs.	President
Univ. of Montana	2	2–5	1–3 yrs.	Chief Academic Officer
West Va. Univ.	2	2	2-3 yrs.	Chief Academic Officer

a   UG = undergraduate; G = graduate

REFERENCES

• • • • • • • • •

AAUP, *American Association of University Professors Policy Documents and Reports* Washington, DC: AAUP, 1990.

AGB Report. *Trustees and Troubled Times in Higher Education.* Washington, DC: Association of Governing Boards of Colleges and Universities, 1992.

Ackoff, R.L. *A Concept of Corporate Planning.* New York: Wiley & Sons, 1970.

Alpert, D. "Performance and Paralyses: The Organizational Contexts of the American Research University." *Journal of Higher Education* 56(3), 1985, pp. 241-81.

Austin, A.E. and Gamson, Z.F. *Academic Workplace: New Demands, Heightened Tensions.* ASHE-ERIC Higher Education Report No. 10. Washington, DC: Association for the Study of Higher Education, 1983.

Baldridge, J.V. and Okimi, P.H. "Strategic Planning in Higher Education: New Tool—or New Gimmick?" *AAHE Bulletin* 35(10), 1982, pp. 15-18.

Baldridge, J.V. "Shared Governance: A Fable about the Lost Magic Kingdom." *Academe* 68(1), 1982, pp. 12-15.

Baldridge, J.V. and Deal, T. *The Dynamics of Organizational Change in Education.* New York: McCutchan, 1983.

Bean, J.P. and Kuh, G.D. "A Typology of Planning Problems." *Journal of Higher Education* 55(1), 1984, pp. 35-55.

Bennis, W. (Ed.) *Leaders on Leadership.* Boston: Harvard Business Review, 1992.

Bess, J.L. *University Organization.* New York: Human Sciences Press, 1982.

Bess, J.L. *Collegiality and Bureaucracy in the Modern University.* New York: Teachers College, 1988.

Birnbaum, R. "Responsibility without Authority: The Impossible Job of the College President." In J. Smart (ed.) *Higher Education Handbook, Theory and Research.* Vol 5. New York: Agathon, 1985.

Cameron, K. "Strategic Responses to Conditions of Decline." *Journal of Higher Education* 54(4), 1983, pp. 359-80.

Cameron, K. and Tschircharet, M. "Postindustrial Environments and Organizational Effectiveness in Colleges and Universities." *Journal of Higher Education* 63(1), 1992, pp. 87-108.

Chaffee, E.E. "Successful Strategic Management in Small, Private Colleges." *Journal of Higher Education* 55(2), 1984, pp. 212-41.

Chaffee, E.E. "The Concept of Strategy: From Business to Higher Education." In J. Smart (ed.) *Higher Education Handbook of Theory and Research.* pp. 133-72. New York: Agathon, 1985.

Chaffee, E.E. and Sherr, L.A. *Quality: Transforming Postsecondary Education.* ASHE-ERIC Higher Education Report No. 3. Washington, DC: The George Washington University School of Education and Human Development, 1992.

Chemers, M.M. "An Integrative Theory of Leadership." In M.M. Chemers and R. Ayman (eds.) *Leadership Theory and Research: Perspectives and Directions.* New York: Academic Press, 1993.

Cohen, M.D. and March, J.G. *Leadership and Ambiguity: The American College President.* New York: McGraw Hill, 1984.

Cole, J. "Balancing Act: Dilemmas of Choice." *Daedalus* 122(4), 1993, pp. 1-36.

Coler, B. J. "An Attribution Theory of Leadership." In B. Shaw and G.R. Salancit (eds.) *New Directions in Organizational Behavior.* Chicago: St. Clair Press, 1977.

Cope, R.G. *Opportunity from Strength: Strategic Planning Clarified with Case Examples.* ASHE-ERIC Higher Education Report No. 8. Washington, DC: Association for the Study of Higher Education, 1987.

Corak, K.A. "Do Big Decisions Committees Work?" *Planning for Higher Education* 21(1), 1992, pp. 20–24.

Corak, K.A.S. "Governance Models at Work on the Campus: Goal Setting and Decision Making in 'Joint Big Decision Committees.'" Ph.D. diss., San Diego State University, San Diego, CA, and The Claremont Graduate School, Claremont, CA, 1990.

Covey, S.R. *Principle Centered Leadership.* New York: Simon & Schuster, 1991.

Crossland, F.E. "Learning to Cope with a Downward Slope." *Change* 12(4), 1980, p. 20.

Dill, D.D. and Helm, K.P. "Faculty Participation in Strategic Policy Making." In John C. Smart (ed.) *Higher Education: Handbook of Theory and Research,* Vol. 4, pp. 319-55. New York: Agathon Press, 1988.

Drucker, P. *Managing in Turbulent Times.* London: Pan Books, 1981.

Duryea, E.D. "Evolution of University Organization." In J. Perkins (ed.) *The University as an Organization,* pp. 15-37. New York: McGraw Hill, 1973.

Etzioni, A. *Modern Organizations.* Englewood Cliffs, NJ: Prentice Hall, 1964.

Fiedler, F.E. and Chemers, M.M. *Improving Leadership Effectiveness.* New York: Wiley, 1984.

Floyd, C. *Faculty Participation in Decision Making.* ASHE-ERIC Report No. 8. Washington, DC: Association for the Study of Higher Education, 1985.

Gardner, J.W. *On Leadership.* New York: The Free Press, 1990.

Garvin, D.A. "How the Baldrige Award Really Works." *Harvard Business Review,* 1991, pp. 80-93.

Glenny, L.A. "Demographics and Related Issues for Higher Education in the 1980s." *Journal of Higher Education* 51(4), 1980, pp. 376 ff.

Heydinger, R.B. "Academic Planning for the '80's." *New Directions for Institutional Research No. 7.* San Francisco: Jossey Bass, 1980.

Jones, L.W. "Strategic Planning: The Unrealized Potential of the 1980s and the Promise of the 1990s." In *Strategic Planning: New Directions for Higher Education,* No. 70, Summer 1990. San Francisco: Jossey Bass.

Keller, G. *Academic Strategy: The Management Revolution in American Higher Education.* Baltimore: Johns Hopkins University Press, 1983.

Keller, G. "Academic Strategy: Five Years Later" (an interview with George Keller). *AAHE Bulletin* 40(6), 1988, pp. 3-6.

Kemerer, F. and Baldridge V. "Academic Senates and Faculty Collective Bargaining." *Journal of Higher Education* 47(4), 1976, pp. 391-411.

Kemerer, F. and Baldridge, V. "Senates and Unions: Unexpected Peaceful Coexistence." *Journal of Higher Education* 52(3), 1981, pp. 256-64.

Kerr, C. "Administration In an Era of Change and Conflict." *Educational Record* 54(1), 1973, pp. 38-46.

Kerr, C. and Gade, M. *The Many Lives of Academic Presidents: Time, Place and Character.* Washington, DC: Association of Governing Boards, 1986.

Kotler, P. and Murphy, P.E. "Strategic Planning for Higher Education." *Journal of Higher Education* 52(2), 1981, pp. 470-98.

Lee, B.A. "Campus Leaders and Campus Senates." In R. Birnhaum (ed.) *Faculty in Governance: The Role of Senates and Joint Committees in Academic Decision-Making. New Directions in Higher Education* No. 75, pp. 41-61. San Francisco: Jossey-Bass, 1991.

Lewin, K. *Field Theory in Social Science.* New York: Harper, 1951.

Lozier, G.G. and Chittipeddi, K. "Issues Management in Strategic Planning." *Research in Higher Education* 24(1), 1986, pp. 3-14.

Lozier, G.G., Dorris, M.J. and Chittipeddi, K. "A Case Study in Issues Management." *Planning for Higher Education* 14(4), 1986, pp. 14-19.

Meeth, R.L. *Quality Education for Less Money.* San Francisco: Jossey-Bass, 1974.

Millett, J.D. *The Academic Community: An Essay on Organizations.* New York: McGraw Hill, 1962.

Mortimer, K.P. and Tierney, M.L. "The Three Rs of the Eighties: Reduction, Reallocation and Retrenchment." *ASHE-ERIC Research Report No. 4,* p. 6. Washington, DC: AAHE, 1979.

Powers, D.R. and Powers, M.F. "How to Orchestrate Participatory Strategic Planning without Sacrificing Momentum." *Educational Record* 65(4), 1984, pp. 48-52.

Prestbo, J.A. "Pinching Pennies: Ohio University Finds Participatory Planning Ends Financial Chaos." *The Wall Street Journal,* May 27, 1981, pp. 2, 18.

Rice, R.E. and Austin, A.E. "High Morale and Satisfaction among Faculty." *Change* 20(2),1988, pp. 14-15.

Schmidtlein F. "Responding to Diverse Institutional Issues: Adapting Strategic Planning Concepts." In Schmidtlein & Milton (eds.) "Adapting Strategic Planning to Campus Realities." *New Directions for Institutional Research* No. 67, 1990.

Schmidtlein F. and Milton, T. "College and University Planning: Perspectives from a Nationwide Study." *Planning for Higher Education* 17(3), 1989, pp. 1-19.

Schuster, J.H., L.H. Miller and Associates. *Governing Tomorrow's Campus: Perspectives and Agendas.* New York: American Council on Education/Macmillan Publishing Co., 1989.

Seymour, D. *On Q: Causing Quality in Higher Education.* Phoenix, AZ: American Council on Education/Oryx Press, 1992.

Stamatakos, L.C. and Rogers, R.R. "Student Affairs: A Profession in Need of a Philosophy." *Journal of College Student Personnel* 25(5), 1984, pp. 400-11.

"Statement on Government of Colleges and Universities" by AAUP/ACE/AGB. *Academe* 52(4) 1966, pp. 375-79.

Steiner, G.A. *Strategic Planning.* New York: Macmillan, 1979.

Vaill, P. American Council on Education, annual meeting, San Diego, CA, 1993.

Weick, K.E. "Educational Organizations as Loosely Coupled Systems." *Administrative Science Quarterly* 21(1), 1976, pp. 1-19.

Wildavsky, A. "If Planning Is Everything, Maybe Its Nothing." *Policy Sciences* (4), 1973, pp. 127-53.

Yamada, M.M. "Joint Big Decision Committees, Strategic Planning and University Governance." Ph.D. diss., The Claremont Graduate School, Claremont, CA, 1990.

Yamada, M.M. "Joint Big Decision Committees and University Governance." In R. Birnbaum (ed.) *Faculty in Governance: The Role of the Senates and Joint Committees in Academic Decision Making.* New Directions in Higher Education No. 75, pp. 79-96. San Francisco: Jossey Bass, 1991.

Yukl, G.A. *Leadership in Organizations.* Englewood Cliffs, NJ: Prentice Hall, 1981.

INDEX

• • • • • • • • •

by Linda Webster

213

Georgia Southern *(continued)*
  founding of, 121, 205
  governance of, 121-22, 124,
    127-31
  organizational climate of, 132-33
  planning at, 123, 131-32
  staff of, 130-31
  Strategic Planning Council at,
    131-32
  students of, 122, 123
Georgia Southern Institutional
    Planning Council (IPC)
  communication and, 132
  decision making by, 128-29,
    133-35
  dissolution of, 181, 186
  effectiveness of, 133-38, 191
  establishment of, 181, 206
  governance and, 127-31
  historical background of, 123-26
  impact of, 127-33
  membership of, 126, 136, 206-07
  organizational climate and, 132-33
  planning and, 131-32, 184
  purposes and arrangements of, 126-
    27, 136
  schedule of meetings, 126, 127
  as strategic planning council,
    122-38
Goheen, Robert F., 32, 33, 46
Governance. *See also* Strategic
    governance
  challenges in, 6-7
  coordination needed in, 21
  criticisms of, 9-10
  as crucial element in strategic
    governance, 180-83, 199
  differing perspectives between
    planning and, 25-26
  expansion of administrative
    positions in higher educa-
    tion, 7
  faculty attitudes about, 8
  of Georgia Southern, 121-22, 124,
    127-31

  linking of planning with, in
    strategic governance,
    197-200
  of Northwestern University, 49-63,
    180
  of Ohio University, 83-96, 180
  participatory governance in higher
    education, 14-17
  of Princeton University, 32-48,
    180, 181
  of Shippensburg University, 139-
    40, 145-49, 153
  strategic planning councils and,
    180-83
  of Teachers College, 66-79, 180,
    181
  tension between planning and, xi,
    7, 9-10, 22-26, 193-96
  tension between superficial
    representation and genuine
    participation, 25
  of University of Montana, 99-100,
    106-08
  of West Virginia University, 159-
    60, 164-65

Higher education. *See also* Strategic
    governance; and names of
    specific colleges and universi-
    ties
  adaptation needed, to changing
    environment, 18-19
  collegial management style of, 3-4
  corporate mode of decision
    making in, 4
  efficient management of, 17-18,
    22-24
  environment for, 4-7, 18-19, 24-25
  expansion of administrative
    positions in, 7
  faculty attitudes about administra-
    tion and governance in, 8
  imperatives for decision making in,
    14-20
  leadership in, 19-20, 23-25
  megatrends in, 5

Teachers College *(continued)*
  Faculty Executive Committee at,
    66, 67-70, 72-73
  faculty of, 65, 66-79, 186-87, 205
  Faculty Personnel Committee at,
    66
  Faculty Salary Committee at, 66
  founding of, 64, 205
  governance at, 66-79, 180, 181
  planning at, 74
  students of, 65, 66, 67, 72, 78
Teachers College, College Policy
    Council (CPC)
  academic affairs governance and,
    68-71
  administrative/financial affairs
    governance and, 71
  budget and, 71
  campus climate and, 74-75
  changes in governance and, 71-74
  communication and, 75-76
  dissolution of, 79, 181
  effectiveness of, 76-79
  establishment of, 66, 180, 206
  factors limiting effectiveness of,
    77-78
  impact of, 68-76
  membership of, 67, 206-07
  planning and, 74
  responsibilities of, 66-67, 69
  schedule of meetings of, 68
Timpane, P. Michael, 65
Total Quality Management (TQM),
    3, 13, 17, 194
TQM. *See* Total Quality Management
    (TQM)
"Turfism," 7

Unions, 16, 20, 50-51, 92-93, 100,
    140, 143, 146-47, 156, 158,
    160, 188
Universities. *See* Higher education;
    Strategic governance; and
    names of specific colleges and
    universities

University of Montana
  academic affairs at, 107-08, 110,
    117-18
  academic programs of, 99
  administrators of, 101-02, 111-15,
    117-18, 187
  Associated Student of the Univer-
    sity of Montana at, 100, 102
  budget of, 103, 105-06, 117, 184
  communication and consciousness
    raising at, 110-11, 185
  Council of Deans at, 107
  enrollment of, 99, 103, 205
  faculty of, 101, 102, 103-04, 106-
    07, 186, 205
  Faculty Senate at, 100, 101, 102,
    103, 106-07, 186
  founding of, 99, 205
  governance at, 106-08
  governance of, 99-100
  organizational climate at, 111-12
  planning at, 108-10
  Staff Senate at, 102, 108
  students of, 99, 100, 102, 108
  University College at, 110, 118
  University Teachers' Union at, 100
University of Montana University
    Planning Council (UPC)
  communication, consciousness
    raising and, 110-11
  constraints on, 116-18
  decision making by, 113-17
  dissolution of, 181, 186
  effectiveness of, 112-20
  establishment of, 103-04, 181, 206
  evolution of, 103-06
  governance and, 106-08
  historical preconditions for, 101
  impact of, 106-12
  membership of, 100, 102, 206-07
  organizational climate and, 111-12
  planning and, 108-10
  positive contributions of, 118
  purposes and processes of, 103
University Planning and Advisory
    Council (UPAC). *See* Ohio

JACK H. SCHUSTER—is professor of education and public policy at The Claremont Graduate School and currently chairs its Faculty Executive Committee. A former administrator at Tulane University and assistant to the chancellor and lecturer in political science at the University of California, Berkeley, he served as legislative and administrative assistant to Congressman John Brademas. A member (and former chair) of the American Association of University Professors Committee on Governance, he has written widely on the faculty, campus governance, professional development, and education politics.

Dr. Schuster earned a B.A. in history from Tulane University, a J.D. from Harvard Law School, an M.A. in political science from Columbia University, and a Ph.D. in higher education from the University of California, Berkeley.

DARYL G. SMITH—is associate professor of education and psychology at The Claremont Graduate School. Dr. Smith also has an extensive background in college and university administration, having served 23 years as a dean and vice president in such areas as student affairs, institutional research, and planning. She serves as a consultant to colleges and universities in areas related to institutional planning, diversity, accreditation, and institutional management. Dr. Smith is currently involved in research projects related to planning and governance, the impact of women's colleges, the organizational implications of diversity, and adult development. She has published in each of these areas.

Dr. Smith received a B.A. in mathematics from Cornell University, an M.A. from Stanford University, and a Ph.D. in social psychology and higher education from The Claremont Graduate School.

KATHLEEN A. CORAK—is dean of undergraduate studies and director of institutional research at Minot State University, North Dakota. An associate professor of interdisciplinary studies, she is also involved in curriculum development aimed at attracting promising undergraduates to career opportunities in higher education. Dr. Corak has held a variety of responsibilities in college, university, and state system-level academic administration in Montana, Virginia, and North Dakota. Her current research projects and recent publications are concerned with leadership and strategic planning, outcomes assessment and curricular reform, and institutional research and organizational change.

Dr. Corak received a B.A. in psychology and a M.A. in counseling from the University of Montana and a Ph.D. in higher education from San Diego State University and The Claremont Graduate School.

MYRTLE M. YAMADA—is director of administrative services of the College of Education, University of Hawaii at Manoa. She has served for over 20 years as a university administrator, including serving as associate director of the College's organized educational programs. Dr. Yamada is currently involved in research projects on evaluation and assessment of educational programs.

Dr. Yamada received a B.A. in mathematics and an M.B.A. from the University of Hawaii at Manoa, and a Ph.D. in higher education from The Claremont Graduate School.

ISBN 0-89774-847-6

90000

9 780897 748476